Alternatives to Capitalism in the 21st Century

Series Editors: **Lara Monticelli**, Copenhagen Business School, and **Torsten Geelan**, University of Copenhagen

---

Debates about the future of capitalism demonstrate the urgent need to envision and enact alternatives that can help tackle the multiple intertwined crises that societies are currently facing. This ground-breaking new series advances the international, comparative and interdisciplinary study of capitalism and its alternatives in the 21st Century.

Forthcoming in the series:

Remaking Money for a Sustainable Future
By **Ester Barinaga Martín**

Prefiguring Utopia:
The Auroville Experiment
By **Suryamayi Aswini Clarence-Smith**

Find out more at
bristoluniversitypress.co.uk/
alternatives-to-capitalism-in-the-21st-century

Alternatives to Capitalism in the 21st Century

Series Editors: **Lara Monticelli**, Copenhagen Business School, and **Torsten Geelan**, University of Copenhagen

---

Advisory board:

Wendy Harcourt, Erasmus University Rotterdam, Netherlands
Vasna Ramasar, Lund University, Sweden
Tom Malleson, King's University College, Canada
Silvia Federici, Hofstra University, US
Richard D. Wolff, The New School for Social Research, US
Nancy Fraser, The New School for Social Research, US
Luke Martell, University of Sussex, UK
Laura Basu, openDemocracy and University of Utrecht, Netherlands
Juliet Schor, Boston College, US
Isabelle Ferreras, Université Catholique de Louvain, Belgium
Göran Therborn, University of Cambridge, UK
Gar Alperovitz, The Democracy Collective and the Next System Project, US
Francesca Forno, University of Trento, Italy
Flor Avelino, Erasmus University Rotterdam, Dutch Research Institute for Transitions, Netherlands
Emanuele Leonardi, University of Parma, Italy
David Bailey, University of Birmingham, UK
Ashish Kothari, Global Tapestry of Alternatives, India
Aris Komporozos-Athanasiou, University College London, UK
Arturo Escobar, University of North Carolina, US
Albena Azmanova, Brussels School of International Studies, Belgium

Find out more at

bristoluniversitypress.co.uk/
alternatives-to-capitalism-in-the-21st-century

FROM CAPITAL TO COMMONS

Exploring the Promise of a World Beyond Capitalism

Hannes Gerhardt

First published in Great Britain in 2025 by

Bristol University Press
University of Bristol
1-9 Old Park Hill
Bristol
BS2 8BB
UK
t: +44 (0)117 374 6645
e: bup-info@bristol.ac.uk

Details of international sales and distribution partners are available at bristoluniversitypress.co.uk

© Bristol University Press 2025

British Library Cataloguing in Publication Data
A catalogue record for this book is available from the British Library

ISBN 978-1-5292-2453-5 hardcover
ISBN 978-1-5292-2454-2 paperback
ISBN 978-1-5292-2455-9 ePub
ISBN 978-1-5292-2456-6 ePdf

The right of Hannes Gerhardt to be identified as author of this work has been asserted by him in accordance with the Copyright, Designs and Patents Act 1988.

All rights reserved: no part of this publication may be reproduced, stored in a retrieval system, or transmitted in any form or by any means, electronic, mechanical, photocopying, recording, or otherwise without the prior permission of Bristol University Press.

Every reasonable effort has been made to obtain permission to reproduce copyrighted material. If, however, anyone knows of an oversight, please contact the publisher.

The statements and opinions contained within this publication are solely those of the author and not of the University of Bristol or Bristol University Press. The University of Bristol and Bristol University Press disclaim responsibility for any injury to persons or property resulting from any material published in this publication.

Bristol University Press works to counter discrimination on grounds of gender, race, disability, age and sexuality.

Cover design: Liam Roberts Design
Front cover image: Zualidro

This book is dedicated to all those (compeerists) who still see the benefit in sharing, collaboration, and care, even if it doesn't pay

Contents

About the Author   viii

Introduction   1

PART I   Contemporary Capitalism and the Promise of the Digital Revolution
1. Theorizing Capitalism and its Demise   17
2. The Digital Commons' Elusive Potential   35
3. Taking Back the Internet   56

PART II   The Material Economy and Commons
4. Democratizing Infrastructure   75
5. The Promise of 'Design Global, Manufacture Local'   93
6. Contending With the Limits of Our Natural World   113

PART III   Money and Value
7. Coping With Money's Monopoly on Value   137
8. Reinventing Money's Role in the Economy   155

PART IV   In Pursuit of a Post-Capitalist Future
9. Compeerists of the World Unite!   175
10. A Compeerist Society   198

Conclusion   217

References   222
Index   252

About the Author

Hannes Gerhardt is Professor of Geography at the University of West Georgia. His research spans a range of topics within political geography and geoeconomics. His most recent area of scholarly interest centres on the relationship between technology, the commons, and capitalism.

Introduction

Many reading this book will have heard some approximation of the quip, 'It is easier to imagine the end of the world, than it is to imagine the end of capitalism' (Fisher, 2009, p 2). The origin of this line can be traced back to Fredric Jameson's (1996) *Seeds of Time,* but it is probably most closely associated with Slavoj Žižek, who has been fond of making the claim in various ways. In a 2005 documentary, for instance, Žižek proclaims, "Thirty, forty years ago, we were still debating about what the future will be: communist, fascist, capitalist, whatever. Today, nobody even debates these issues. We all silently accept global capitalism is here to stay" (in Taylor, 2005, np). Mark Fisher has even coined a term to capture this sentiment of inevitability, 'capitalist realism', describing it as the 'widespread sense that not only is capitalism the only viable political and economic system, but also that it is now impossible even to *imagine* a coherent alternative to it' (Fisher, 2009, p 2).

Awareness of a mass resignation of society to the inevitability of capitalism is not new. It was already captured in Friedrich Engels' (2000) comments on 'false consciousness', later honed by the likes of Antonio Gramsci (2011) and Theodor Adorno (2015) to explain the working class's complacency towards their own exploitation. Yet what seems to have changed is that the political left has now also fallen prey to capitalist realism as evidenced, for instance, by the almost complete incapacity to envision and pursue societal wellbeing in a way that does not depend on ever-expanding business revenue and a rising stock market (Jackson, 2017). Hence, while some socialist and green-minded movements can point to isolated political victories, in the end, they have been unable to tap into or develop any inspirational ideas to effectively challenge the deep sense that our current organization of the world, despite its many intractable problems, is more or less as good as we can ever hope for. Clearly, for those who truly believe 'another world is possible', something new is needed to wake us from our dogmatic resignation.

In this book we delve into one proposition seeking to do just that. It is a different way of seeing and doing that is predicated on the increasingly popular conceptualization and enactment of the 'commons', a third space distinct from markets and governments where resources are maintained, generated, and managed as a shared endowment by and for the people. More specifically, it is a proposal, backed by unfolding efforts around the world, focused on the potential of new, digitally based technologies to expand these commons en masse to achieve a more fair, sustainable, and prosperous, post-capitalist order for all. As such, it is rooted in the idea that our current state of economic and technological development makes the adoption of openness, cooperation, and shared ownership/governance a more rational economic choice in meeting the needs and wants of humanity than one based on competition, artificial scarcity, and the pursuit of profit. In this book we will critically assess, organize, and hone this emerging framework and movement, which we will come to call 'compeerism'.

Visions of overcoming capitalism and their limitations

A critical starting point for much of the relevant work informing the compeerist proposition is the conceptualization of a currently dominant post-Fordist, cognitive capitalism in which growth and profits have become increasingly dependent on knowledge and information (Dyer-Witheford, 1999; Gorz, 2010; Rifkin, 2015; Mason, 2016). It is an economic condition that was already pondered by the early Marx (1973) in *Grundrisse*, where he posited an open and accessible 'general intellect', understood as society's accumulated skills, understandings, and interactions becoming a critical force of production. With an expanding general intellect, Marx argued, the achieved productivity gains would make physical labour increasingly obsolete at which time knowledge, and not labour, would become the primary basis of value. Importantly, in Marx's vision, this general intellect is seen as a form of commons, accessible to each worker, 'in whose head exists the accumulated knowledge of society' (Marx, 1973, p 712). The upshot of this thinking was that the commons-centred general intellect would be the basis of a new way to organize production, liberate workers, and rob capitalists of their ability to accrue profit, thereby blowing the foundations of capitalism 'sky high' (Marx, 1973, p 706).

While it certainly could be asked how anyone in the mid 19th-century could access, let alone store, all of society's accumulated knowledge in their heads, today, with the dawn of the digital revolution, this type of access is no longer inconceivable. The digital revolution is here understood to entail the transformational ability to digitize, store, transmit and process almost any form of information (knowledge, code, data and audio/visual media) across a publicly accessible network. It is this technology that makes the actual storage and availability of at least the more tangible aspects of society's, and indeed all of humanity's, general intellect a true possibility. Consequently, and following in the footsteps of the Marx of *Grundrisse*, there has been a blossoming of the idea that this digitally enabled freeing up of knowledge and collaboration is leading to critical openings for non-capitalist forms of production and social organization.

Yochai Benkler (2006) was one of the first to realize that something important was unfolding in the way the internet was enabling mostly unpaid, crowdsourced work to create impactful forms of production for the commons, with open-source software and Wikipedia being the prime examples. He called this economic activity 'commons-based peer production', describing it as, 'radically decentralized, collaborative, and non-proprietary; based on sharing resources and outputs among widely distributed, loosely connected individuals who cooperate with each other without relying on either market signals or managerial commands' (Benkler, 2006, p 60). Benkler came to see this new form of production as highly innovative and productive, as well as inherently non-capitalist, despite being in a continuous give-and-take relationship with capitalist interests.

Beyond the initial focus on software and online platforms, scholars began to notice a host of other collaboratively produced, freely offered digital value as evidenced by activities and mobilizations around open research, open education, open-design, and open-source hardware (see O'Neil et al, 2021 for a broad overview). Indeed, Jeremy Rifkin (2015) has argued that one reason for diminishing GDP rates across the world is due to the increase in volunteered, digital forms of production that slip under the radar of traditional market exchange. Yet, while Benkler's final conclusion from his work was the need to find the right regulatory means to ensure a productive co-existence between commons-based and capitalist production, others soon began to offer a different conclusion.

Looking at the same phenomenon, a number of more critically oriented academics and activists have argued that any commons at the root of commons-based peer production is, in its very nature, inherently incompatible with 'capital' in the long run, where capital is understood as the deeply rooted, yet humanly embodied and enacted force within capitalism that seeks to transform everything into a money-making commodity. Consequently, if the commons realm is to truly thrive and meet its full potential, it must find a way to delink from, and eventually overcome, capital. This more explicitly counter-capitalist interpretation has found varying forms of expression, ranging from anarcho-Marxist to more recent, reformist approaches linked to the P2P Foundation (referred to here as the P2P approach). Within this broad spectrum, a common thread has been the emphasis on the potential of the commons and 'commoning' (the process of creating and maintaining the commons) to usurp capital, and ultimately capitalism.

This book builds on these approaches while also addressing their current shortcomings by providing a more holistic analysis of the many technological, economic, and political shifts that would necessarily be involved in a commons-centred trajectory out of capitalism. Hence, the starting point for this endeavour is to home in on the four most fundamental and difficult to crack obstacles that stand in the way of such a commons-based transition. These are:

1. capital's cooptation and subsequent prevention of a fully freed, digitally empowered general intellect;
2. capital's continued control and exploitation of the material basis of the economy;
3. the difficulty of establishing commons-based social relations and forms of production given that value is monopolized by markets and money; and
4. the lack of a coherent political framework and mobilization that could succeed in bringing about positive systemic change.

It is worth reviewing these, and the perceived inability of current commons-based theorizations to deal with them, before summarizing compeerism's own particular positionality.

The hurdles facing a capital to commons trajectory

To begin, the digital revolution's promise of liberating a turbocharged, commons-based general intellect must be acknowledged as far from inevitable. In fact, while the abundance associated with crowdsourced and freely accessible digital knowledge/code/data poses a potential threat to the mediation of scarcity on which capitalism largely depends, it appears that capital as a whole has effectively adapted to the new technological environment and, indeed, has turned it to its benefit. This coup has been achieved in a variety of ways.

For one, capital has engaged in a fierce battle to keep its own digital productions artificially scarce through intellectual property protections while increasingly making use of the digital commons for free, valuable content and inspiration. Additionally, capital has managed to corral digitized, proprietary and volunteered material through internet platforms that act as rent-seeking gatekeepers. These platforms, furthermore, have become a critical source of data extraction, offering an entirely new realm of highly profitable marketing information. Not least, the decentralization and modularization of work enabled by digital networks, heralded as a way to foster geographically distributed collaboration, has been tapped by capital to acquire a pliable and easily exploitable pool of labour, as is well documented in the so-called gig economy (Woodcock, 2021).

Looking to the future, capital is already engaged in shaping and subverting the next wave of digital technologies to open further profit frontiers. This is most clearly seen in the embrace of encrypted ledger technologies, such as blockchain, which enable secure and theoretically infallible digitally logged records of ownership and transactions. Blockchain can hence be used to digitally capture and monetize activities and productions that were previously outside the reach of commodification (Swan, 2015). One example is the proliferation of non-fungible tokens, or NFTs, which allow for the secure marketization of a broad range of digital media by making these into artificially scarce 'property' managed on the blockchain. Thus, in short, while the digital revolution may have changed the way capitalism works, it has not made it weaker – if anything, the opposite appears to be true.

The second major obstruction to a digitally empowered usurpation of capitalism pertains to the fact that the underlying materiality of the economy is still primarily in private, profit-seeking hands. Hence, even if a liberated general intellect mediated through the digital commons is accepted as a possible challenge to capital in some areas, it is fair to doubt that this would be enough to precipitate the demise of the entire capitalist 'mode of production', that is, the overarching organization of our labour and resources (Marx and Engels, 1965). This is because the assumption of potential abundance linked to digital value, which is the cornerstone of the argument that commons-based peer production maintains an advantage over capital, does not apply to the material realm, which is characterized by clear physical limitations and, indeed, scarcity.

In the absence of a commons-oriented takeover of material assets and resources, therefore, these will go on being employed in the pursuit of extractive and exploitative profits. In the digital economy, this means capital will resume leveraging its ownership of the undergirding material infrastructure to control and limit access to what could theoretically be infinitely reproducible information/knowledge. Capital will also retain control over the physical resources and added value entailed in the unending amount of material things we want and need, from food and clothing to all the electronic devices that enable and harness the internet's value. Not least, due to this control, capitalist actors and their interests will continue to define humanity's currently dysfunctional relationship to the environment. The overarching question when faced with these realities, then, is how commons-based rationales and values could break through and become dominant not only within the digital realm, but also in areas such as infrastructure, manufacturing, and resource/environmental management.

This brings us to the third foundational challenge, which gets to the very heart of why both the digital and material commons struggle to assert themselves, namely, capitalism's ability to reduce almost everything of value to a market-based, money-denominated good or service. With money here becoming a stand-in for value, it also becomes the de facto means for accessing almost anything tangible that is worth having. As such, as long as access to the goods and services required for living are denominated in tokens that can generally only be acquired through work, people will continue to depend on remunerated (paid) employment to live. Indeed, this is how labour is so easily coopted and exploited by capital, and, subsequently, disallowed from significantly contributing to the commons. For instance, in terms of the promise of freeing digital abundance (the general intellect), we are reminded of Apple co-founder Steve Wozniak's well-known statement at the first Hacker Conference of 1984, where he opined that 'information should be free but your time should not' (Brand, 1985, p 49). In other words, digital producers also want to be paid (and software companies want to make profits).

Faced with the underlying reality of the monopolization of market-centred value, a natural conclusion could be that actors seeking to expand the commons and commons-forms of governance have no choice but to engage markets in order to fund the labour and resources needed for their activities. This approach, however, comes with a host of additional difficulties and conundrums, such as dealing with the apparent contradiction involved in striving to provide something as a commons-based good that is, at the same time, intended to generate revenue. Additionally, the commons-oriented entrepreneur must compete within a price-oriented marketplace that can clash with their adopted principles of production, such as sharing innovations, investing in the community, and worker-empowerment. Some even argue that engaging in commodity exchange and money leads to an inevitable condition in which the worth of resources and labour can only be understood through the lens of markets, hence making a path out of capitalist rationales and actions impossible (Pitts, 2018a).

Lastly, turning to the final major obstacle facing a capital-to-commons trajectory, there is the overarching question of what political action would be required for the needed shift in social relations to become dominant, and if successful whether the subsequent governance regimes would be preferable to what is being replaced. Regarding this latter issue, for instance, critics like to point out the haphazard and sometimes autocratic managerial cultures evident in the production of the digital commons (Pentzold, 2021). Additionally, and focusing on commons-based peer production in particular, some scholars have pointed to the lack of intentional, bureaucratic governance structures in these endeavours, making them unqualified for handling complex, long-term and inherently political projects involving multiple external stakeholders (Kreiss et al, 2010). In other words, it is one thing to crowdsource an encyclopedia for the commons, but it is a very different thing, for example, to organize universal access to the internet.

Even if an effective and just commons-centred form of governance can be achieved at scale and across economic sectors, however, we are still left with the question of how to get there. In other words, how would a mass, commons-based transition out of capitalism unfold politically, and, more to the point, what role would the state, as a bulwark of the current mode of production, play in such a process? The question of a counter-capitalist movement's relation to the state finds multiple, divergent answers by proponents of a commons-centred systemic transition, ranging on a spectrum from calls to ignore, engage, and capture the state. Neither of these, however, has proven to be broadly convincing for the politically left-leaning populace as a whole.

Anarchist inspired visions of a bottom-up replacement of the existing order through concerted, locally-driven prefigurative actions that circumvent the state appear overly idealistic, while a revolutionary, physical capture of the levers of power is largely dismissed as anachronistic, violent, and ultimately doomed to failure. Yet, engaging the state to effect systematic change from within is also met with scepticism due to the state's deeply ingrained and institutionalized marriage to capital. Any chance to significantly break this bond, if possible at all, would require a socio-political upheaval within society, giving rise to a well-organized social movement with the means and patience to systematically claw away at capital's power over the economic, political, as well as cultural realms of society. The problem, however, at least from the view of sceptics, is that there is little evidence of such a political movement, let alone one that is unified around the promise of the commons.

Compeerism as a path from capital to commons

Despite the many challenges just identified, which are the undergirding buttresses of capitalist realism, this book aims to show that a systemic shift from capital to the commons is, nonetheless, still achievable. The starting point of such a proposal, broadly in line with the reformist P2P approach linked to Michel Bauwens and other academics associated with the P2P Foundation, holds on to the idea that a technologically enhanced commons sphere could be leveraged to counter and eventually overcome capital's dominance in the political economy (Bauwens et al, 2019). We will return to the specific case made for this position shortly, when we summarize the broad argument made in the upcoming chapters. First, however, we must introduce the term 'compeerism', which is used as a guiding concept throughout the book.

We can begin by first noting that the terminology of 'commons-based peer production' (or just 'peer production'), still widely embraced by P2P theorists, is inadequate in capturing the proposal actually being offered. The main issue here is that it is unclear whether the concept refers to a supplement to capitalism, as per Benkler, or to an upstart form of production challenging capital, as posited in the P2P approach. Homing in on the second of these meanings, the term 'compeerism' is offered as a related yet still distinct outlook, ultimately consisting of an amalgamation and finessing of existing theorizations of a commons-based transition out of capitalism.

The label of compeerism is apt as it combines the commons and the 'peer to peer' focus into one, while adding a dimension of political intentionality by making the term an 'ism'. Compeerism also encapsulates and puts an emphasis on the commons/community and implies sharing in the word 'peer', reflecting a commitment to counter-capitalist 'commonification', that is, the process of shifting critical assets into the commons realm (Broumas, 2020). Furthermore, the actual word 'compeer' is defined as 'an equal' or 'peer', with the archaic verb meaning 'to be equal to'. This connotation is fitting as it points to the need to enable equitable opportunities to produce, access, govern, and collaboratively use the commons.

Lastly, compeerism, as a word, is succinct and evocative, and hence more likely to inspire a call to action than the rather stale label of 'commons-based peer production', or even worse its commonly used acronym 'CBPP'. Consider, for instance, this adaptation of Hélder Câmara's famous quote: "When we purchase goods for the poor, they call us saints; when we ask why the commons aren't used to eliminate poverty, they call us compeerists!". If we were here to substitute 'compeerists' with 'commons-based peer producers', the quote would clearly lose its force.

Moving forward, the term compeerism explored and advanced in this book denotes two interrelated conceptualizations. On the one hand, it references a broad theoretical framework to make sense of the current and potential future relationship between the state, capital, and the commons. This assessment pays special attention to how capital has been, is being, or could be exited and replaced with commons-oriented forms of production and governance. On the other hand, compeerism also designates a political-economic positionality that embraces specific, non-capitalist values. Indeed, the compeerist proposition is not just about theorizing a technologically enabled reworking of how production is organized, as per Benkler, but rather how a completely new organization of society could come about, and, critically, why such a transition is worth pursuing.

The conception of value and values inherent in compeerism, broadly shared by the counter-capitalist approaches from which it is inspired, goes a long way in illuminating its underlying drive and fundamental clash with capital (De Angelis, 2007; Arvidsson and Peitersen, 2016). Consider, for instance, that capitalism's quintessential character is that it reduces all value in the world to money-mediated exchange-value, that is, what you can get for something in the market. Capitalists claim that deferring all economic decision making to the dictates of exchange-value frees them of the inherently subjective task of deciding what or how goods and services should be produced; the free market knows best. Yet this position belies the many hidden assumptions (and ultimately values) that are, nonetheless, at work here. This includes the deep-seated acceptance of a world characterized by pervasive scarcity and the naturalness of individualized competition to acquire compartmentalized property claims. In rebutting any sense of community ownership or stakeholdership, it is an outlook in which secrecy, possessiveness, and mistrust become intuitively rational, as is the concomitant demand for a counterbalance in the form of a patriarchal state.

On the flip side, in compeerism value is not viewed first and foremost in terms of what price any given good or service can fetch on the market but rather, based on Marx's original exposition of the term 'use-value', on the ability of something to assist in meeting people's basic needs and aspirations (Bauwens, 2005; Birkinbine, 2021). Building on this focus, and in line with Eleonor Ostrom's (2015) Nobel Prize winning work on the effective governance of the commons, emphasis is placed on the shared ownership and management of resources and assets as the most effective approach with which to systemically pursue such valuation. Finally, in the compeerist outlook, the creation and management of commons-based use-value is, ideally, not compelled by the force of markets, but rather propelled by self-motivated and permissionless labour via networked, horizontal coordination.

The compeerist approach to production described here then also tends to foster values of openness, cooperation, and, more broadly, a sense of working and being in common (Pazaitis et al, 2017). Importantly, the commitment to shared ownership and collaborative, democratic production also frequently goes hand in hand with a preference, when feasible, for decentralization and localization over more macro-level, and often hierarchical, forms of organization (Carlsson and Sandström, 2007; Dafermos, 2012; Kostakis et al, 2015). The broader philosophical outlook underlying this geographical proclivity, furthermore, which is explicit in many commons-oriented governance approaches, is a deep-seated scepticism towards dogmatic universal doctrines, let alone expansive institutions empowered to pursue them (Ostrom, 2009; Levy, 2010). As such, community-based self-determinism and pragmatic problem-solving are favoured over universal ideology and state-level micromanagement (Bollier and Helfrich, 2019; Ramos, 2020).

To be clear, the 'compeerist' outlook described here is by no means a fully-fledged, 'new' theory or political subjectivity. Rather, it is a proposition in the making and a call to action that reflects and builds on existing conceptual and practical commons-based work, grounded in a wellspring of historical, current, and latent counter-capitalist sentiments and values. Compeerism thus also signifies a nascent social movement whose seeds and budding expressions can be found all around us. In this sense, many of us can already be considered compeerists; and many more can be seen as embryonic, compeerists-in-waiting. Hence, the compeerist perspective and subjectivity presented in this book is best understood as still evolving and, thus, prototypical, with its potential mature form – if it comes about at all – hinging on an array of complex internal and external factors.

We should, nevertheless, acknowledge from the start that attention in the upcoming chapters will fall primarily on the high-income countries of the so-called global North, recently relabelled by some the 'Minority World' (Alam, 2008). The reason for this geographical focus is that it is in this Minority World, and especially in the cities, that we find the greatest concentration of resources, technology, and general intellect to be commonified, as well as the presence of already existing compeerist-aligned movements. Furthermore, given their affluence and power, a case can be made that it is in Minority World societies where the modelling of entirely new forms of production would be most impactful, with potential rippling effects across the globe. Nevertheless, compeerism is not unaware of the presence and importance of commons-based efforts in the poorer, global South, or 'Majority World', and some of these will also be addressed in subsequent chapters. Indeed, in the long run, achieving a truly global post-capitalist political economy will require the mobilization and synergizing of compeerist efforts the world over.

The forthcoming argument

The chapters following this introduction are an exposition of the compeerist idea and movement outlined thus far. They seek to tap into the strengths and address the weaknesses of existing commons-oriented theorizations, while drawing lessons from the experiences of actual commons-aligned actions and mobilizations. As a whole, the aim is to address, and find possible responses to, the four major hindrances facing a commons-based, post-capitalist trajectory summarized earlier.

In the first part of the book, the digital revolution and the subsequent establishment of a post-Fordist economy is explored in terms of affording new openings for counter-capitalist, commons-based forms of production. Chapter 1 commences by laying out the theoretical foundation on which the rest of the book relies, presenting a capitalism that is turning increasingly to 'engineered scarcity' to ensure profits (Kostakis and Bauwens, 2014). The chapter then turns to the question of possible systemic change. The compeerism framework is here shown to be aligned with, but also distinct from, the nascent P2P approach, with the major difference being compeerism's supplemental incorporation of autonomist Marxists' theorization of capitalism. As such, the prototypical compeerist outlook presented both embraces Hardt and Negri's (2009) call for a bottom-up 'exodus' out of capital, while also recognizing the need to engage 'the market' and 'the state' if capital is ever to be fully overcome. The role of digital technologies is presented here as an important tool that nonetheless only affords certain possibilities; nothing is predetermined.

Chapter 2 then delves into the question of how, given capital's cooptation of the digital revolution, the expansion of commons-based digital value production can nonetheless progress and lay the foundation for a knowledge-based commons sector that could eventually outcompete capital, as per Marx in *Grundrisse*. Non-capitalist forms of digital commons contributions are presented, including from government, non-profits, and cooperatives. The cooperative framework and movement, with its commitment to devolving ownership and management to a set of localized and relevant stakeholders, is shown to be particularly aligned with compeerism, a recurring theme throughout the book. The key takeaway from Chapter 2, however, is the need for commons-based digital value producers to engage in greater solidarity, or 'boundary commoning', in order to significantly boost the expansion of the digital commons (De Angelis, 2017b). Especially important here is the establishment of a peer-property regime that can protect commons-sourced digital value from unwanted exploitation, thus enabling the producers of this value to challenge capital in a market context.

Next, Chapter 3 goes on to study the various options to exit and overcome the organization of the current internet, that is, a transactional cyberspace that has given rise to an increasingly powerful and all-consuming platform capitalism and an emerging 'data colonialism' (Couldry and Mejias, 2019). The chapter considers the promise and challenges involved in 'taking back' the internet via 'platform cooperatives' and a movement to reclaim private and commons-sourced data. This includes efforts to establish a 'self-sovereign id' and the creation of a data commons. Within these efforts the important role of the state, and especially municipalities, comes to the fore.

The next part of the book moves on from the digitally based economy to tackle the challenge of translating compeerism to the material realm. Chapter 4 focuses on the electricity and information technology (IT) infrastructures on which the digital economy depends. Immediate forms of exit such as opting out of the electrical or internet 'macrogrid' are considered, before possible longer-term options for decapitalizing critical infrastructure are explored. Compeerism here seeks alternatives to the top-down, centralized arrangements prevalent in the delivery of IT and electricity services by promoting localized, smaller operators and 'prosumers' (individuals participating in production) that would enable greater community autonomy and control. At the same time, limits to localization are identified, pointing to the need for state engagement to pursue a decapitalization of larger-scaled infrastructural assets. The creation of networked and highly democratized stakeholder cooperatives are presented as the most promising organizational approach to commonifying the trans-local, material basis of our electricity and internet delivery systems.

Chapter 5 continues the consideration of the material economy by looking at the organization of manufacturing. The focus here falls on the 'design global, manufacture local' (DG-ML) model espoused by some P2P theorists as a way to achieve a greater democratization of the means of production (Kostakis et al, 2015). The blossoming of open-source design, open-hardware, and versatile makerspaces and fab labs are taken up first as short-term, localized forms of exit. The analysis then moves on to the challenges and potentials inherent in a larger scaled, integrated network of community oriented, democratized small-scale factories. Possible management arrangements for such commons-oriented facilities are then assessed and compared, ranging from state-run to various cooperative/collaborative forms of organization.

Next, Chapter 6 delves into the foundational basis of any economy, that is, the renewable and non-renewable resource sectors and the underlying natural planetary systems to which they are bound. This chapter therefore deals with the overarching challenge of establishing a more resilient and environmentally sustainable economy within a broader commons-based governance regime. The DG-ML model is here shown to be particularly suited for the needed shift to a truly circular economy. The chapter also focuses on agriculture as a quintessential case of renewable resource management, and a design global, farm local (DG-FL) model is proposed and explored as part of the broader aim of achieving a compeerist approach to feeding the world.

In each of the previous three chapters, the argument is made that greater inter-commons solidarity and commons-friendly state policies are essential if capital's decisive control over the material economy is to be overcome. It is also recognized, assuming the desirability of maintaining advanced and materially prosperous societies, that complete localization is untenable as some upscaling would still be called for in the pursuit of efficiencies and comparative advantages. This would, then, also mean a continuation of some longer distance trade. Finding a compeerist-aligned approach to trans-local interactions thus becomes critical, especially when it comes to the postcolonial, exploitative exchanges that continue to define Minority–Majority World connections. This challenge is taken up explicitly in Chapter 6, with emphasis placed on the need to localize the control and governance of material assets/resources in the Majority World while simultaneously empowering their communities via access to a vibrant, expansive digital commons.

After the first six chapters, it becomes clear that compeerist efforts to boost the commons are fundamentally bogged down by market-based money's monopolization of all value designation, a defining feature of capitalism. This condition calls forth two essential factors required for a compeerist trajectory to go forward. First and foremost, in order to fund themselves, compeerist-aligned actors must adapt to the current, exchange-value centred economic environment without 'selling out'. Yet, a second, more long-term imperative entails challenging and ultimately fully overcoming the current system of valuation altogether, replacing it with one that is more in line with compeerist values. Part III considers both of these efforts.

Chapter 7 begins by making the case that there currently is no real exit for the commons from a certain dependency on money. Consequently, various adaptation strategies by commons-oriented actors are explored, including the pursuit of exit from capital through collaborative consumption, dependency on gifting from the populace and government, and lastly, by engaging markets. The case is then made that the only way to truly challenge capital is via the latter, market-focused strategy. As such, various mechanisms are reviewed that could be adopted to assure corruption in such an approach is avoided. Additionally, two monetary/finance specific efforts are considered that could assist commons-based producers in going toe-to-toe with capital. One centres on finding savings and credit arrangements that could internalize the circulation of money within the commons, and the other deals with the use of alternative cryptocurrencies to help build, manage, and facilitate engagement with the commons-based 'subeconomy'.

Chapter 8, in turn, focuses on the broader compeerist task of fully replacing the current organization of money creation and distribution. The need for such a move is highlighted by the fact that the banks' control over the issuing of debt-based money, conjured out of thin air, has led to the funnelling of investments into exploitative and unsustainable commercial endeavours while governments are left unable to address the increasing dysfunctions precipitated by their economies. By taking up emergent, unorthodox approaches to monetary theory, the argument is made for the state to reclaim its sovereign position as money creator and distributor. Such a shift, especially if matched with a greater commitment to commons-friendly policies, would be a crucial coup for the compeerist project. However, given that states may not be willing to go down such a path, the chapter ends by also considering macroscaled efforts and potentials to use commons-controlled, crypto-based monies as a way to help establish sizable, autonomous, non-capitalist economies.

Lastly, the final part of the book turns to the political mobilization and organization that would be called for to truly achieve a post-capitalist trajectory along compeerist lines. Chapter 9 thus proceeds by making the case that such a political-economic upheaval would depend on the emergence of an intentional, commoner consciousness that could inspire a mass political 'movement of movements'. Yet for such a movement to outcompete other, more destructive discourses and mobilizations that are likely to emerge as capitalism's failings mount, will depend on being able to deliver actual benefits from the commons and commoning. Harnessing a mass mobilization to compeerist ends is thus presented as necessitating both bottom-up forms of exit and targeted 'hit-and-run' demands on the state. This latter focus on the state is based on a long-term commitment to improve the chances of localized, compeerist initiatives to form and coalesce to the point where they can effectively challenge capital.

After having remained squarely focused throughout the book on a presentation of compeerism within the context of the current capitalist mode of production, Chapter 10 concludes by looking at what a fully-fledged compeerist economy, released from the fetters of capital dominance, could look like. Importantly, no universal prescriptions are offered, seeing that a compeerist society can have multiple configurations. Nevertheless, the chapter offers a basic outline of the major issues involved in pursuing a commons-oriented governance of the market, money, and property. Then, to offer a bit more tangibility, the chapter proceeds to lay out just one case of a hypothetical compeerist future. Careful consideration is here given to the interconnected and mutually reinforcing organization of both the economic and political spheres of society.

As the book comes to an end, the reader should be left with a better understanding of the compeerist promise and its challenges. The focus will primarily have been on the techno-economic dimensions of what a commons-based transition out of capitalism would involve, with some attention also given to the political breakthroughs that would be required. As such, the book will have addressed the fundamental question of whether a post-capitalist future is possible that is not only prosperous but also just and sustainable. The answer to this question is, in the end, a conditional but insistent 'yes', if societies can find the needed motivation and method to put the various pieces of the compeerist puzzle together.

PART I

Contemporary Capitalism and the Promise of the Digital Revolution

1

Theorizing Capitalism and its Demise

What would it take for a commons-centred, collaborative form of production to supplant capitalism? That is the central question of this book. In approaching this query, it is necessary to first establish a basic understanding of what capitalism is, how it currently works, and the inherent challenges involved in overcoming it. In doing so we can also get a better sense of the proposed compeerist framework, and how it is reflected in, yet also partially distinct from, a number of existing theoretical offerings.

It makes sense to start by viewing the economy as a mode of production, since this is how capitalism is often framed by those espousing its replacement with a new mode centred on commons-based, collaborative forms of socio-economic organization. A mode of production is here understood as a fully-fledged, values-laden arrangement of a society's productive forces (labour and machines) and productive relations (the organization of property, law, and social interactions) in the pursuit of economic output (Marx and Engels, 1965). It is this arrangement that fundamentally determines the accumulation and distribution of material wealth within a society. The starting point of this mode is the privatization of the means of production, enabling individuals who gain access to these means the ability to use them in the pursuit of personal wealth. Importantly, for Marx, this foundational basis of the capitalist mode of production is also directly linked to the emergence of a host of injustices and conflicts.

To begin, Marx (1992) pointed to how capitalism's origins are rooted in a type of thievery, expressed in the enclosing and privatization of communal lands and assets, leading to the entrenched haves and have-nots on which capitalism depends to establish a working class reliant on wage labour. It is the exploitation of this labour (surplus labour) that then established what Marx (1992; 1993) identified as the foundation of industrial profit (surplus value) and the concomitant amassing of wealth in the hands of the relatively few. Furthermore, as this process of privatization and the establishment of waged labour unfolded, money, which is used to mediate property and labour exchange in an open market, begins to function as a stand-in for all value. In doing so an underlying mindset is created that reduces the social and environmental relations involved in production to the commodities themselves, a phenomenon Marx termed 'commodity fetishism' (1992).

As a consequence of this narrow exchange-value thinking, we become increasingly incapable of valuing those things that are not easily or effectively captured as a commodity, yet that nonetheless are critical to humanity's wellbeing, like ecosystem services, positive inter-human relationships, and good health. It is then also this bracketing out of all that cannot immediately be transformed into exchange-value that has allowed capital to externalize so many of the real costs associated with their production, from polluted natural environments to physically and mentally degraded workers. In other words, producers are not held responsible for these impacts as there is not an immediate, literal price to pay; and costs that do eventually arise, like environmental clean-ups or medical procedures, are pushed onto others. This reality is well captured by the maxim of capital privatizing profits while socializing risks and costs (Chomsky, 2006).

A further effect of commodity fetishism is that workers, who are erased from the perception of a commodity's worth, become alienated from the work they do, which otherwise would be a fundamental aspect of their identity. On the flip side, consumers lose any sense of relation to the people that source the commodities they purchase. It is ultimately a combination of the drive to absorb, exploit, and commoditize, and the subsequent inequality and alienation that follows, that is blamed by critical social scientists for a class-based society rife with a host of dysfunctions such as poverty, depression, addiction, crime, and corruption (Peet, 1975; Swedberg, 2005; Wilkinson and Pickett, 2010).

Beyond the noted negative social consequences, Marx and subsequent Marxists have also pointed to inherent, economic contradictions within the capitalist mode of production that can lead to even more far-reaching destabilizations. Arguably the most fundamental source of these contradictions is the underlying, continuous demand for economic growth. This growth is needed on the macro level to avoid unemployment, tax shortfalls, and wealth shrinkages, yet it is largely driven on the micro level by the pursuit of profitability and reinvestment in an environment of never-ending market competition (Marx, 1992). In the end, however, this competition-fuelled growth imperative threatens capitalism and its societal order with a number of undermining crises, two of which are particularly noteworthy.

First, over time, the unfettered pursuit of profit can lead to supply outpacing demand (underconsumption), where the subsequent overcapacity then expresses itself, paradoxically, in dwindling revenue and the lack of viable investment opportunities. Such a condition has been shown to be especially intractable in modern, industrial economies, which have been faced with long-term stagnation and bouts of economic and social hardship (Brenner, 2006). A related and exacerbating development in this dynamic has been the continuous push for higher productivity, that is, producing more with less labour, expressed as automation. This effort, however, which is aimed at recapturing a competitive edge through lower prices in a difficult market environment, is a short-sighted solution as productivity gains, increasingly rooted in knowledge/information (the general intellect), ultimately give rise to the long-term eroding of what Marx saw to be the underlying source of profit to begin with: the exploitation of 'surplus labour'. In other words, as the innovations entailed in automation are adopted and diffused across the economic spectrum, the eventual outcome is reduced profit for everyone and possible unemployment (and hence more underconsumption) (Marx, 1993).

The second key problem, which is becoming increasingly pronounced, is that the imperative for continuous growth comes with the concomitant need for the expansion of material throughput linked to making ever more stuff. This reality has resulted in the increasing degradation of the planetary ecosystems on which human civilization depends (Schor, 2010). Given that present competition demands trump any thought of a 'distant' future, however, means that little is being done (because 'it can't be done') to circumvent the massive ecological upheavals and subsequent economic – not to mention human – costs that lie just around the corner.

We should, lastly, note that the proneness to crises linked to the growth imperative outlined here has been significantly intensified by the global monetary order that came into shape after the US abandoned the gold standard in 1973, after which the major economies of the world moved to freely floating, fiat currencies. The consequence of a turn to money that is not backed by anything material (like gold), combined with banks that have been allowed to issue credit without significant reserves (fractional reserve banking), has been a nearly exponential growth of the money supply. This credit/debt linked monetary expansion, in turn, can be directly related to a compounding of competition and growth demands. In other words, the continuous release of money that requires more money to be returned predictably leads to the requirement that the future economy be much bigger than the present one (Werner, 2014; Harvey, 2015).

Theorizing the current state of capitalism

It is in light of the difficulty in appeasing the relentless and expanding growth imperative within capitalism, combined with the emergence of a digital revolution that threatens to bust the scarcity conditions that create market value, that we must place capital's most recent profit-seeking innovations and interventions. We can here identify three new, or renewed, interconnected profit extraction strategies: the imposition of engineered scarcity, commons enclosure, and financialization.

In terms of scarcity, controlling material supply, where this is competitively feasible and legal, has long been a capitalist strategy to boost prices, as in the production of oil. Yet, the pursuit of imposed, manufactured scarcity has become most critical in the realm of immaterial, and theoretically infinite, (digital) value, which now comprises the brunt of the post-industrial economy. Consider, for instance, that intangible assets, which include research and development, code, data, and other intellectual property are estimated to make up 90 per cent of the S&P 500's value (Durden, 2020). These assets are intentionally kept scarce, mostly through the use of copyrights and patents, to preserve their profit value for the capitalist owner. In some instances, as with technical know-how, these protections are meant to keep certain competitive advantages secret, while in other cases, as in end-user products (consumer goods), the aim is to extract royalties and rents.

The process of making scarce is also directly related to the strategy of enclosure. Here value is captured from currently non- or under-monetized assets within communities and nature with the intent to privatize and repackage them as something in short supply that needs to be purchased. Since the turn to neoliberalism, which entailed the ratcheting back of the state to allow capital greater control of the economy, this process has taken the form of a renewed 'accumulation by dispossession' (Harvey, 2013). This is often done by disempowering targeted populations, largely through monetary and financial means, at which point capital swoops in to control and privatize critical resources and services. Examples include the continuous expansion of resource extraction into Indigenous lands, the privatization of essential services, and the copyrighting of biological genetic code. Now, digital technologies are being developed to expand this enclosure. For instance, blockchain-enabled smart-contracts, which are executed when if-then conditionalities are met, can be used to commoditize urban resources that were previously considered 'public', such as establishing microcharges for the individual usage of roads, parks, bridges and other urban infrastructure (Garrod, 2016).

Yet, the enclosure of resources goes beyond just the physical realm; it also encompasses social and cultural productions, interactions, and information/knowledge, much of which is being facilitated and captured in digital form. This is essentially the general intellect that exists as commons. Here too capital is continuously on the march to capture and transform anything innovative or useful into profit (Hardt and Negri, 2009). This can include, for instance, copyrighting and patenting work that has been communally produced, or using commons-sourced labour and data on digital platforms to garner advertising revenue (Vercellone et al, 2019). Capital has also begun to incorporate and profit from commons-based forms of organization, such as crowdsourcing innovation and engaging in other peer-production methods (Papadimitropoulos, 2018; Birkinbine, 2021). In this sense, the digital commons serve as an increasingly important area of growth potential, offering a wellspring of value to be harnessed and enclosed in the form of carefully managed commodities.

A final way in which capital has responded to its current predicament of mounting, yet difficult-to-achieve growth demands, has been the expansion of the finance and banking sector, which have evolved far beyond the role of simply greasing the wheels of productive capitalist endeavours. Going back to the work of Magdoff and Sweezy (1987), financialization is seen as the process of using banking/finance to counteract the diminishing rates of profit in production. One obvious opening for capital here pertains to the profitability of interest-bearing credit, the need for which increases as carefully managed scarcity pushes prices higher. Beyond banking, however, another key opening pertains to the widespread adoption of financial instruments, referred to by Marx (1993) as fictitious capital. What Marx meant is that these paper assets, such as stocks, are not productive, they are merely claims on the wealth of future production. In creating such financial instruments, then, opportunities are not only created to raise capital, but an entirely new financial realm of speculation and risk management is brought about with its own significant prospects for accruing profit without actually having to produce anything.

Yet, an important development worth noting here has been that the claim to revenue generating future production, generally associated with fictitious capital, has itself been increasingly replaced by a claim on the ability of specific corporations to simply manage scarcity and manipulate demand to profitable ends (Gorz, 2010). This situation is well captured in the concept of an 'asset-based economy' where power and wealth are not measured in terms of actual productive capabilities, but on the capacity – denoted in financial assets – to garner profit through such extractive, yet ultimately nonproductive strategies (Adkins et al, 2020). Indeed, the growing disconnect between stock-market capitalization and GDP appears to be indicative of this trend (World Bank, 2021).

Clearly, the establishment of such an asset-based economy represents the complete neglect of use-value in the economy. In other words, if the actual production of goods/services is not the path to greatest profit, it will not be pursued, even if these goods and services are needed. The ultimate consequence of this predicament is a massive misallocation of resources and the ossifying of wealth differentials within society (Adkins et al, 2020).

Nonetheless, despite the increasingly abstract and ephemeral qualities that characterize contemporary capitalism, as just laid out, it is important that we do not completely dismiss the role being played by the traditional capitalist exploitation of labour in actual production. Indeed, the continued use of sweatshops in the Majority World and the rise of low-paying service-sector jobs in the Minority World; the related emergence of easily exploitable gig workers; and the enclosure of the general intellect via a highly skilled, white-collar workforce are all a testament to labour's continuing importance, even if this importance is slowly eroding. More specifically, it is essential to acknowledge here that engineering scarcity and subsequently capturing higher prices, rents, fees, interest and royalties are still rooted in actual material things and services. The point being made, therefore, is not that traditional capitalism, and its foundational ability to exploit labour, has ceased to exist, rather it is that this capitalism, which has begun to reach certain internal limits, now depends on a massive superstructure of scarcity, enclosure, and finance to keep profits flowing.

Capitalism as process and lines of flight

Having established a basic outline of how contemporary capitalism works, the next question has to be how it can be challenged and overcome. Communists and anarchists of old would tend to answer this question with the call to 'revolution', even if their ideas of what happens afterwards varied. As the 20th century unfolded, however, insurrectionary tactics were increasingly abandoned. While revolutionary Marxists persist, often in the limited realm of academia, their numbers have significantly dwindled; and on the anarchist side the singular focus on class and the need to rise up in revolt has given way to more countercultural areas of attention and the aim to 'prefigure' systemic change from within (Cornell, 2016).

The increasing unpopularity of revolutionary demands to 'smash the system' coincides with a theoretical shift in ontological thinking (the basic assumptions of what reality is) rooted in the post-structural dismissal of deterministic, inflexible frameworks. In this view the Marxist reification of monolithic structures such as 'capitalism' or 'the state' are viewed as fundamentally wrongheaded. It is not possible to topple capitalism by capturing the state, because 'capitalism' is not a 'thing' that can simply be undone, nor is the state. These so-called 'systems' are better understood as complex phenomena composed of numerous interacting parts, both physical and mental, with which we, as subjects, are intimately intertwined.

Directly related to this assessment, critical scholars and activists have also challenged classical Marxist thinking for being inherently disempowering (Gibson-Graham, 2010). In other words, when capitalism is conceived as a colossal, reified thing with a more or less determined trajectory, it leaves people with little sense of agency; revolution becomes a waiting game for the all-encompassing system to reach an apex of inevitable internal crisis. While such crises are often presented by Marxists as imminent in economic downturns, when capital then nonetheless regains its footing, these same prophets succumb to dismay and resignation. Consequently, there has been a concerted turn in recent decades towards approaches and conceptualizations that posit a much more indeterminate and malleable reality, one that leaves more room for political action here and now.

One way to capture this flexibility is through the concepts of 'assemblage' and 'apparatus' (Foucault, 1980; Deleuze and Guattari, 1987; Agamben, 2009; Legg, 2011). While the terms have been used in disparate ways, an assemblage/apparatus can here be understood as the never fully stable arrangement and articulation of multiple animate and inanimate forces and potentials that interact to achieve specific outcomes. Importantly, this conceptualization of reality is one of flux, determined by the relations between things rather than by their essences. Yet, at the same time, assemblages/apparatuses still manage to bring about a distinct order, as, in the words of Agamben (2009, p 14) they maintain 'the capacity to capture, orient, determine, intercept, model, control or secure the gestures, behaviours, opinions, or discourses of living beings'.

In terms of conceptualizing capitalism, a productive use of assemblage/apparatus can be found in the work of Deleuze and Guattari (1987) who present the various defining features of our socio-economic condition as being continuously de- and reconstructed to ensure the overarching logic of capital accumulation. Especially instructive is their rethinking of Marx's (1993) trinity formula as the 'three-headed apparatus of capture' (three apparatuses in one), understood as the intertwined forces that manage to continuously reinvent the governance of land (property), labour, and money in the service of profit. Thus, in its original iteration commons land and serf labour were set free from their positionalities within the feudal mode of production, only to be recaptured and reconstructed through the mechanisms of rent and wages to become the privately owned factory and the industrial worker. Underlying all of this, however, is money, which enables the commodification of property and labour in the first place. Money is brought under control via the assemblage/apparatus behind the execution of taxation, where the obligatory payment of a specific tender grounds this money's worth and gives it the power to become the de facto measure of exchange-value in the market more broadly.

Hence, in Deleuze and Guattari's approach, Marx's conceptualization of a capitalist mode of production, and more particularly the submission to an exchange-value framework, as captured in the idea of commodity fetishism, is still present, yet the underlying forces creating this reality are now seen as being part of a more indeterminate process of deconstruction, recapture, and reconstruction. This 'process' of capitalism, furthermore, is continuous, as we can see, for example, with the industrial worker (labour) and the factory (land) being de- and then reconstructed as the gig worker and the server farm. Or, for that matter, how money was de- and reconstructed to become an unbacked fiat currency that could expand exponentially in the pursuit of growth via fractional reserve banking.

Returning, then, to the question of achieving systemic change, we can make use of two further concepts from Deleuze and Guattari, namely 'lines of articulation' and 'lines of flight'. Lines of articulation can be understood as the way assemblages/apparatuses channel inherent potentials to maintain the functioning of a given organizational stability. Lines of flight, in turn, have been described as 'bolts of pent-up energy that break through the cracks in a system of control … they reveal the open spaces beyond the limits of what exists' (Rayner, 2013, np). Deleuze and Guattari suggest that lines of flight may combine with others to ultimately bring about the destabilization of an entire 'system', referring to this as 'a whole generalized conjunction that overspills and over-turns the preceding apparatuses' (Deleuze and Guattari, 1987, p 452). On a large enough scale, then, such a generalized conjunction could, theoretically, spell the end of the capitalist mode of production, at least as it is currently conceived.

Arguably, the most critical lines of articulation within capitalism are rooted in the apparatus of capture, where the commodification of everything, including labour, pulls subjectivities into the overarching logic of exchange-value calculations and hence capital accumulation. Lines of flight, in turn, can have various expressions, including haphazard ones, but from the perspective of actively pursuing systemic change, the most relevant lines of flight take the form of prefigurative acts of resistance – where prefiguration is defined as 'those forms of social relations, decision-making, culture, and human experience that are the ultimate goal' (Boggs, 1977, p 100). In essence, prefiguration is an action of being the change you want to see, which, by being embodied and performed, creates a line of flight that makes a different world suddenly seem possible.

Significantly, however, Deleuze and Guattari see these rebellious lines of flight, including intentional forms of prefigurative resistance, as remaining mostly imperceptible from within the status quo. In other words, those controlling and embracing the currently dominant operating procedures and discourses are blind to these prefigurations, either because they are intentionally hidden from view, or because their logic makes no sense from the given set of assumptions within the current assemblages/apparatuses at work. For those familiar with Star Trek, this is akin to the Borg, a hive collective of cybernetic beings who do not acknowledge outsiders beaming onto their spaceship until they are explicitly identified as posing a danger. In the case at hand, lines of flight can be seen expressed in the various forms of commons-based peer production, and commoning more generally. Until quite recently, these lines of flight have largely gone unnoticed, operating in the shadows, overlooked or seen as hardly noteworthy.

Yet, to bring about change will eventually require coming into the light. Indeed, the point of the prefigurative is not, as Thomas Nail (2015, p 99) helpfully explains, 'to relish the theory of an impossible and invisible revolution, but rather to "bring the imperceptible to perception" by changing the dominant conditions for visibility'. In this sense, lines of flight are like rockets seeking to break free from the fetters of gravity; they are continuously pulled on until they fall back to the ground, unless they have the power to break out of the conditions of visibility that define our world. What this means in terms of achieving a commons-based mode of production is the need to overcome the nearly inescapable apparatus of capture, which comprises the dominant conditions for visibility that render transgressive lines of counter-capitalist possibilities, like the commons, not only invisible, but largely dysfunctional, especially at larger scales.

But what would a generalized conjunction of lines of flight that could topple the apparatus of capture actually look like? Is it even possible? The answer to these decisive questions hinges on how the alternative economic activities and relations being posited (the lines of flight) are understood in relation to the currently dominant capitalist mode of production. When considering the commons and commoning as this alternative, we find a number of conflicting approaches.

Theorizing capital–commons relations and systemic change

Starting with Ostrom's innovative and empirically documented work, the commons realm is presented as more than a free, unmanaged resource condemned to unsustainable exploitation (Ostrom, 2015). Instead, with the administration of sound, place-specific governance, the commons can, and often do, serve as a shared good that can be made sustainably and equitably accessible to the whole stakeholder community. Given such governance structures, Ostrom presents the commons as a valuable economic realm that can productively co-exist with capital. It is a position that Yochai Benkler (2006b) later adopts in developing the concept of commons-based peer production within the digital realm.

For proponents of a commons-based trajectory out of capitalism, however, this liberal position is rejected (see, for instance, Caffentzis and Federici, 2014). The view here, as noted in the introduction, is that the commons, and the various lines of flight that they launch, will remain subservient to capital until the overarching assemblages/apparatuses at the heart of capitalism are overcome, that is, when the conditions of visibility have been fundamentally altered. Yet, differences persist as to how exactly this can be achieved. We can identify four broadly distinct approaches here, each with their own strengths and weaknesses.

First, in the autonomist Marxist view, the commons, and the 'general intellect' specifically, are seen as an increasingly critical source for new commodification and subsequent profit for capital. It is precisely for this reason that the commons are considered the natural site from where capital must be challenged (Hardt and Negri, 2005; 2009; Ruivenkamp and Hilton, 2017). Hardt and Negri see such a commons-based campaign to oust capital as comprising an economic and social exodus, which they describe as 'a process of subtraction from the relationship with capital' (2009, p 152). The vision here is one of a mass movement of people, 'the multitude', successfully navigating the wholesale exit from capital in favour of commons-based socio-economic relations. Such an exodus would amount to the 'whole generalized conjunction' identified by Deleuze and Guattari as being necessary to bring about a new order. Yet the question still begged in this is whether such an exodus would proceed as an event or a process, that is, as revolution or evolution.

This question is one of the autonomists' biggest conundrums. On the one hand, there is still a deeply rooted Marxist understanding of capitalism as an all-encompassing system, meaning any compromise or give-and-take that the commons may negotiate with capital is generally considered 'selling out' to, and ultimately strengthening, capitalist rationales. Within such an outlook, the event scenario appears to be the only option out. Indeed, this is the position taken in the early works of Hardt and Negri (2001; 2005), arguably the most influential of the autonomists. Thus, as in classical Marxism, the internal contradictions within capitalism are seen as eventually leading to a breakdown of its internal logic, at which point the 'proletariat', or in this case the much broader conception of the multitude, will rise up and smash the system in one furious affair.

Yet, on the other hand, there is the realization that such a position leads back to the numerous issues noted earlier with regard to the pursuit of overly rigid, teleological systems that allow for little agency. We should also not forget that history is littered with past revolutions in which the levers of state power were captured, only to see the promises of the rebellion never come to fruition. A convincing explanation for this is that the lines of articulation were never fully overcome, largely because the initiated lines of flight were not adequately developed and combined prior to the taking of power, leaving an inadequate foundation for a new socio-economic order to take effect.

It is perhaps with these arguments in mind that another faction of autonomist-aligned thinkers of the commons have, instead, adopted the idea of systemic change as process, that is, evolution marked by occasional, seismic ruptures (Dyer-Witheford, 2015; De Angelis, 2017b; Holloway, 2019). This is also, incidentally, the direction that Hardt and Negri (2009; 2017) subsequently adopt in their later works. Nonetheless, many of these autonomists, and Hardt and Negri in particular, still struggle with the consequences of their Marxist theorization of capitalism as penetrating practically everything. This position then makes it difficult to see how the multitude, as well as the various commons more generally, can ever break from their relationality to capital (Gibson-Graham, 2010; Southall, 2011). In other words, there is no clear way of thinking through how the commons can ever manage a prolonged, winning contest with capitalism when lines of flight seem destined to always get pulled back down to earth.

The anarchist response to this conundrum, which represents the second main approach to a commons-based transition, is simply to reject the notion that there cannot be a vibrant 'outside' to capitalism. Indeed, these anarchists claim that this outside, in the form of non-capitalist behaviours and actions, such as in the organization of mutual aid, is evident all around us (Springer, 2016; White and Williams, 2016; Kropotkin, 2022). This outlook, then, relies heavily on prefiguration as a political strategy in which this external space, as embodied in the commons, can be fostered and used to present and inspire an alternative to capitalist and authoritarian assemblages/apparatuses (van de Sande, 2015). These prefigurative challenges to the status quo, furthermore, are generally conceived as intensely and deliberately local, where they must continuously strive to stay under the radar of coercive power.

The reason for this local focus is that any engagements with more macro-level structures of authority, such as law or government, are understood to legitimize and strengthen these oppressive arrangements, and in doing so, they diminish the force of the prefigurative (Gerhardt, 2019). As such, however, this anarchist approach again appears to be overwhelmed by the dominant 'conditions of visibility', making it difficult to explain how the various localized prefigurations could ever establish sufficient momentum to create the 'whole generalized conjunction' needed for systemic change – for instance in the form of a macro-level exodus out of the apparatus of capture. Hence, while this apparatus may be identified and resisted at the localized level by 'squatting land, hacking power lines, engaging in barter, etc.', such actions, while important, generally remain limited to 'targeting only the local expressions' of the apparatus of capture, not the apparatus itself (Gerhardt, 2019, p 6).

A third option, which breaks with both the autonomist and anarchist frameworks, is to embrace the state as an instrumental actor in liberating and then harnessing the commons to bring about a seismic shift out of capitalism. This mostly reformist approach is well captured in the work of Paul Mason (2016), who views the potential of a scarcity-busting freed general intellect primarily through the lens of state-based leadership and command. Mason's focus therefore quickly turns to the need for large government-driven programmes involving the breaking up of monopolies and targeted nationalizations, hi-tech macroeconomic planning, debt management, and a top-down effort to tackle climate change. In taking this position, however, the bottom-up impetus of commons-based peer production, where 'the state' is generally viewed with a good deal of scepticism, is mostly abandoned. Instead, Mason falls back to a politics and economics that are largely in line with standard democratic-socialist discourses.

While this direction is probably the most likely to be adopted by leftist politicians and parties today, it also has its share of serious pitfalls. Autonomist and anarchist scholars of the commons, for instance, adamantly argue that the state is hopelessly intertwined with the dictates of capital, forming a capital-state nexus that renders any vision of a state-led evolution out of capital an unrealistic fantasy. A further and more immediate challenge, however, especially considering its more mainstream, change-from-within outlook, is that socialist discourses are largely failing to garner the electoral support they would need to pursue the envisioned unleashing of the commons. This is likely the result of these discourses having increasingly lost touch with the changes taking place in capitalism and the subsequent shift in the workforce and labour's self-perception. The failure of socialist parties, organizations, and unions to prevent the eroding of the middle class amidst widespread deindustrialization undoubtedly has also played a role. In this sense a general scepticism has set in towards the idea of 'the state' as a representative of the people's will, reflecting to some extent the anarchist/autonomist position noted earlier.

Within this context, then, it should not be surprising that the increasingly dominant post baby-boom generation finds itself largely unconvinced by suggestions of shifting economic control from capital to the state, that is, exchanging one distant, hierarchically organized form of decision making with another. In Europe this generational attitude is reflected in the plummeting of traditional party membership and, more particularly, the broad implosion of the socialist left, where, with a few exceptions, neither moderate nor more radical leftist parties can gain much electoral traction (van Haute, 2011; Taylor, 2018). In the US, in turn, while younger adults appear to be warming somewhat to the term 'socialism' (the term is generally not defined in polls), there is, at the same time, a deep lack of confidence in government in general (Jones and Saad, 2019; Pew, 2021). Given these trends and attitudes, rooted in the reality of a capital-state nexus that takes more than an election to overcome, it is difficult to see how a post-capitalist political-economy could effectively spawn from a big-government, socialist platform.

This brings us, lastly, to the fourth option, what we have come to call the P2P approach, and which is also the most closely aligned with the compeerist proposal presented in this book. Here, the digital revolution is seen to be creating the conditions for more collaborative and shared forms of production – undergirded by a massive repository of abundant, commons-based digital value – that can pave the way to a bottom-up driven, post-capitalist future. It is, in essence, a radicalization of the commons-based peer production idea offered by Benkler, yet where, contrary to many

Marxists, the conflictual capital–commons relationship is not understood to be a de facto losing game for the commons. In this way, Hardt and Negri's multitude is replaced by a more concrete and identifiable collection of expanding, increasingly decentralized communities pursuing resilience through collaborative peer production, shared governance, and open access resources and services (Kostakis and Bauwens, 2014).

It is in these communities, and the work spearheaded by those within (referred to as commoners), where the true potential for capital exodus is thought to lie. Importantly, while immediate and clandestine exits and hacks can be a part of the envisioned commons transition, its ultimate success is understood to hinge on the ability of commons-centred activities to successfully contend with and engage markets while establishing non-capital-oriented alternatives. The final goal of such a market-engagement strategy is to replace capitalist relations with commons-based ones, hence commencing a fundamental shift in ownership and control (or 'transvestment') of wealth and assets from capital to the commons (Kleiner, 2016; Bauwens and Niaros, 2017; Bauwens and Pantazis, 2018).

We should note, however, that this proposal of a commons-based economic sector giving capital a run for its money is exactly the kind of feat Rosa Luxemburg (2011) cast doubt on, over one hundred years ago, when she disparaged, in particular, the counter-capitalist potential of cooperatives. Following Luxemburg, cooperatives' refusal to exploit labour and achieve maximum efficiencies in production leads to inevitable limits to expansion; and with limited reach the cooperative economy does not possess the productive capacity to actually decouple from, let alone capture, capitalist markets. In this view, the evolutionary vision of a transvestment of resources from capital to the commons is an impossibility, given the way exchange-value mediating markets work.

P2P theorists would undoubtedly push back here by arguing that market viability for commons-based entrepreneurial actors is, counter to Luxemburg's outdated position, enabled today by the massive potential of abundance and innovation inherent in the digital revolution. More specifically, the ability to fully harness this potential depends precisely on employing non-capitalist modes of operation, including sharing and collaboration. Still, while this perspective offers a refreshingly hopeful and pragmatic angle to pursuing a commons-based world beyond capitalism, underlying questions remain as to whether this optimism can be justified. Simply pointing to the ability to tap into digital abundance and crowdsourced innovation is not sufficient. A more coherent answer is still needed for how to contend with capital's market advantages and its documented power to enclose and coopt the commons, especially in the digital realm. We address these apparent shortcomings in the P2P outlook in more detail next, as part of the presentation of compeerism's own positionality.

The compeerist (r)evolution

As noted in the introduction, compeerism comprises a prototypical work in progress that amalgamates and moulds existing scholarly work and disparate commoning efforts in an attempt to create a more holistic, grounded, and hopefully compelling framework. Particularly influential, and serving as compeerism's starting point, is the P2P approach just outlined. Both are interested in the role that a digitally empowered general intellect, as a harbinger of new forms of production and social relations, could play in a shift to a new mode of production; and both advocate for the leveraging of the commons to engage with markets, and ultimately also the state, to truly challenge capital. Yet there are also a number of important departures and enhancements that make the compeerist approach distinct.

For one, beyond the choice of terminology (compeerism over commons-based peer production or just peer production), compeerism, as a theorization and label, intentionally cross-fertilizes commons-oriented efforts and imperatives across the entire economy, including in the digital, material, and financial/monetary realms. While P2P analyses have moved far beyond their original focus on digitally facilitated, collaborative production – another reason why the digitally focused 'peer production' terminology is problematic – these various forays, usually in the form of limited reports sponsored by the P2P Foundation, have not yet been assembled and brought into relation with each other to form a coherent whole. For the other, however, and more substantively, P2P and compeerism maintain different theoretical groundings, which then come to bear on their respective conceptualizations of the capital–commons relationship.

A recurring critique of the P2P literature has been that it does not engage Marxist/anarchist/socialist theory enough, leading to a relatively shallow conceptualization of capitalism and, ultimately, an unpersuasive vision for how a commons transition can be achieved (Lund, 2017; Kioupkiolis, 2020c). At least one relevant factor for this shortcoming can arguably be traced to its ontological foundation, presented in the self-proclaimed manifesto of the P2P approach (Bauwens et al, 2019). It is, in the end, a philosophical and rather grandiose view of the world based on Kojin Karatani's work on historically evolving exchange systems, hence bestowing a structural, quasi-teleological undertone to P2P's envisioned post-capitalist trajectory. Thus, even with the manifesto's claims that a commons transition hinges on a people-driven mobilization, it still is conceived as part of a broader 'historical succession of systems' and hence a transition that is already initiated and locked into a specific, even if not preordained, trajectory (Bauwens and Gerhardt, 2019, np).

In contrast, the compeerist outlook, arguably shared by most people engaged in commoning and commons expansion, considers progressive change as a much more indeterminate process contingent on the will of the people. More in line with post-structural thinking, 'structures' and 'systems' are here regarded as pliable agglomerations of people, discourses, and materialities (assemblages/apparatuses) that must be worked on through meticulous and intentional action from the ground up in order to give them a new direction, or, in the long term, to fundamentally recast them altogether. In embracing this view, it is worth noting that the use in this book of the terms 'capitalism' or 'capital', as well as the frequent references to 'the state', should be understood primarily as heuristically helpful denotations that assist in making sense of forces and processes that are recognized as being much more complex and fluid in actuality.

This difference in ontological underpinnings between P2P and compeerism, then, also comes to the fore in the distinct ways that the shared themes of markets and technology are conceptualized and approached. Turning to markets first, we can start by pointing to compeerism's alignment with the P2P position that money-mediated markets can and must be engaged, tamed, and ultimately made subservient to more commons-centred forms of economic interaction. However, rather than grounding this stance in an ontology of historically evolving exchange systems, as P2P does, compeerism seeks to position itself in relation to the established discourses on the political left, where we can find a rich engagement with the challenge of capital's intractable dominance.

Hence, the first critical move for compeerism in staking out its position is to explicitly reject the proposition, based on the commodity fetishism concept, that the production of commodities and the use of money forces us to *only* comprehend the world through the lens of exchange-value. Instead, compeerism firmly embraces the idea, well theorized in the 'diverse economies' literature, that subjects and their doing can, in fact, be formed 'against and beyond' the various political and economic assemblages/apparatuses that are dominant at any given time (Holloway, 2010, p 915; see also Gibson-Graham, 2010; Gritzas and Kavoulakos, 2016). In other words, as we will see in upcoming chapters, compeerism touts the possibility and actual enactments of economic modes of operation that are based on values distinct from those of capital. On a more systemic level, this means that market exchange mechanisms can also be made to function in productive ways within non-capitalist, or 'barely capitalist' environments, hence aligning compeerism with aspects of mutualist and market socialist theory, especially where the cooperative ownership of the means of production are espoused.

At the same time, compeerism also acknowledges that overcoming the current organization of the market is a monumental challenge. This is because it remains firmly entwined in the three-headed apparatus of capture, where it is employed to facilitate the monopolization of valuation by exchange-value. Indeed it is largely for ignoring the underlying 'heads' of property, labour, and money that the P2P approach is critiqued, because it then misses the inherent forces that continuously work to coopt and absorb the commons and commoning.

To avoid such criticism, compeerism proceeds from the foundational understanding that current markets are dominated by capital, which is continuously on the prowl to enclose and/or disallow the commons. Along the same lines, Luxemburg's argument that less efficient, values-oriented forms of production are inherently disadvantaged in a capitalist economy is made the starting point for any consideration of commons-centred market engagement. In doing so, compeerism seeks to offer more specific, and hopefully more helpful, insights into what a commons-based transition out of capitalism would require.

This more critically reflective approach to the capital–commons dynamic also comes into clear focus when considering the role of technology in progressive change. P2P scholarship, for instance, is rooted in the underlying conviction that digital technology maintains positive transformational power. Yet, to counter any sense of techno-determinism, and again referring specifically to the P2P manifesto, an intentional effort is made to present the digital revolution as just one component of the currently emerging, commons-centred exchange system that is presented as being next in line to succeed capitalism (Bauwens et al, 2019). Still, in being a fundamental part of this historical trajectory, technology remains entwined in its overall teleologically leaning character. It is therefore not surprising that some scholars still see P2P as maintaining at least a 'mild-techno-determinist view' (Kioupkiolis, 2020c, p 74).

In contradistinction, and again in line with its more post-structural outlook, compeerism accepts that technology possesses latent, disruptive forces, but these potentials are understood to be myriad and capable of going in any number of directions. This view is perhaps best captured through the lens of 'abstract hacktivism', where technology is presented as being interlinked with the various assemblages/apparatuses that undergird any particular socio-economic-political reality (von Busch and Palmås, 2006). Importantly, however, and following von Busch and Palmås, this 'reality' is always in flux and open to change, which is where technology can play an important role. Indeed, in their view we are currently in the process of a technology-induced, societal shift in thinking (a de- and reconstruction), switching from an older mechanical paradigm linked to motorized machines to one that is shaped by the 'abstract' mechanism of computers, that is, the digital. Critically, despite having certain potentials that serve as a background agency, the technology involved here is conceived as neither inherently undermining or bolstering when it comes to the dominant assemblages/apparatuses undergirding capitalism more broadly. Instead, it is accepted as contested, as shaping and being shaped.

Within this view, the task of the intentional abstract-hacktivist, and also the aligned compeerist, lies in disallowing capital the ability to fully coopt the new, paradigm-shifting technologies by finding ways of hacking and redirecting these towards non-capitalist ends (Terranova, 2014; Lovink and Rossiter, 2018). From a compeerist perspective, if such interventions, or lines of flight, could be significantly upscaled and cross-synergized, they could provide the impetus for a mass exodus out of capital-controlled markets and relations. Given compeerism's acknowledgement of capitalism's intransigence, however, it is also understood that while the broader shift to digital forms of organization and thinking may provide openings to challenge capital, in the end the success of such challenges is far from certain.

Nonetheless, recognizing the difficult position the commons and commoning are in vis-à-vis capital – whether in the realm of technology, markets or elsewhere – does not lead compeerism to a position of despair or to frustrated calls for the violent overthrow of all societal institutions. Backed by a theoretical foundation that sees indeterminacy – and hence openings for lines of flight – from within dominant assemblages/apparatuses, compeerism still recognizes the possibility for change. In this sense compeerism represents an embodiment of the Proudhonian vision that 'a new society be founded in the heart of the old society' via a *longue-durée* evolutionary transformation (Proudhon, 2011, p 321). For such an evolution to transpire, however, depends on the right, deliberate impetus, which itself is rooted in commoning and commoner consciousness. In other words, it will require effort and, indeed, a concerted mobilization to be able to go against the force of the prevailing headwinds.

It is this inherent pragmatism that then also dictates compeerism's broad tactical outlook, which is where alignment can again be found with P2P thinking. More precisely, compeerism accepts the importance of prefiguration, as emphasized by anarchists, yet then also insists on the need to cohere these prefigurations into more inter-commons forms of meso-level solidarity. Furthermore, compeerism then calls for this united, commons-based political force to pursue state-based concessions and interventions. The state, however, is not, as per Mason (2016), posited as the source and eventual centre point of a commons transition and society. In the short to medium term, any engagement with the 'oppressive arrangements' of the current capital-state nexus, for instance via the push for classic social-democratic market interventions, must be understood as means to a more far-reaching, commons-oriented economic reorganization.

While such a reorganization may contain 'public' (state-run) components, compeerism here is nonetheless most in line with the vein of market socialism that espouses direct worker/member control and/or ownership of the means of production. This position, increasingly also emphasized in P2P scholarship, is ultimately grounded in an embrace of commons-centred forms of governance – where operational management is characterized by decentralized, bottom-up and inclusive decision making – as the most effective way to ensure production is not beholden only to the pursuit of exchange-value. In this light, it then also follows that the longer term, compeerist objective is to break the undemocratic capital-state nexus altogether. Yet the point here is not to create a hierarchically ordered socialist state that takes a top-down lead to restructuring the economy, but rather to recast 'the state' into what P2P scholars refer to as a 'partner state', made subservient to the decentralized/localized needs of the commons and commoners (Bauwens et al, 2019).

In sum, then, the compeerist proposal presented here can be understood as an application of the P2P approach to a more anarcho-Marxist foundational outlook, with the aim to help theorize more thoroughly the promise and challenges inherent in a commons transition to a world beyond capitalism. Still, it is also important to recognize that what is offered in the following chapters is only an incomplete part of what must become an even more expansive project/movement. More specifically, the predominately techno-economic focus offered here would greatly benefit from supplementary efforts that addressed in more detail how to contend with capitalism's sociocultural hegemony, meaning that capital and its underlying assumptions and rationales are still deeply and unreflectively embraced and enacted by the populace at large (Gramsci, 2011; Kioupkiolis, 2021). For now, however, a first important step is to provide a convincing presentation of the basic political-economic interventions and mechanisms that could, if effectively and broadly pursued and implemented, enable a commons-based economy to emerge, grow, and ultimately outcompete capital.

2

The Digital Commons' Elusive Potential

In basic terms, compeerism aims to harness the digital revolution to unleash the general intellect, hence triggering a gradual shift from a mode of production aimed at engineering scarcity to one committed to serving the most pressing needs and wants of humanity. Yet, capital's continuing efforts to privatize knowledge/information via intellectual property protections and the pilfering and coopting of the digital commons has thus far stymied any designs on blowing the foundations of capitalism 'sky high', as per the early Marx. This chapter, therefore, explores the proposition that a compeerist-aligned movement can still succeed in creating a digital commons that could serve as a repository and incubator of a capital-challenging, liberated general intellect. Before delving into such potential, and the various barriers that need to be overcome to realize it, we must review in more detail the current state of commons-based digital value production and its relation to capital.

The digital commons and copyleft

In conceptualizing the digital commons, it is important to distinguish between labour-derived, curated content, on the one hand, and raw, collected data, on the other. Digitized data, which is still unprocessed, is a different form of information that we will deal with in the next chapter. For now, we can stay focused on labour-derived, intentionally assembled digital value, which is entangled in a number of other pivotal issues that require our attention, including property and remuneration for work. We begin by considering code and other creative/cognitive media, which gave rise to the first commons-oriented property protections, before turning to the challenges and promise entailed in commons-based research and applied knowledge (design).

Code and software offered the first glimpse of an organized demand for the creation and protection of a digital commons. Richard Stallman, a pioneer of the hacker movement, developed the idea of the 'four freedoms' of code, namely that code should be open and free to use, study, manipulate, and distribute (GNU, 2021). These freedoms then became the rallying call for the free open-source software (FOSS) movement. Since its inception, there have been many widely cited cases of successful FOSS projects in which a community of 'geeks' comes together to collaboratively develop a particular code which not only is free and open-source but is of equal or superior quality to any proprietary options (Benkler, 2006).

The Linux kernel operating system and various specialized distributions of this code, such as Debian, is a favourite example of successful commons-based peer production as it has been adopted on a massive scale in computers of all sizes. Similarly, the Apache server program, Python programming language, and WordPress content management are all open-source code productions that have become critical components to the organization and execution of the internet. On the end-user (consumer) side, while much more limited, there are also instances of free, collaboratively produced software options, especially for the most popular paid-for software, such as Microsoft's Office (LibreOffice), Intuit's QuickBooks (GnuCash), and Adobe's Photoshop (GIMP). LibreOffice, for instance, which offers all the main applications included in the Microsoft Office suite has over 200 million users (Watkins, 2018).

The burgeoning of this quality, commons-oriented code is often attributed to the existence of a strong hacker community and culture that highly prizes meritocratically based reputation (Benkler et al, 2015). Contributors are frequently computer programmers with extra time on their hands, motivated by a sense of camaraderie and the desire to have their skills recognized and appreciated. To the extent that these projects achieve significant collaborative buy-in, furthermore, they benefit from Linus's law (named after Linux's founder), which states that 'given enough eyeballs, all bugs are shallow'. In other words, crowdsourced innovations and improvements are here deemed to be superior to individual or small group efforts. Yet, arguably the most critical component of FOSS's success has been the establishment of an alternative property regime geared to protect and foster the commons-sourced value being produced.

This development can be traced back, once again, to Richard Stallman, who had an epiphany in 1980 when he was unable to access the software to a newly installed printer he wanted to modify. The fact that he had helped design the code from which he was now barred did not sit well, leading him to the realization that the commons needed protection from capital's tendency to enclose and make scarce. The outcome of this experience was the development of the GNU General Public License (GPL), designed specifically to encourage fully open-source, free software. The key tenet of GPL is that the code being produced may be seen, used, altered, and distributed by anyone as long as it is also filed under the same licensing. As such, GPL was the first model for establishing a legally binding 'copyleft' alternative to copyright.

As it turns out, however, protecting the commons is not synonymous with excluding capital. In fact, a key contributing factor for why GPL licensed software has been so successful is that it has managed to garner significant contributions from capital. This is not surprising as many of the corporate tech giants are reaping the benefits of commons-derived, open-source code. More specifically, given that there is no restriction on using GPL licensed code within what is otherwise a commercial product, it makes this code a valuable, yet mostly free resource. These companies thus happily support this code within the copyleft parameters given. IBM, for instance, has long supported the development of the Linux kernel, committing over US$2 billion in labour power to the project (Benkler et al, 2015). Today, more and more firms are joining the bandwagon, with Microsoft, the long-time curmudgeon in the open-source software world, being the latest to accept the value of FOSS software and committing to help in its development (Barnes, 2020). In this sense, software offers the perfect case for Benkler's liberalist view of the commons and capital representing distinct but potentially mutually beneficial economic spheres.

Nevertheless, it is important to recognize that this embrace of open-source code by capital is mostly limited to producer-oriented software, meaning it is programming that primarily serves as a means to a further removed end, namely, an end-user commodity. The Linux kernel, for instance, is the bare bones of an operating system, facilitating the interface between software and hardware. This kernel has now become the basis of the majority of mobile-phone operating systems (Android) as well as that of high-powered mainframes. As such, the Linux code is essentially a means of production, used to build the specific functionalities employed in a host of market-oriented goods and services. Hence, for capital, quickly advancing such commons-based production capabilities, which cannot be done as effectively in isolation, is desirable as it facilitates the rapid development and production of protected (copyrighted) consumer goods on which profit can then be made (Kleiner, 2010).

The story, however, is different when it comes to more specialized, end-user code that is itself a consumer product, such as application software and video games. Here, capital generally sees FOSS as competition and its support of such efforts is distinctly absent. Furthermore, end-user code typically has smaller user populations and there tends to be a greater premium on aesthetic and artistic input, which also makes collaborative crowdsourcing more difficult to achieve (Hill and Monroy-Hernández, 2012). As a consequence, despite some isolated successes, end-user, open-source software often finds itself struggling to keep up with capital due to the lack of adequate support to maintain, secure, and update this code. Not least, copyrighted, profit-oriented software and hardware is often intentionally designed to be incompatible with outside products, making it even more onerous for open-source applications to break through.

Beyond code, there is also an expansive realm of creative digitized media in the form of text, sound, and video that faces its own unique sourcing and property dynamics. Certainly, much of this end-user production, as with application software, is done by waged workers, where the ideas and creations remain in the proprietary realm of private, often massive media and entertainment companies. There are, however, also digital creators who are not immediately controlled by capital who must decide for themselves how they wish to make their work available. Some of these still seek to 'earn a living' or at least supplement their income, while others, in line with the earlier noted free-time coders, are mostly motivated by a number of non-monetary reasons to create digital value, which they are then generally happy to release to the commons.

With the dawn of the digital revolution, independent creative workers saw huge potential in achieving enhanced, autonomous production capabilities and, of course, boundless internet-based distribution. For independent income-seeking creative workers, in particular, there appeared to be an opening to overcome the dependency on capital-controlled production companies, which had long been associated with exploitation and invasive measures to control the creative process. Yet, with the establishment of the internet also came ubiquitous piracy, plagiarism, and a host of other forms of unintended use and abuse of creative work. As a consequence, creators quickly found themselves in a revamped relationship with producers, with capital regaining control over creative work via digital, mediating platforms that could guard digital value and enable profit, either by charging rents, as with Spotify, or through advertising, as with YouTube.

In this context, one far-reaching response aimed at enabling creative workers to exert more control over their own production has been the establishment of creative commons (CC) licensing. This licensing regime was the brainchild of Lawrence Lessig who has long championed the need for an open and accessible digital commons (Lessig, 2004). CC licensing focuses on creative and artistic work, emphasizing the rights of creators to determine how their work will be used. Several types of CC licenses have since been developed, offering different combinations of 'rights' with regard to copying, attributing, changing/mixing, distributing, and using for commercial purposes. There is also a popular 'share-alike' option that, as with FOSS, requires any changes made to share-alike digital content to also fall under the same property rules.

Importantly, since its inception, CC licensing has become widely adopted beyond the original focus on the artist to include other individual and collaborative work. Perhaps most impactful here has been its use in the realm of knowledge and skills communication (education broadly defined) which represents one of the most critical factors in actualizing the potential of the general intellect. We can here find a wide range of free and abundant resources employing some form of CC licensing, ranging from the plethora of do-it-yourself (DIY) webpages and videos to the more formal educational content to be found, for instance, in Kahn Academy tutorials or university-based massive open online courses (MOOCs). Wikipedia, however, which uses the most lenient form of CC restrictions, is undoubtedly the poster child for how knowledge curation and delivery can become a fully commons-based, crowdsourced endeavour. With nearly 60 million articles (over six million in English) in over 300 languages, and being the seventh-most visited internet site in the world, Wikipedia has singlehandedly made for-profit, knowledge-guarding encyclopedias an anachronism (Wikipedia, 2022).

Nonetheless, despite becoming the most ubiquitous, non-code copyleft arrangement, CC has also garnered its share of detractors. We can note here that a key aim for Lessig was to re-establish a read-write culture, meaning that anyone accessing CC digital content would be able to use it in various creative ways, hence transforming the consumer to a producer-consumer, or 'prosumer' (Lessig, 2009). An expansive and active prosumer populace using, mixing, and adding on to commons-based digital content would be the ultimate enactment of a liberated general intellect. For critics, however, CC licensing fails to advance this vision as its à la carte approach to adding use restrictions still facilitates a clear producer-consumer dichotomy, which can include the pursuit of commercial gain by the license holder (Kleiner, 2010). Yet, to be fair, we should acknowledge that the aim of the non-profit Creative Commons organization was never to disallow the pursuit of exchange-value or to challenge capitalism more broadly; it was, instead, always more modestly focused on empowering the creative worker to effectively function within this existing arrangement.

Research/design

While the review of GPL and CC licensing in the previous section revealed a number of promising ways that important digital value (particularly code and media) can be fostered and at least partially protected as a commons resource, in the realm of actual research and the development of new innovations, which comprise a critical component of the promise of a liberated general intellect, such outcomes are often difficult to achieve. This is particularly an issue when it comes to innovative, applied knowledge, or what we can call 'design', where the information being created often offers a competitive edge in markets (or geopolitical relations). Yet even in the realm of academic knowledge, or knowledge for its own sake, the traditional ideals of openness, sharing, and collaboration are also becoming increasingly compromised. Nevertheless, in both instances, there are also significant initiatives underway aimed at bringing the process of creating, and then accessing, new knowledge/innovation into the digital commons.

Turning first to academic knowledge, many point to publicly funded universities and research centres as the quintessential example of commons-oriented, peer production. Yet the historically rooted, noble endeavour to pursue knowledge for the 'common good' has also become increasingly siloed and proprietary as universities and related institutions succumb to the business model. In this model, research is guided by the prioritization of money-making synergies with capital while a laser focus is kept on individualized and institutional academic productivity in competition with others. Consequently, the majority of research activities, which otherwise would benefit from Linus's law of many eyes, are being conducted by isolated and highly guarded groups and individuals (Milham and Klein, 2019).

The response by commons advocates to this situation has been multifaceted, with the most obvious demand being for governments to financially and ideologically support universities and public research centres as institutions mandated to pursue knowledge as a commons-based, collaboratively achieved good. Beyond this more top-down focus, however, and motivated by the FOSS movement, there has also been an expansion of so-called 'open research' or 'open science', now facilitated by digital, open, online research platforms (Densmore, nd). In the case of Figshare, for example, an online networking tool is offered that allows data and findings within an ongoing research project to be easily shared and discussed across a boundless digital network, thus enabling much larger communities, beyond the confines of universities and labs in the Minority World, to participate and assist in all stages of the research process in real time (WIRED, 2014). Based on these capabilities, the potential for expansive crowdsourced or 'citizen science' initiatives are greatly enhanced. These commons-based endeavours are characterized by individuals volunteering their time or resources (like computing power) to assist in the collecting and processing of data, and sometimes also in the framing of the research question, for the sake of a specific scientific project, from cancer studies to the search for extraterrestrial life (Franzoni et al, 2021).

Apart from the actual doing of science, however, a further fundamental barrier to commonifying emerging, cutting-edge academic knowledge lies in the issue of access to published research findings, primarily rooted in restrictions maintained by for-profit publishing companies. Today, five companies control half of all published academic articles (Larivière et al, 2015). In the face of this challenge there has been a rigorous push to break down the walls maintaining this artificial scarcity. The Budapest Open Access Initiative, for instance, is committed to making academic production 'available to anyone with internet access', which could then radically accelerate and deepen the pursuit of knowledge by unleashing the many eyes of the crowd (BOAI, 2022).

Currently, the main way this aim is being realized is by garnering funds for authors and libraries to pay publishers to adopt some version of CC licensing for their publications. In this way the open-access initiative has managed to place roughly half of all published research under some form of copyleft rules. This is, indeed, a significant win, yet we should nonetheless acknowledge that in most instances these gains do not truly represent an exit from capital, as publishers are essentially only being bought off, paid by a source other than the final consumer. A preferable arrangement, therefore, can be found in the numerous examples of non-profit, commons-oriented outlets that aim at circumventing capital altogether by facilitating the release of open-access research and scholarship within a freely accessible commons (mostly digital) realm. These efforts, however, also tend to struggle with chronically limited funding and subsequent resource challenges, meaning they have thus far struggled to break through as a widely established alternative.

Moving from academic knowledge to design, understood to encompass the broad field of innovatively applied information/knowledge, we find a form of digital value that has long been pursued and carefully guarded by capital. Yet, at the same time it also harbours tremendous commoning potential. To begin, we should note that commons-based, digitally captured design is multifaceted and difficult to place in terms of existing copyleft regimes. For instance, digital information intended to guide manual forms of production can fall under CC licensing agreements, while programmed instructions in digital manufacturing are essentially code, which could be captured under GPL. In this sense it can also be difficult to clearly establish digital design as a means of production or an end-user good. In the end – at least from capital's perspective – this designation will largely be contingent on the role this design plays within a broader market strategy.

In focusing a bit more on this dynamic, we can note that, as in open-source software, capital has moved to embrace a commoning of design in some special cases. In 2014, for example, Elon Musk revoked all of Tesla's electric car patents, imposing a pledge that any company using its technology would not be sued if they equally dismiss any patent claims on their own electric-car related technology – essentially establishing an internal 'share-alike' regime (Hirsch and Hsu, 2014). In a symbolic show of this new commitment, all of Tesla's patents that had been prominently displayed in the lobby of their Palo Alto headquarters were taken down. Musk can here be seen as acutely aware of the squandered ingenuity caused by intellectual property restrictions, and he is gambling that an opening of the gates will launch the still limited e-vehicle market that he sees Tesla dominating. Similar moves can be identified in a number of other industries, where the rationale, again, centres on how crowdsourced design can be used to help create or improve a certain, profitable end-user commodity.

This openness, however, is certainly not the norm. In most cases, from engineering to pharmaceuticals, the designs developed and employed, even in means-of-production applications, are deemed too valuable, and hence the de facto strategy is one of secrecy. The expansion of a design-focused commons, as with much code, therefore often falls back to the work of commoners, unaided by the help of capital. Yet, even without this assistance, some see open-design as having the potential to replicate the intense activity within the more utility focused code production associated with FOSS (Chaves, 2021). Indeed, a FOSS equivalent 'geek' community within the nascent open-design movement is evidenced by the long-established, commons-oriented DIY/ maker culture, the widespread popularity of maker faires, and the rapid growth of makerspaces and fabrication labs (fab labs) across the world.

Regarding this connection between design and making/fabricating we can point out that a natural offshoot from the open-design effort is a commitment to open-source hardware, that is, where the digital means for building the actual tools and machines needed for making stuff is made fully accessible as a commons resource. The pursuit for open-sourced hardware can here be seen, as Marx had envisioned in *Grundrisse*, as the productive potential of the general intellect becoming both materially manifested in actual machinery and commonified as a public asset. To offer just one remarkable effort in this vein, consider Open Source Ecology, a commons-oriented non-profit committed to creating what it calls the Global Village Construction Set, described as a 'high-performance platform that enables the relatively easy fabrication of the 50 different Industrial Machines that it takes to build a small, sustainable civilization with modern comforts' (OSE, 2014, np). If we then take this access to open-sourced means of production together with the growing store of free and unrestricted end-user designs, we can see the conditions beginning to coalesce that would enable significantly enhanced, commons-based material production, from basic tools and furniture to automobiles and houses.

Finally, it should be noted that in some few instances government support has also been forthcoming in commoning efforts around design, reflecting the possibility of rewarding synergies between the two. A case in point is that of pharmaceutical design, which has become the focus of a movement, motivated by FOSS and open-research initiatives, that seeks to make work-in-progress pharmaceutical 'designs' fully open-source. Instead of code as the focus, the aim is to garner large-scale, digitally enabled collaboration on the discovery, testing, and improvement of medicinal molecular sequences. Given that such a project requires significant resources and funding, yet where the product is clearly directed at the common good, it is an ideal candidate for government partnership. One example of such a synergy coming to fruition can be found in the pioneering, India-based Open Source Drug Discovery (OSDD) project, dedicated to the crowdsourced discovery of new and cheap pharmaceuticals for afflictions largely ignored by big pharma (OSDD, 2013). With a dedicated digital infrastructure that connects nearly 8000 participants across 130 countries, the OSDD project is a prime instance of government-supported open research and open-source designs in the pursuit of use-value expansion.

Contending with capital

There is undoubtedly significant potential in the various digital commoning efforts reviewed thus far, yet it is also equally clear that these initiatives remain deeply constrained by limited resources and a broader political-economic context that generally favours capital. More specifically, commons-based digital producers, especially those refusing to engage as market participants, often lack a sufficient supply of donated labour and resources to adequately support their operations. The most effective response to this condition, however, is a matter of considerable disagreement.

Many advocates of a vibrant digital commons are animated by the ontological position that the 'authors' of any creative/cognitive work, regardless of whether it is code, art, research, or design, are not singular intellects; rather they are channelling and feeding off of the cognitive/cultural productions of society as a whole (the general intellect) (see Kleiner, 2010 for a review; also Smiers and van Schijnde, 2009). Proponents of a radically free digital commons thus bristle at the prospect of imposing any restrictions on access to digital value. Many also see remuneration for digital commons contributions as a corrupting of the commons ideal. While compeerism ultimately shares the underlying sentiment giving rise to these positions, it simultaneously recognizes some debilitating limitations when this outlook is applied to current realities.

Consider, for instance, Wikipedia's conscious decision to not pay its content contributors with the annual revenue it garners because, it is argued, such a move would destroy the commons-production culture that Wikipedia is trying to foster (Lund and Venäläinen, 2016). This culture is also evident in the FOSS movement, which sees commons production as an endeavour that should exist fundamentally outside the logic of markets and money, focused instead on the simple aim, as per Richard Stallman (2021), to 'make our society better'. On the face of it there is a certain anarchist, mutual-aid feeling behind these views. Yet, the flip side to a free, accessible digital commons that we can all benefit from is that those freely giving their time and know-how still need to figure out how to feed themselves.

In short, the vision of a commons produced solely by volunteers ignores the impact of the apparatus of capture, that is, the commodification of everything and the subsequent need to sell one's labour. What the culture of commons production really reveals, therefore, is a dependence on people that have the luxury to contribute their time because they can find access to market-acquired money elsewhere, usually a 'day job' linked to capital. This form of the digital commons, then, does not represent an alternative to capitalism, rather, it is a relatively small, subservient economic activity, squaring with the original formulation of commons-based peer production maintained by Yochai Benkler.

Hence, from a compeerist perspective, the result of casting the digital commons outside the realm of money/markets is that most of the digital productive capacity held by capable workers, who must pay their bills, will be sucked into capitalist forms of production. As such, while compeerism accepts that volunteer labour can be an important means to boost the commons, there is also a tactical acknowledgement that it should not, if the commons are to truly expand, be the only source. The issue of remunerating creative/cognitive work by and for the commons must therefore be addressed. We revisit this matter as part of a more in-depth consideration of the challenges and options entailed in contending with the overarching dependency by the commons on market-based resources in Chapters 7 and 8. Nonetheless, it is helpful to offer a brief overview here of the specific funding realities involved in pursuing an expanded and vibrant digital commons. We will do the same when covering other sectors of the economy throughout the book.

To begin, and in line with the more purist views of the commons, various forms of freely donated monetary support can be pursued to pay for some labour and other expenses, as is often done within non-profit organizations. As per the Fast Forward's 'non-profit tech directory' there are hundreds of digital value producers registered as non-profits, driven by the aim 'to scale social impact', and many of these will undoubtedly be reliant on some form of donation model (Ffwd, 2022, np). Wikipedia, however, remains the classic example of the donation approach to expanding the digital commons, managing to garner over US$150 million in revenue each year, with an average contribution sum of $15 (Wikimedia, 2022). Wikipedia then uses this revenue for operational expenses, including the payment of over 500 staff members, but, importantly, not content suppliers.

A second option, popular within the established socialist left, is for the state to use its tax revenues for the purpose of directly engaging in commons-based digital value production. In the realm of media and culture the state often still maintains a significant budget with which to pursue this aim. A noteworthy effort here has been the digitization and commoning of critical cultural assets held by state-owned galleries, libraries, archives, and museums (GLAM) (Wallace, 2020). There are also a growing number of public broadcasters committing to making their productions available under

CC licensing, as Germany's biggest broadcaster ZDF has done with a wide range of its productions (Dobusch, 2020).

With regard to science and scholarship, in turn, many still point to state-sponsored academia and research as a model. Mariana Mazzucato (2015), for instance, has made a compelling case for the pervasive impact that US government sponsored science and engineering has had in fostering innovations with tremendous economic repercussions. The amount of funds being committed by governments is also nothing to be dismissed, with the US still spending just shy of three per cent of its total budget on research and development (OMD, 2022).

Lastly, a final route to fund the expansion of the digital commons is to engage markets through some form of entrepreneurial production that nonetheless aligns with compeerist principles. As we have established, this is a critical component of compeerism's vision for replacing capital in the *longue durée*. Undoubtedly the most proven execution of a values driven, yet viable production form within the broader context of capitalist markets can be found in the more intentional iterations of the cooperativist model. Traced back to the Rochdale Principles for cooperatives laid out in 1844, the cooperative outlook, which emerged as a direct response to the negative impacts of capital's dominance within markets, includes a commitment to openness, democratic participation, fair remuneration, solidarity, and a concern for the community (ICA, 2018). When true to these principles, especially if pursued as a way to exit capital and foster the commons, cooperatives can be seen as inherently compeerist in nature.

While early cooperatives focused on offering non-exploitative access to goods and services to their members via member cooperatives, these were soon followed by worker and stakeholder co-ops where emphasis was placed on the shared ownership and management of the means of production by members or by a worker-member-stakeholder alliance. In the digital realm, the cooperative model is mostly associated with resistance to the service-centred gig economy, which we will return to in the next chapter. However, there is also a growing presence of commons-oriented cooperatives working in digital value production. This includes enterprises engaged in code and design (for example, worker co-ops like Hypha and Gnucoop), news and media (as with member co-ops such as the German Tageszeitung or stakeholder co-ops like the British-based Ethical Consumer magazine), and cultural production (such as the New York-based worker co-op Meerkat Media). These cooperatives, and many more like them, align well with compeerist principles as they maintain various commitments to expanding the commons while also pursuing 'meaningful livelihoods' and empowerment for their workers (Townson, 2021, np).

Along similar lines, yet focusing particularly on design, a further possibility to engage markets with commoning intent can be found in the still nascent model of open-value-networks (OVNs). The pioneer behind this approach, Canadian-based Sensorica, is an online incubator for the generation of design-focused projects centred on sensor and sensing equipment, with the designs usually being offered under share-alike CC licensing. In the words of Sensorica's founder, the basic idea behind open-value networks can be simply summed up as, 'people creating value together, by contributing work, money and goods and sharing the income' (Brastaviceanu, 2016, np). In this way, the capitalist boss is explicitly cut out of the production equation.

In essence, OVNs work by allowing anyone who feels so inclined to assist in a project by contributing time and/or resources. While there is a project leader, decision making and pay is 'distributed' and decentralized based on an agreed upon, algorithmically-enabled calculation that seeks to measure the overall value of any particular contribution. Everyone who signs onto a project can see exactly how it is organized and how decision making and payment rights are determined – these are also generally open to continued democratic revision. In most cases, even work done on a project that fails to garner revenue can end up being remunerated if this work is incorporated into a later endeavour that does find market demand.

We should note that open-value-networks, as well as intentional cooperatives, are increasingly enabled by a growing number of sophisticated tools that can assist in their management aspirations. Backfeed, for instance, was an early pioneer in creating digital, blockchain-based solutions for networked, collaborative organizations, offering 'decentralized management tools, equity-sharing schemes, crowdsourcing mechanisms, and instruments for the collaborative evaluation and curation of content' (P2PF Wiki, 2019a, np). Even more ambitious is the project Backfeed ultimately morphed into, DAOstack. The focus of DAOstack is the creation of democratic and equitable decentralized autonomous organizations (DAOs), understood as comprehensive production environments consisting of coded missions, rules, and operational procedures governed by blockchain-enabled if-then smart-contracts (Banov, 2018). These digital environments are ultimately intended to create a smooth and seamless production process that stays true to a set of intentional operating procedures. As such, it is not difficult to see how such blockchain-empowered management infrastructures could become critical future enablers of compeerist-aligned, values-oriented production in the digital realm and beyond.

Persistent challenges

The various funding options just outlined are ultimately responses to the recognition, counter some commons-based activists, that the promise of the digital commons cannot be achieved by only harnessing volunteered labour on the basis of mutual aid, play, or self-promotion. Yet each of these avenues for soliciting external funds also faces significant hurdles, all of which are related to the overarching political economic context defined by the apparatus of capture and the subsequent dominance of exchange value rationales.

Thus, relying on gifting leaves commons producers vulnerable to the demands of the often capital-oriented giver, and, in the end, establishes more of a dependency on capital rather than offering an alternative. State support, in turn, which ultimately also hinges on the siphoning of capitalistically derived wealth via taxes, is hobbled by its weakened fiscal position and the increasing internalization of capitalist rationales within government institutions. Lastly, and most pertinent to the compeerist strategic outlook, market engaged non-profits, cooperatives, and open-value-networks face serious difficulties navigating a competitive, price-focused environment in which they seek to service the commons while also fairly remunerating their workers. This is a challenge, related directly to Rosa Luxemburg's critique of cooperatives covered in the previous chapter, that we will continuously grapple with throughout this book.

For compeerist-aligned entrepreneurs committed to providing digital value to the commons, the task at hand is to find a reliable source of revenue that does not fully enclose the value being produced. The standard approach employed here is to make a large portion of the digital goods or services provided open to the commons, while restricting just a small, choice portion to be sold at a premium. Alternatively, additional, optional perks, for example related to 'product support', could be offered for a fee. In the case of Sensorica, for instance, while their designs are freely available and open-source, revenues are pursued through extra customization and targeted customer services (Brastaviceanu and Bergeron, 2015). Yet, while this business model could work very well if it were adopted by everyone, it becomes much more difficult to execute in a context where most actors are capitalistically driven, meaning they tend to take and profit from the digital commons while making their own advantageous digital value costly to acquire or entirely off limits.

As an example, consider Local Motors, a specialized automotive company (now defunct) that organized public, collaborative design initiatives seeking to tap into innovative ideas and work from an unpaid, commons-sourced 'crowd'. Yet, Local Motors then proceeded to use restrictive CC licensing that prevented these designs, or altered versions of them, from being openly distributed, thus actively preventing the commons and commoners from benefiting. Marcin Jakubowski, founder of Open Source Ecology, noted earlier, took public offense at this practice, particularly because Local Motors billed itself as being committed to open-source design. In an online post, Jakubowski (OSE, 2019, np) wrote, 'Local Motors is not open source. ... This is pointed out because such confusion weakens the case for real open source. At stake is the transition to the true open-source economy, a prerequisite to ending artificial scarcity'.

Another good example of this dynamic can be found in the story of MakerBot, one of the first and most innovative manufacturers of 3D printers. While MakerBot was established as a for-profit enterprise, it maintained a productive synergy with the commons by open-sourcing its designs and thus benefiting tremendously from crowdsourced innovations coming from an eager, maker community. Yet once the company had managed to produce a significant amount of innovation-based value, MakerBot was bought out by its larger competitor Stratasys, which promptly proceeded to close MakerBot's open-source commitments in order to patent the technology and keep it from the commons (Zaleski, 2016).

In short, then, with some exceptions, capital is very good at taking from but not giving back to the commons. This reality not only hurts the cause of commons expansion but gives capital an unfair advantage in relation to commons-oriented digital value producers who refuse to engage in such self-centred, extractive tactics. Further exacerbating this situation is the fact that even if copyleft licensing is employed, it is often insufficient in truly protecting commons-based digital value from being coopted by capital. For instance, as noted earlier, while GPL offers some assurances against its code being made proprietary (even if altered), it still allows this code to be freely incorporated into products that can be enclosed through other intellectual property barriers (Papadimitropoulos, 2018).

Faced with the various challenges noted here, compeerists will ultimately be forced to engage two fronts of activism to ensure the digital commons can reach their full potential in fostering, capturing, and sharing the world community's general intellect. On one front, it will be necessary to pressure the state, wherever it is most feasible, to establish concessions and actions aimed at creating a political-economic environment that supports the production of commons-centred digital value, whether sourced from civil society, the state, or the market. On the other front, and related to the market in particular, much more concerted inter-commons cooperation and mobilization are called for that could empower commons-oriented actors to effectively go toe to toe with capital. We will consider both of these imperatives next, placing greater emphasis, however, on the inter-commons dimension, and especially the use of peer property, as this tactical component of a commons-based transition is still relatively unexplored and overlooked.

The compeerist pursuit of an expansive digital commons

While the state, in its current form, is not in a strong position to spearhead a publicly funded expansion of the digital commons, state engagement is by no means a lost cause. Even if certain seismic shifts in governance seem distant today, it is important to keep in mind that over time, conditions and realities do change. In the meantime, there are several important concessions and interventions that could still be squeezed from variously scaled tiers of government, especially in those windows of opportunity when a commons-friendly administration is in power.

Regarding the digital realm, in particular, compeerist political engagement would most directly translate into demands to establish and expand government involvement in the production and dissemination of commons-based digital value, including in the GLAM and public broadcasting realms. Similarly, pressure could be exerted to increase support for publicly funded research institutions, with calls for the explicit commitment to greater openness and collaboration in the research process and an insistence that all academic work be released to the digital commons. Additionally, appeals could be made for the delivery of grants, tax breaks, and other financial assistance to external actors engaged in commons-based digital production, ranging from transnational initiatives such as the Open Source Drug Discovery (OSDD) project to smaller local cooperatives focused on various forms of place-specific, commons-based digital value production.

Lastly, compeerists could home in on the significant role the state plays in the determination and execution of intellectual property laws. In response to this power, there is a long established and growing movement of both copyright reform and outright copyright abolition as the intellectual-property regime is viewed by an increasing number of people as leading to an unjust 'intellectual monopoly' (Lindsey and Teles, 2017, np). While getting the state to abandon copyright protections altogether is undoubtedly unrealistic in the near term, clear demands relating to intellectual property are mounting, for instance from the likes of the Access to Knowledge movement and anti-copyright Pirate Parties (Timmermann, 2014; Cammaerts, 2015). These demands include the suspension of intellectual property on goods linked to humanity's inalienable rights, shortening the expiration dates of standard patents and copyrights, and establishing greater transparency and contributor rights in the assignment of patents. Additionally, given that the state also plays a critical role in overseeing and enforcing copyleft alternatives, compeerists will naturally insist that the relevant state institutions enforcing and adjudicating these cases apply the same type of rigour and commitment as they do when dealing with copyright infringements.

Following compeerist thinking, however, while concerted, state-based initiatives are an important way to support the digital commons, in the end, they are insufficient on their own. This is because, for the general intellect to truly become liberated – and hence reach its full counter-capitalist promise – requires the populace itself (the true source of the general intellect) to be the driving force behind the commoning of information/knowledge. In other words, it is up to commoners to foster and expand the digital commons into a vibrant, enabling space by and for the people, unrestrained or corrupted by the extractive tendencies of capital. At the same time, as we have seen, this is a tall order considering the broader context where the apparatus of capture significantly limits people's ability to engage in commons-based work.

Massimo De Angelis has written at length about the importance of leveraging synergistic relations between commons-oriented entities themselves, to create a more concerted impetus for commoning from the bottom up. More specifically, he refers to a commons ecosystem that can be strengthened and expanded through what he terms, 'boundary commoning'. According to De Angelis (2017b, p 287), boundary commoning 'activates and sustains relations among commons thus giving shape to commons at larger scales, pervading social spaces and intensifying the presence of commons within them'. In this sense we are dealing with a meso-level form of economic/political organization that aims to cohere local, prefigurative commons-based initiatives into a more unified force in the face of macro-level assemblages/apparatuses undergirding the capital-state nexus. There are, ultimately, numerous ways that such boundary commoning can express itself, from variously formal arrangements facilitating the pooling, management, and sharing of resources to establishing commons-oriented guild-like organizations that work to enhance both the economic and political power of their members (Arvidsson, 2020; De Moor, 2008; Kostakis and Bauwens, 2019).

In terms of the aim of expanding the digital commons, then, an important boundary-commoning initiative that comes to the fore is that of establishing a more proactive and solidaristic form of commons-based digital property governance, that is, peer property. The emerging concept of peer property denotes an alternative to both top-down state ownership and fully individualized property rights (Bauwens, 2009; Kleiner, 2010). Instead, peer property is 'commons property', understood in the vein of Ostrom (2015) as being produced, maintained, and governed by a particular community and made available, as any well-functioning commons, according to particular rules, norms, and restrictions. In this sense property must also be grasped, as commons advocates David Bollier and Silke Helfrich (2019) insist, as relational, not something to possess but rather something to negotiate.

In the digital realm, GPL and CC are the two major alternatives to proprietary property laws, with each approaching copyright's deficiencies in different ways: while GPL emphasizes the expansion of the commons, CC focuses on the empowerment of creative/cognitive workers. What is needed, however, is a licensing arrangement that can do both more effectively, that is, one that can further the commons while also supporting the right of the digital value producer to not only control their work, but to be remunerated for it. This goal can ultimately be achieved by making free access to commons-sourced value conditional. Bauwens et al (2017, p 38) present the matter quite plainly by stating that 'while knowledge sharing should always be maintained, we should also demand reciprocity for the commercial exploitation of the commons'. In essence, then, peer-property licensing reverse engineers existing copyright and patent laws to form a contingency component to the license, where use rights change depending on how or by whom the peer-property asset is used.

In this way, if you are in the commons in-group, you may use the peer licensed asset freely, including commercially. If you are in the capital out-group, any use is either prohibited or comes with the mandate to pay some form of compensation. Enforcement would here be based on commons-based actors using the legal status of peer-property in litigation suits against offenders, just as capital pursues the enforcement of copyright. Hence, by demanding that capital pay something for its use of commons-sourced digital value, a transference of much-needed resources into the commons is created. Such an arrangement would then open the opportunity to actually pay commons workers and cover other operational costs, thus offering a partial reprieve from the dependency on capital and facilitating the production and dissemination of commons-based digital value.

Yet, a key question here is how the in- and out-groups and their subsequent rights are to be determined. One approach, termed 'coopyright', has sought to build a reciprocity-like license using already existing CC licensing as a foundation (P2PF Wiki, 2019b). Being grounded in the globally recognized and fully open-sourced Creative Commons regime, the terms of the license can be easily modified to include a dual mechanism in which a restrictive, non-commercial use license is primary (including unaltered use within other commodities), while a more open license becomes operational if certain commons-contribution criteria are met. In this sense, while similar to a reciprocity demand, the key issue is not so much one of share-alike, but rather share-with-whom.

What ultimately counts as an adequate commons-contribution would be left to the issuer of the license. While one option would be to institute some form of tit-for-tat condition, which would require quantifying what is taken and what is returned to the commons, a simpler alternative would be to make the commons contribution criteria linked to some form of membership. This is the approach taken by FairShares, self-described as the 'association for multi-stakeholder cooperation in member-owned social enterprises' (FairShares, 2017). FairShares has thus embraced coopyright in a way where the digital resources produced by FairShares are available for a wide array of uses, including commercial ones, to active, contributing members of the association while non-members must pay fees, regardless of whether their interest in the resource is commercial or not. Establishing clear in-group privileges in this way helps not only to overcome questions of how to determine reciprocity, but it minimizes the difficult task of needing to oversee and enforce commercial use conditionalities, a recurring burden within CC licensing.

Taking the idea of membership beyond a relatively confined in-group, Copyfarleft, developed by Dmitry Kleiner, stipulates a peer property regime in which the digital asset under its license is open and free of intellectual property protections, unless it is used with the primary intent to achieve profit, in which case some form of payment is required (Kleiner, 2010). This approach has since been adopted by the P2P Foundation as Copyfair licensing, where the in-group is now defined to include all intentional, worker-empowered enterprises, hence again dealing with the issue of difficult-to-adjudicate profit intentionality. Some, however, have argued Copyfair's operationalization is too strict, preferring an expansion to include the commons-aligned 'social and solidarity economy' (SSE) (P2PF Wiki, 2019b, np). Indeed, if the aim is to create a large enough commons sphere to where peer-property can offer a significant benefit, it would make sense to also include non-profits and intentional member cooperatives. Importantly, each of these also maintain recognized legal status, thus creating clear and indisputable distinctions in determining in- and out-group designations.

Regardless of its eventual form, a peer-property licensing regime that could reach adequate scale holds the potential of creating a massive collection of open-source code, design, know-how, and other digital content that would be guarded from capitalist extraction. While some critics on the left argue that the bounding of resources in this way is contrary to commoning and ultimately reflects capitalist, market-oriented thinking, it is an argument that compeerism firmly rejects (Rigi, 2014). As we have seen, compeerism regards successful market engagements as a necessity if economic and political power are ever to be transferred from capital to the commons, and peer property is a valuable tool to achieve this aim. Furthermore, as the upcoming chapters make clear, the way true compeerists, in the digital realm and beyond, interact with markets is rooted in fundamentally non-capitalist values and modes of operation. Indeed, it is due to the embrace of these values that significant market disadvantages arise, which is precisely why establishing an expansive and robust peer-property regime is so important.

Consider, as an example here, the Wikimedia Foundation behind the Wikipedia project, which has long been committed to a fully open digital commons. As such, they have willingly worked with capital to secure donations and establish strategic partnerships, as for instance with Alphabet (Google). More recently, however, there have been grumblings from the Foundation that tech giants are not adequately paying back to the commons, leading to the exploratory development of a commercial service that private entities would be required to pay for in order to receive access to streamlined and vetted Wikipedia content (Cohen, 2021). The Wikimedia Foundation ultimately presents this move as providing a service, not as a forcing to pay.

Yet, consider the ramifications if the Foundation had gone even further to adopt a full-blown peer-property licensing model, where most capital-oriented enterprises were prohibited from the free commercial use of its content. Not only would such an arrangement establish a competitive edge for the commons-oriented in-group that makes use of Wikipedia, but the Wikimedia Foundation itself could now count on a steady revenue stream from capital. This more reliable and sizable inflow of money could then be used to expand Wikipedia's contribution to the informational commons, for instance by garnering a larger pool of contributors who are offered fair remuneration for their work.

Looking ahead

Beyond Wikipedia, which is already quite well endowed, there are collectively thousands of non-profits, cooperatives, and open-value-networks supplying important digital value that could greatly benefit from a peer-property revenue boost. Imagine, then, that these actors established a sweeping interconnected peer-property regime extending over a significant swathe of digital value, including code, media, and design. This would force digital-oriented entrepreneurs into a choice. One option would be to pursue the commons route, for instance by establishing a worker-owned cooperative within a larger guild-like organization made up of similar enterprises committed to economic democracy, fair remuneration, community service, sustainability, and commons expansion. In being part of this in-group, the commons enterprise would gain free and unconstrained use of a large trove of critical peer-property licensed digital value, hence offering a significant boost to their competitiveness in the market.

A second option would be to go the capitalist route, where there is the possibility of high profits and personal wealth, but where the odds for failure would also be quite high, especially as the size of the enterprise diminished. In this scenario, the capitalist entity would be forced to compete as a lone wolf not only with other capitalists, but also with an increasingly formidable and united commons sector. Critically, for the capitalist, the expansive and invaluable digital content falling under peer property protections would not be freely accessible, and all digital value employed within the goods or services being offered for sale would come at a cost, posing significant competitive disadvantages.

Yet, in taking a step back here, it is not unfair to ask whether such an imagined trajectory is actually realistic. Copyright academic turned blogger, Alan Toner, argues that there simply is not enough political intentionality to make peer-property licensing very popular. According to Toner, people dabbling in commons production like to rally around loose pro-piracy and anti-industry ideas because these can be construed as non-ideological and centred on individual freedoms, but that is as far as they will go. In his words, 'Try and interest the same people in drawing up a political programme that addresses the complexity of modern social organization and you'll retain the attention of about .1% of them. Maybe 1.1%, if you can make them laugh with reasonable frequency' (Toner, 2007, np). In other words, in a world where capitalist realism has become the norm, many producing digital value for the commons enjoy taking jabs at capital here and there, but there appears to be relatively little appetite for systemic confrontations.

The lack of a truly counter-capitalist attitude within the digital commons sphere is evident on multiple levels. Individuals offering free labour to help crowdsource digital value for capital, for instance, are motivated by a variety of reasons, including the opportunity to learn, 'be discovered', or simply because they enjoy the challenge and camaraderie of solving problems and being creative in a team (Spaeth and Niederhöfer, 2021). In many of these participants' minds, it does not matter much if this work is eventually coopted by capital. Large, non-profit commons producers, like Wikipedia and Linux, in turn, maintain cooperative relationships with capital as they are attracted to the funding and other resources that come with corporate connections, even if we are starting to see some isolated examples of push back.

Clearly, from a compeerist perspective, a more conscious and organized resistance to capital is called for. We will return to how a compeerist-aligned mass movement could emerge and mobilize to resist capital's power over the commons more broadly, later in the book. Yet, for now, we should keep in mind that the commons-oriented 'ecosystem' that could benefit from an expansive peer-property regime is already sizable and growing (Salamon and Newhouse, 2020). Furthermore, from the perspective of the market-engaged non-profits and cooperatives making up this ecosystem, peer-property licensing does not necessarily require an immediate embrace of a rigid, confrontational political platform. Rather, this commons-based licensing regime can be viewed first and foremost as a pragmatic boosting of these non-capital oriented actors' power and independence in a tough market-based environment.

Indeed, in the final analysis, asking why the commons ought to freely give to capital when capital does not return the favour should not be considered a radical question. Ostrom's (2015) work on the commons makes very plain the requirement for effective commons governance, which often includes the need for imposing restrictions. For Ostrom, such restrictions were often based on innate scarcity or limits, as with particular natural resources. Within the digital commons, where scarcity is less of an issue, the rationale for restrictive governance is, instead, rooted in the imperative of being able to maintain generation, that is, economic sustainability within an environment determined by the apparatus of capture. For the individual and society, furthermore, the benefits of supporting a vibrant, accessible digital commons are not difficult to fathom. It should then also not be a stretch to view peer-property, which is an enabler of this commons, as being an inherently sensibleand fair arrangement, motivated by a pursuit of the common good.

Yet, while the effort to build a vibrant digital commons continues, the internet, which is a key technology in this pursuit, has itself become much more than a tool for building and sharing digital information/content and capabilities. It has steadily been transformed into a space aimed at facilitating transactions and mediations, while simultaneously becoming a massive data collection assemblage/apparatus, all of which has been sponsored and exploited by capital. It is this development within the digital revolution, and its implications for a compeerist transition, to which we must turn next.

3

Taking Back the Internet

Proponents of the view that commons-based peer production represents an alternative paradigm for organizing the economy like to point to how the steam engine ushered in the final death knell of feudalism. Why should it not be possible, then, to harness the digital revolution in a similar way to bring about another fundamental shift, this time out of capitalism? The internet's power to capture and disperse the digitized general intellect could here be the impetus for a transition to a commons-based, collaborative economy characterized by the abundance of digital information/content and massive leaps in the quality and efficiency of material production (Arvidsson, 2020; Mason, 2016).

As the previous chapter revealed, however, there are many obstacles that still stand in the way of achieving a liberated general intellect for which the internet could serve as a facilitator and conduit. Apart from these constraints, which centre on capital's ability to enclose and commoditize digital value, it is, however, important to acknowledge that the internet itself has become a controlled, cyber infrastructure in the service of capital. With the establishment of the more interactive Web 2.0, and Web3 on the horizon (based on blockchain-enabled smart-contracts), the capitalization of people's use of cyberspace has taken centre stage. This reality poses novel and difficult challenges, but also some openings, for a compeerist-aligned evolution to a new, post-capitalist mode of production.

We can begin by reiterating that compeerism views the liberatory potential of the digital revolution with a great deal of caution. While technological upheavals can challenge capital, capitalism has been historically adept at bringing any lines of flight back into the fold of wealth-extracting commodification. More to the point, as Dmytri Kleiner, a long-term (h)activist and disabused believer in the revolutionary potential of the internet put it: 'so long as capitalism is the dominant mode of production, it will produce platforms that reproduce it' (Wilson and Kleiner, 2013, np). Kleiner refers specifically here to the 'client-server-capitalist state', an arrangement engineered to control and centralize what would otherwise be a decentralized and free network of information and exchange. In this way the internet has been reconfigured into a set of interlinked assemblages/apparatuses composed of technologies, 'providers', and 'consumers' that make up the basis of capitalism's latest wave of renewed profit and growth. Indeed, the digital economy, including spillover effects, is now estimated to make up nearly 20 per cent of the Minority World's GDP (UNCTAD, 2019).

Arguably the biggest coup for capital in terms of coopting the internet for the sake of profit has been the ability to control and profit from digital content, cyber interactions, and data extraction through the establishment of dominant web platforms. These platforms have essentially become an immaterial form of real estate, or 'cyber estate', which serve as the locations where users interface with the internet's content and services. As such, these can be seen as the latest iteration of space's de- and reconstruction in the service of capital. In the face of this state of affairs, compeerists are tasked with the imperative to hack and ultimately decapitalize a significant portion of the interactional/transactional dimension of the contemporary internet, reclaiming it for the commons.

Platform capitalism

Capital's new realm of profit making via the use of cyber estate is well captured in the term platform capitalism (Langley and Leyshon, 2017). The success of this arrangement is evidenced by the fact that the big tech corporations have catapulted themselves to the top tiers of the stock market, with the platform-based companies Alphabet and Amazon firmly ensconced in the top ten most capitalized businesses (Marketcap, 2022). It is, furthermore, estimated that in the next few years the major platform companies will be mediating close to a third of all economic activity (Gurumurthy and Chami, 2020).

There are four basic platform models we can identify (Vercellone et al, 2019). The first focuses on capitalizing on the prosumer nature of the internet, which includes social network platforms used for advertising and data mining once they are populated with freely provided content, for example Facebook, YouTube, and Google. A second model is that of the middleman, linking providers of a particular service to users, such as Uber and Airbnb. Here, the providers are generally accessed not as employees but as independently contracted labour (gig workers, share workers) with minimal company obligations with regard to remuneration or worker benefits (Jiménez, 2020; Woodcock, 2021).

A third approach is the establishment of gateway interfaces controlling access to copyrighted content via specific fee arrangements, as with Spotify and Netflix. It can be noted here that video content in this platform model has been increasingly characterized by gatekeepers offering their own original content, while big content providers, such as Disney, are opting to become their own gatekeepers. It is this gatekeeper platform arrangement that ultimately plays a pivotal role in the enclosure and scarcity management of creative digital value covered in the previous chapter.

The final platform arrangement is the virtual marketplace (e-commerce) where goods can be bought from the platform company or secondary sellers. Amazon is far and away the most important player here, leveraging its retail platform to expand into integrated sectors, from logistics and artificial intelligence to the production of digital content and hosting cloud storage. As a result, Amazon now maintains monopoly-like conditions in the e-commerce realm, where secondary online retailers become dependent on the Amazon platform, whose rules and conditions ensure there is no room for serious competition. Indeed, where upstart online market sellers have tried to find their own retail cyber-estate niche, Amazon has responded with prolonged, below-market pricing to force the competitor to fold (Mitchell and Knox, 2021). Furthermore, Amazon is increasingly using its retailing dominance to enter the realm of production, making their new product lines competitive by using consumer data (based on mostly non-Amazon products) collected on its expansive platform.

Platform capitalism reveals a number of unique qualities (Jiménez, 2020). For one, the need for labour is greatly diminished; the employee to profit ratio in most tech companies (Amazon is an exception) is miniscule compared to other businesses, with much of the value being generated by prosumers and outsourced workers. This latter category often takes the form of contracted gig workers, who represent a new realm of exploitative possibilities for capital. The struggle facing Uber drivers, to be recognized as employees in order to garner basic employer benefits and the cut-throat, demeaning environment that characterizes the menial digital tasks farmed out through Amazon Turk are just the most obvious and publicized examples (Scholz, 2017; Berry, 2019).

Competitive internet platforms are also characterized by Metcalfe's law, which states that the value of a platform is proportional to the number of its users squared. This, in turn, means that once a platform is widely embraced, it can quickly establish dominant, possibly monopolistic status. The need to attract and maintain users is related directly to the revenue model of these platforms; many are dependent on advertising, and most are engaged in valuable data mining, that is, the collection and use of the endless streams of user information that platform engagement generates. In other words, Facebook knows what you like, Google knows what you search, and Amazon knows what you buy. Such data is valuable to capital actors as it helps them in the development, delivery, and targeted marketing of their goods and services. Data can here be used by the platform directly, packaged as part of data-based services, or it can be sold raw to companies or data brokers.

The growing importance of information gathering and use has led some to claim that 'data is the new oil' (Kuneva, 2009, np). While this is not a perfect analogy, as data is renewable and can be shared infinitely while oil cannot, the comparison helps in pointing out how critical data has become for corporate actors. The global collection and use of personal data is a business that involves hundreds of billions of dollars, where each internet user's data is estimated to be worth up to US$1000 per year (Madsbjerg, 2017). Meta (Facebook), for instance, makes almost all of its money selling targeted ads based on data it has collected, but they have also discussed selling 'user' data directly for cash (Seetharaman and Grind, 2018). Meta also maintains data sharing agreements with apps that use the Facebook login as an identity checker, which is how Cambridge Analytica got hold of 50 million users' data to assist in targeted pro-Trump messaging in the 2016 US election.

Taking data to the next level

Looking towards the future, data collection for capital (and the state) will become increasingly ubiquitous and important. Beyond being tracked and logged in our engagement with the internet, we are seeing an expansion of data collection opportunities in our everyday interactions with 'smart' (networked) devices and sensors. This includes our phones, cars, and appliances that can track our behaviours and routines as well as the digital wearables, and soon 'digestibles', that can track our body. Importantly, even if we own these devices, we generally do not own the data they collect. There is also a quickly growing array of cameras and other sensing instruments in the public and private domain that track our movements, activities, and environments.

Today, much of the collected data on individuals exists as a hodgepodge of stored, raw information across multiple sites. However, with the continued expansion of data and processing power, it is fair to wonder how long it will take before there are detailed, individualized profiles and ID systems beyond our control. In China we can already see a state sponsored version of this, where its Social Credit System establishes an intricate scoring scheme for its citizenry based on social behaviour captured in various ways, from surveillance cameras to digital payments (Kobie, 2019). While the Chinese Communist Party is seeking to create a veritable panopticon of self and peer regulation, in the hands of capital similar registries of personalized profiles could eventually be used to pursue a range of profit opportunities (Lyon, 2019). All the while, the amount of data keeps growing.

Many now believe that the culmination of the increasing mass of interconnected information from the explosion of smart appliances and gadgets will be the creation of an internet of things (IoT), in which billions of networked and interconnected devices will blanket the globe, turning 'reality' into a continuous data stream, thus supercharging the digital revolution. The IoT, of course, has some distance to go before becoming reality, with various obstacles still standing in the way – from ensuring security against malicious hacks to achieving the computing capabilities to make constructive use of all this data. Yet, while many of these challenges have seemed insurmountable in the past, today they appear much less so. This progress is particularly evident in the realm of high powered, data-crunching capacity. Artificial intelligence (AI), for instance, has evolved to the point of being able to autonomously learn from its errors and continuously improve in its data processing tasks. In combination with the expanded power of networked cloud computing, and even quantum computing, AI will likely soon have the capability to make sense of, learn from, and respond to the massive digitization of reality that the internet of things promises.

There are obviously numerous interests involved in making the IoT a reality. Capital wants to continue using the explosion of information as a way to further the development and marketing of ever new and 'improved' goods and services; the state wants to maximize the effectiveness of its governance priorities; while the populace, which can see benefits in well-applied data, also harbours growing concerns about how this data could be misused. In some instances, there are openings for triple-win scenarios for all parties involved, such as a car company using collected vehicular data to help improve fuel efficiency, or a municipal government using aggregated traffic data to reduce congestion. Yet there are also significant openings for conflict. For example, the data collected on a network of interconnected smart devices could be used and peddled to help capital manipulate supply and demand at the cost of the consumer (Lyon, 2019). Or, alternatively, as already evidenced in the Chinese case, government can use its expansive sensing and tracking networks to pursue a draconian and invasive law-enforcement regime in which any sense of privacy is completely obliterated.

Couldry and Mejias (2019) have placed capital's push for ever more data in the darkest light by arguing that capitalism is entering a new frontier of value extraction, where every aspect of life, no matter how mundane, becomes a resource to be mined and then used to exploit the very people who are the source of this information. This emerging 'data colonialism' is not presented as simply a matter of privacy; the issue is much deeper and insidious. It is the vision of a new societal order in which the enormous amount of data being produced and collected is used to mould an ever more malleable populace that can be categorized, controlled, and shaped to be maximally aligned with the needs of capital. In the extreme, the creation of a perfectly curated environment for capital would leave practically no room for reflective, autonomous thought, as such autonomy can only come about when our minds have multiple and conflicting sources of information and stimuli to work with.

In sum, given the way cyber estate has been developed and put to use, we see that the internet, which was devised as a decentralized network with the explicit intent of sharing information, is increasingly giving way to assemblages/apparatuses working to engineer scarcity, exploit prosumer and gig labour, establish monopolistic/oligopolistic powers, and achieve ever-greater degrees of manipulative control over the consumer and citizen. At the same time, however, the underlying technology on which these arrangements depend is not predetermined. Indeed, there are numerous abstract hacktivist efforts underway today seeking to redirect and reshape the internet and big data in more commons-oriented ways. Looking ahead, there are two related compeerist imperatives linked to decapitalizing cyberspace and harnessing it for the good of the commons: one focuses on expanding commons-based platforms and the other centres on reclaiming control over data. We can start with platforms.

A compeerist organization of the internet

There are several avenues through which platform capitalism can be challenged. The simplest form is micro-level sabotage, as can be found, for instance, in actively seeking to block ads. The adoption of ad-blocking software has already reached up to 25 per cent in some countries and is estimated to cost online publishers tens of billions of dollars in yearly lost revenue, resulting in a veritable code-based arms-race between ad-blockers and tech-based capital (Davies, 2016). While ad blocking is likely more related to people's disdain for ads than it is to an internalized commitment to overcoming capital, it shows a notable level of frustration with one of platform capitalism's favourite revenue models: advertising.

More conscious efforts to exit the current exploitative/extractive nature of the internet can be found in active decisions to stop supporting the major big tech corporations that dominate it, for instance by not shopping through Amazon or seeking alternative ways to connect with friends online. As has been well documented, however, actually quitting the Big Five (Alphabet, Amazon, Meta, Apple, Microsoft) is extremely difficult due to the ubiquity of their control over a broad range of the digital economy and beyond (Hill, 2021). Thus, while these immediate efforts to exit capital in the realm of cyber estate are valiant, to truly make a difference they would need to be backed by a massive groundswell of intentional resistance and, equally critical, the establishment of viable alternatives.

This need for alternatives is animating a compeerist-aligned push to become more engaged in the service side of the internet. With the tech economy's exploitation of workers and prosumers, it is an effort that has come to be significantly shaped by the established thinking and experience of the cooperative movement, grounded in the mission to establish functional enterprises that actively circumvent capital and its rationales. Trebor Scholz (2017), a pioneer in rejuvenating the cooperative model for the digital age, has thus proposed challenging capital-centred platforms, apps, and algorithms by replacing these with ones emphasizing the wellbeing of workers, the community, and the environment. This idea has been termed platform cooperativism.

Some iterations of platform cooperatives entail traditional, union-oriented organizations seeking to protect the increasingly precarious labour of gig workers, as for instance through the National Domestic Workers Alliance and the California App-Based Drivers Association. Others take the form of producer collaboratives seeking to circumvent middleman platforms. Stocksy, for instance, is a stock-photo enterprise based on co-ownership and profit sharing, while Resonate is a community and artist owned music streaming cooperative. Fairmondo, in turn, is a German user-owned e-commerce site seeking to offer an alternative to Amazon. Commons-oriented labour facilitation platforms are also emerging, such as localized taxi apps or the more expansive Loconomics, a worker-owned platform used by freelancers to find jobs without mediation fees. Along similar lines, and probably the best-known capital-circumventing mediation service was the original Couchsurfing platform, which linked travellers to hosts offering free places to stay.

In the realm of social media, despite the particular difficulty of entry due to Metcalf's law, there are also a number of commons-oriented platforms to point to. Diaspora and Mastodon, for example, aim to be alternatives to Facebook and Twitter, respectively. Both are non-profit initiatives with the mission to create decentralized, cooperatively run platforms to help people connect and organize. An even more ambitious platform cooperative initiative is the French-based Framasoft, which is committed to a wholesale reinvention of the internet's function by fostering free open-source culture and software, while offering a wide range of commons-based services, including search engines, office management systems, and even social media sites.

Platform cooperatives, as the ones just noted, represent a promising effort to establish more just, democratic, and community-oriented digitally mediated services, yet, in the final analysis, they are also faced with daunting obstacles related to the difficulty of competing in a cyber estate environment in which capital has all the advantages. This is especially true if the goal is to actually offer viable alternatives to capital-based platforms, seeing that such an effort would be reliant on significant start-up funds, continuing revenue streams, and, of course, the ingenuity to establish the 'killer apps' that people want. While ingenuity is generally not in short supply within commons-based initiatives, the issue of accessing needed funds is more problematic.

Given that the use of rents/fees, advertising, and data mining run counter to the ideals of the commons and commoning, many online alternatives to the big-capital platforms fall back to a non-profit model dependent on donor-support and volunteer labour. This is the approach taken, for instance, by the alternative social media sites Diaspora and Mastodon, as well as in many of the commons-oriented mediation services, including the original Couchsurfing platform. As we have seen with digital commons production more generally, however, garnering the needed labour and revenue in this way over a prolonged period has significant limits, not to mention that these donated resources are still predominately linked to capitalist sources. Hence, in the Couchsurfing case, for instance, the lack of a reliable income stream ultimately became untenable as the service boomed in popularity and use. Much to the dismay of its early supporters, the decision was then made to make Couchsurfing a for-profit entity with significant investor buy in.

Acknowledging the frustrating dynamics involved in such cases, compeerism, as we know, prefers a commons-centred tactic that actively engages markets in order to circumvent any compromising resource challenges from the outset. Such a strategy means that a more intentional pursuit of market-based income is called for, as is already being done in some commons-based, online services. In this way, the organization behind the Couchsurfing site could have been made into a member-based platform cooperative, staying true to its peer-to-peer principles while managing to sustain itself by imposing limited fees, or pay-what-you-can requests, on those who successfully connect to a host. In the case of social media platform cooperatives, in turn, carefully controlled advertising and aggregated data mining could be adopted, for example by making these services only available to other compeerist-aligned actors. In other words, along the lines of peer property, it would be the establishment of an in- and out-group mechanism that determines with whom business can be done, where efforts would be made to establish compeerist-based alliances within an ever expanding yet vetted in-group.

Building on this line of reasoning, we can note here that while platform cooperatives certainly have their share of challenges in going head-to-head with capital, they also maintain some inherent advantages. First and foremost is the ability to pursue price competitiveness by not needing to reap big profits for investors. Scholz (2017, p 173) argues that platform cooperatives focused on fair remuneration can achieve business viability by garnering a relatively modest 10 per cent profitability rate, as opposed to the standard 30 per cent espoused by their capitalist counterparts. There are a number of boundary-commoning options that can then be initiated to help achieve this profit target. We will return to the essential area of mutual financial support within the commons-centred economy more broadly in Chapter 7. What we should highlight here, however, is the importance for platform cooperatives to foster and harness the free, open-access resources of the digital commons.

Indeed, Bauwens and Kostakis (2014) specifically call for the pursuit and expansion of what they term 'open cooperativism', where the burgeoning cooperative and solidarity economy synergizes with the peer-production movement linked to the digital commons. The use of free, open-source code for platform cooperatives is particularly pertinent here as relevant code is often the most fundamental and expensive aspect of platform operations. Yet, to truly leverage the benefits of this resource would, as explained in the previous chapter, ultimately require the institution of a broadly embraced peer-property regime, where profit-focused platforms were forced to work only with their own, internalized, and closed-off capabilities. With time, this arrangement could create a significant market disadvantage for these capital-oriented entities because, as research has shown, environments characterized by collaboration and sharing, especially in areas like code writing and design, are often far superior in generating innovative breakthroughs than those where actors are isolated and information is guarded (Benkler, 2002; 2006). Taking advantage of this protected but internally open digital-commons realm is a strategic imperative for compeerists that we will continue to see highlighted throughout this book.

The clash over data

The pursuit of an expansive, commons-oriented cyber estate explored in the previous section is directly related to the issue of data management, which has become a central component of big tech's dominance. The private holding of massive amounts of data derived from personal and public activities for the sake of profit or surveillance clearly conflicts with compeerist principles. Hence, the second major compeerist imperative in taking back the internet consists of democratizing and commonifying data collection while ensuring individual rights to privacy. We can make a distinction here between data that is specifically applied to an individual and data that is aggregated on the basis of large populations, even if this is not always an easy line to draw. The main concern with both is the mining and use of data to pursue data colonialism, yet solutions will vary as we are dealing with two different property dynamics.

Turning first to personal data, compeerism aligns with the overarching commitment to establish the right of individuals to reclaim ownership over their personal information. Many are already engaged in simple hacks, such as assiduously tweaking platform settings to limit their invasiveness. Others are turning to alternatives, to the extent that these are present, where data mining is intentionally disavowed. In search engines, for instance, a growing host of Google competitors, such as DuckDuckGo, makes the absence of data collection its primary selling point. While many of these are still for-profit entities, others, such as YaCy and Framasoft's Framabee, are more intentional, committed to open-source software and the decapitalization of user data.

Beyond search engines, the various platform cooperatives explored earlier generally disavow the collection of personal data. Data privacy here offers a certain competitive niche for compeerist-aligned actors. However, it is also likely that capital would begin addressing privacy concerns if these alternatives started to impact market share. Google, for instance, has committed to (yet also repeatedly delayed) the banning of third-party cookies that enable the tracking of users across multiple sites, although numerous other data collection mechanisms have been left unaddressed (Morrison, 2021).

Still, for many engaged in the movement to reclaim data, user/consumer or government attempts to tame market actors will never be sufficient. What is needed, instead, is a technologically enabled solution that could help ensure data cannot be taken from individuals in the first place. This is the vision of a decentralized, blockchain-enabled self-sovereign identity (SSI) (Preukschat and Reed, 2021). To understand what would be involved in such a solution, we can begin by considering a person's basic public identity, which includes things like age, ethnicity, education, employment, familial relations, residences, income, credit reports, and criminal records. Governments and capital actors regularly demand some of this information and most of it is assembled, shared, and digitally stored by multiple entities.

Then, on top of this basic profile, it is possible to place further layers of information, including internet browsing histories and interactions, consumption habits, detailed fitness and health data, activities engaged in, places visited, accomplishments, and social interactions. Most of this information, depending on your use of smart devices, also already exists, either explicitly or latently. Achieving an SSI, then, means establishing ownership over all of these forms of personal information within a highly secure, decentralized verification system controlled by each individual. While sneaky corporate requests for information would still need to be kept in check, an SSI would ultimately empower individuals to share only portions of their information depending on the interaction, with the additional right to disallow the storage or further sharing of this information by others.

Compeerism naturally aligns with the establishment of an SSI as it would not only significantly hamper capital's exploitation of the increasing range and depth of digitally captured personal information, it would also greatly facilitate commons-based and public-realm transactions and engagements, especially online. For instance, by establishing a trustworthy way to verify one's identity, asset sharing and swaps, as well as online voting and decision-making processes could be made easy and secure. A functional SSI system, however, is still in the early stages of development and the direction it will ultimately take is uncertain, with key issues related to the disparate interests involved in such technology remaining unresolved.

Big corporate players, including Microsoft, are already actively exploring the possibilities of an SSI, most notably through the Decentralized Identity Foundation. Clearly, many capital-oriented entities can also see the commercial benefits from the trust that can be established through a secure system of identity attribution, not to mention the significant profit opportunities in providing various capital-oriented management platforms and hosting infrastructures. On the flip side, of course, some tech actors for whom data collection and exploitation is a key part of their revenue model are adamantly opposed to any identity decentralization technology. For compeerists observing this clash there are two key imperatives that come to the fore. While fully committed to wresting personal data from big tech, it is equally critical that any emerging SSI capabilities do not become fully commoditized. In other words, for the establishment of a self-sovereign identity to deliver on its compeerist promise requires that commons-based, highly functional SSI management platforms become available to everyone at no cost.

Lastly, adding a further wrench into the digital identity issue is what the state's relationship to an SSI would be. While the state can legitimately argue that it has economic, planning, and security reasons to collect and process information on its citizens, the extent of this collection and how it is stored and used are issues that can clearly clash with goals inherent in establishing the right to a self-sovereign identity. In the wake of the Edward Snowden revelations regarding widespread and invasive domestic spying, calls to fundamentally check state surveillance and data collection have grown. Still, it is unlikely that the state will completely abandon its own perceived prerogative to maintain information on its citizens for the sake of governance.

Compeerism does not have a wholesale answer to the underlying tension between individual privacy and state-based data collection pursued in the name of the 'common good'. Taking a primarily pragmatic and decentralized approach to such ideological questions, the extent to which data privacy should be pursued vis-à-vis the state is a decision that is left to the place-specific compeerist movements to make in their own contexts. In the final analysis, however, it is fair to assume that the peoples' attitudes towards state-initiated data collection and use for the purposes of effective governance, especially around security and law enforcement, will be directly proportional to the trust and stakeholdership that they have been allowed to gain in their own government.

A data commons

Turning next to aggregated data we are confronted with different compeerist-aligned priorities, dealing less with privacy rights and more with the demands to have this data become a commons good. Indeed, we are in the midst of a boom in aggregated raw data that has the potential to be immensely beneficial to the populace. For instance, data analytics are increasingly informing practice within governance, as exemplified by the 'smart city' ideal in which real-time big data is employed to monitor, assess, and respond to everything from environmental conditions and traffic to infrastructure use and crime. In the commercial realm, in turn, digitally facilitated data collection, which has become pervasive, is creating breakthroughs and efficiencies across economic sectors, including in engineering, manufacturing, and logistics. While smart-city initiatives have been fairly critiqued as being primarily driven by the needs of capital, and commercial data remains guarded and proprietary for the sake of gaining competitive advantage, compeerism still sees immense potential in the possibility of commonifying aggregated data from municipal and commons-based sources.

There are several emerging initiatives in developing commons-based approaches to data collection and sharing that are worth noting here. A central component to these efforts has been, again, intentional, commons-oriented licensing, such as the Open Database License (ODbL). In ODbL data is allowed to be used, distributed, and worked on by anyone. Importantly, as with the reciprocity demand in GPL licensing for software, any processing of, or addition to, the data must also be made available under ODbL. OpenStreetMap, which developed the Open Database License, is a primary example of how crowdsourced data generation can be made fully accessible to facilitate the creation of use-value, in this case free, open-source, digital maps (Vercellone et al, 2019).

Based on the OpenStreetMap example, especially their development of the ODbL license, and with the continuing growth of commons-oriented apps aimed at facilitating the collection and sharing of open-source data, it is possible to envision a much broader effort to expand the amount of aggregated databases within the digital commons (Morozov and Bria, 2018). Compeerist aligned market actors, for instance, could collect and share important data involved in the design, implementation, and performance of the goods and services they create. This information could prove to be invaluable to fellow commons-oriented cooperatives and open-value networks seeking their own market viability in areas ranging from digitally-based services to manufacturing and farming.

Commons-friendly municipalities and place-based non-governmental organizations (NGOs), in turn, could gather and commonify a wide range of data on various local processes and operations collected via a host of methods ranging from traditional surveys and audits to digitally networked sensing equipment. Such public data would have significant value to civil society more broadly, which could use it to improve its own non-governmental initiatives and maintain oversight over local governments' effectiveness in the domains of social, environmental, and economic governance (Bass et al, 2018). If we then included an emerging, commons-friendly internet of things, with real-time streaming of detailed information from millions of interconnected devices plugged into the digital commons, the potential for commons-based innovation, efficiency, and sound governance becomes exponential (Mason, 2016).

Before becoming prematurely optimistic, however, we should note that non-proprietary data licensing such as ODbL still falls victim to the broader challenges facing copyleft. In other words, even if the data itself cannot be commodified, there are no protections against open-source aggregated data being employed by capital-based or state actors for profitable or nefarious ends that are in direct conflict with commons-centred interest. Indeed, it is important to understand that aggregated data can still be used to infringe on people's self-sovereignty rights despite being anonymous or non-individualized. We can note that Google, in seeking to move away from personal data tracking noted earlier, is now beginning to focus on leveraging precisely this kind of group data instead (Nield, 2021).

A good historical example of the unscrupulous use of aggregated data is how banks in the US correlated data sets for race and geographical location to redline African Americans, preventing them from getting equal access to financial services throughout most of the 20th century. It is with this negative potential in mind, then, that we must approach the pursuit of a digitally accessible data commons. In other words, we must be cognizant of the fact that any data opened to the public can ultimately be sifted through, cross referenced, and algorithmically crunched by capital, the state, or civil society in the pursuit of a number of problematic applications, including the execution of discriminatory and predatory practices (Berry, 2019).

Following from this, a strong compeerist case can thus be made for any commons-derived aggregated, open-sourced data to be placed under more proactive peer-property licensing regimes that limit how and by whom the data may be used. Enforcing such regimes for aggregated data, however, is even more challenging than what is involved with specific, added-value intellectual property. Not only is it difficult to contain and control access to this data once it has been made available to a large number of in-group entities, but proving that it has been utilized by an out-group actor in a specific way is often problematic. Nevertheless, in certain situations, where the misuse of protected data is believed to be especially egregious, targeted legal challenges could be pursued on the basis of the relevant peer-property stipulations in place.

In the longer term, of course, as part of a broader economic shift to the commons, the compeerist aim will be to increasingly diminish the power of capital in all aspects of the economy, including in the area of data collection and use. Still, it is important to acknowledge that such a decapitalization will not automatically deliver us from the ills linked to the use of agglomerated data today. This is because the underlying technology, developed to assist in the functioning of capital-focused assemblages/apparatuses, could still be present, retaining a latent agency that runs counter to compeerist aims. Such agency is particularly evident in capital-sourced AI and algorithms, whose code is full of profit-seeking and class-based/racial biases. Hence, in line with abstract hacktivist principles, this code must be systematically expunged through meticulous rethinking and rewriting.

Yet even then, we must ultimately accept that algorithms can never be fully objective or foolproof; being human constructions they will always be reflective of the prejudices and assumptions inherent in humans and society more broadly (Ntoutsi et al, 2020). Following from this, the enlightened use of digital networks and their trove of endless data will require nothing less than continuous critical, democratically informed oversight and engagement. Couldry and Mejias's (2019) answer to this call is to involve the populace in an ongoing, citizen-based research endeavour that seeks to keep tabs on how digital data-capturing technology works in the real world. To execute such a project, an open database could be maintained that tracks a wide range of important algorithms and their functions, based on people's submitted personal experiences. Ideally, then, where problems are identified, collaborative solutions could be found to restructure the hardware, programming, and the overall governance arrangements overseeing this technology to ensure that any bias or other forms of unfair targeting are purged (Stewart, 2020).

Getting there

In the final analysis, compeerism is committed to the creation of an expansive decapitalized cyber-estate landscape that is open, accessible, and replete with collaborative contributions and interactions that work to expand the commons and commoning. Such an internet would require replacing the various platform-based businesses that prey on prosumer and gig labour, serve as gatekeepers to artificially scarce digital value, establish monopolistic/oligopolistic market conditions, and use the ever-growing amounts of data collected to fully control the demand side of markets. As such, compeerists are here tasked with establishing and supporting alternative platform cooperatives while at the same time pursuing control over personal information and the commonification of aggregated data.

Yet, there are a number of difficulties and contingencies that must be overcome to successfully execute such a transition. For one, as we have seen, compeerist-aligned actors striving to compete with capital would need to engage in a more concerted use of boundary commoning, particularly when it comes to expanding and tapping into the digital commons. Beyond critically important code, relevant digital value here includes that of commons-generated aggregated data, which, as with other commons-based intellectual property, would require peer-property licensing protections that restricted this data's use by capital-based entities. For the other, however, there is also a clear need to shift the broader political-economic context, as the entities seeking to establish a more formidable commons-centred cyber estate are faced with significant market disadvantages vis-à-vis capital.

There are several policy initiatives compeerists could support to address these unfavourable conditions. To begin, on the global, national and federated state level, compeerism falls in line with the growing calls to curtail the extractive power of big tech, whether in the form of pursuing tax liabilities, securing protections for gig workers, or monopoly busting where feasible (van Dijck et al, 2019). There are numerous publicized interventions on this front that serve as promising, if still insufficient, examples. These include the challenge to Uber's revenue model and subsequent operating restrictions in some countries; the EU's multi-billion-dollar antitrust lawsuit against Alphabet (Google); and most recently, the EU's far-reaching Digital Markets Act, which aims to keep Europe's digital markets open and competitive, free from big tech's monopolizing tendencies (Meaker, 2022).

The compeerist cause also overlaps with the building pressure on capital regarding privacy rights. Indeed, given the increased value and importance of our digital interactions, it is likely that the struggle over the rights of our digital selves will be one of the most significant economic, legal, and political battles of the 21st century. The EU's General Data Protection Regulation of 2016, which aims at prohibiting the unconsented collection and exploitation of personal data, was a careful start, but much more is needed. In the longer term, governments will require forceful coaxing to facilitate the establishment of a self-sovereign identity (SSI) arrangement that is free and accessible to all. Furthermore, while not taking an overly rigid position regarding the extent to which state-centred data collection on its citizenry should be sanctioned, compeerism does insist that any such collection must be done with clear, democratically ensured oversight and accountability.

There are also multiple governance issues involved with non-personalized data. From a compeerist perspective, an ultimate goal is the commonification of all such assembled information, as well as, and perhaps even more importantly, the opening up of any data processing algorithms for everyone to see (Simons and Ghosh, 2020). As part of this commonification, however, there is also a particular need to restrict capital in how it collects, accesses, and ultimately makes use of such aggregated data. This imperative could most effectively be addressed through law, with state-based entities tasked with oversight and enforcement, backed by the power, if needed, to pry open a corporation's datasets and processing codes to ensure compliance. Thus, just as redlining has been made illegal as a practice by banks, so too can certain forms of data collection and algorithmic functions be barred from being employed in market analysis, advertising, and discrimination.

Yet, while national government involvement has the most far-reaching potential to restrict and even challenge platform capitalism and data colonialism, it is also often the hardest to come by. Thus, turning to the often more promising municipal level, it is possible to identify multiple opportunities for active, commons-oriented actions that elude the macroscaled state. Indeed, as local communities begin to grapple with the impacts of platform capitalism, it is increasingly municipalities that are, under pressure, stepping up to respond. In this way we have already seen cases where Airbnb and Uber have been banned in some cities, while local governments are increasingly receptive to making their aggregated data publicly accessible via open database licensing (Morozov and Bria, 2018). There are also instances of municipal-commons collaborations aimed at achieving greater technological independence, or sovereignty, where various exits from capital are pursued in the digital realm as a way to garner savings and greater control over the digitally based tools and services being employed in governance.

A case in point is the Barcelona en Comú political coalition, which, after gaining the mayoral seat in 2015, commenced an active campaign to achieve 'technological sovereignty' (Lynch, 2019). This goal was pursued by instituting open-data and software policies, including a switch from using proprietary software on government computers to open-source alternatives, as well as establishing contracting benefits for local cooperatives committed to using open-source technology (Lynch, 2019). A further effort was the initiation of the DECODE project, which uses an open-source, online participatory democracy tool, Decidim, to garner public engagement on how to pursue city data management that incorporates public input and whose aggregated data is placed in the digital commons (Bass et al, 2018). The Barcelona case shows that a commonification of critical aspects of the internet, and support for the digital commons, can be pursued effectively by local government. If adopted by enough urban centres across the world, such efforts could offer a significant stumbling block to the digital-colonial designs of big tech and provide the inspiration for a commons-based alternative.

Thus, in sum, while this chapter has shown that platform capitalism is still firmly entrenched, the numerous examples demonstrating resistance and alternatives to this arrangement also point to a possible way out. At the same time, in the final analysis, 'taking back the internet' cannot simply be reduced to reclaiming cyber estate, de- and re-programming code, and commonifying data. This is because the content, data, and processing associated with the internet ultimately depends on an underlying materiality, opening up a number of questions on how accessible or autonomous non-capital-oriented digital value and services can be when housed and run through capital-controlled hardware. Indeed, as long as the physical means of production, including those to produce digital value, remain firmly in the hands of capital, the promise of the digital revolution and a liberated general intellect will remain unfulfilled. It is, therefore, this materiality that we must turn to next.

PART II

The Material Economy and Commons

4

Democratizing Infrastructure

There is a good chance that readers of the first part of this book, in line with the closing thoughts of the last chapter, became increasingly aware of an unaddressed elephant in the room, namely the unspoken fact that any compeerist potential in the digital realm is impossible without an underlying, supportive foundation rooted in the material world (Vadén and Suoranta, 2009). Importantly, compared to digital value, the economic dynamics of material resources and assets are different, as these come with built in limits and breaking points. Within this context, the compeerist issue of interest is not as much about freeing artificially constrained abundance, as in the digital realm, as it is about finding a collaborative, commons-oriented approach to the optimal use of the scarce and constrained material means of production, including infrastructure, manufacturing capabilities, and natural resources. Critically, the pursuit of the 'optimal' here must again be viewed as driven by compeerism's commitment to use-value, that is, of first and foremost servicing the most fundamental needs and wants of humanity.

To achieve this use-value oriented aim, compeerism's commons-based focus centres on the need for greater economic democratization to ensure that the relevant stakeholders within the material economy, from workers to end-users, all have a seat at the table when it comes to determining how resource use and production are to be organized (Alperovitz, 2005; Schweickart, 2011). As with most digital value, however, the current control over infrastructure, factories, and land remains firmly in the grips of corporate capital. This control is further extended to the governance regimes overseeing the natural and increasingly fragile environmental systems within which these assets and their use are embedded. In addressing this challenge, mostly by seeking to expand commons-based forms of economic activity in an effort to supplant capital-based ones, we are confronted by an underlying tension.

On the one hand, compeerism is drawn to decentralized and localized forms of production as a way to enable greater stakeholder empowerment and, hence, better conditions for pursuing commons-centred, democratized forms of production. Yet, on the other hand, in an effort to be economically effective and viable in the face of market pressures, we are now forced much more into calculations of 'efficiency' in a world of de facto scarcity, which often calls for more macro-level approaches to organizing and governing production.

A fundamental question to be answered, therefore, is how, or to what extent, decentralization/localization can be adopted in the pursuit of a compeerist-aligned material economy that can effectively compete with capital. What would the management of resources and labour look like in such downscaled arrangements? Furthermore, where clear limits to such a scalar preference are uncovered, what would the alternative be? We begin in this chapter by considering the material infrastructure without which the digitally based economies covered in Part I could not function, that is, the physical hardware responsible for electricity and internet provision. The two subsequent chapters then address manufacturing and raw materials.

Electricity: the original client-server system

Over half a century ago the Canadian philosopher Marshall McLuhan claimed, 'electricity does not centralize, but decentralizes', by which he was suggesting that electricity empowers people to do anything almost anywhere (McLuhan, 1964, 68). Yet for electricity to deliver on this promise it needs to be accessed, and this access, in turn, is based not on decentralized systems but rather on an arrangement akin to that of the client-server model in computing, where networked "clients" are dependent on a centralized source (the server) for a needed resource. In the case at hand this takes the form of customers on a grid being dependent on large-scale, centralized power plants. The practical monopoly that ensues from this infrastructure is what then empowers large for-profit energy companies to inflate prices while avoiding innovations and upgrades, which is precisely why most energy sectors are regulated by the government (Friedman, 2005). At the same time, however, a variety of technologies have emerged that would allow for the creation of increasingly decentralized energy systems, based on locally produced, renewable energy. While these systems are currently being pursued for the sake of achieving savings and meeting greenhouse gas emission quotas within a still capitalist framework, they also offer an opening for immediate, individual, or community-based forms of exit from capital.

On the household level, for instance, it is now feasible for many to completely opt out of the corporate supply of electricity, by setting up micro-solar and/or wind generators with batteries for storage. Estimates indicate that nearly two million people currently are living voluntarily off-grid in the US, with numbers steadily rising (Rosen, 2014). This has been enabled primarily by the dramatic fall in prices for solar energy and battery storage, as well as the wide array of DIY information online. The tiny-house movement, for instance, which is committed to supporting a viable path to a simpler, more sustainable lifestyle, offers countless forums and open-sourced designs aimed at helping people build and maintain a house that can deliver all the needed amenities of modern life while still being off grid.

The potential to exit energy capital is not restricted to tiny houses, however. To get a sense of the expanding possibilities we can take the average German household's electricity consumption as a starting point, which is about 300 kWh per month (only a third of the US average). To cover this amount of electricity with self-generated solar energy, assuming relatively stable consumption and production, would require about 200 square feet (roughly the area of a soccer goal) of solar panels along with 10 kWh of battery storage. The price for this number of solar arrays today, right out of the factory and without installation, would be just over US$1,200; 20 years ago, it would have been closer to $15,000 (Feldman et al, 2021). The factory-based price for the required battery, in turn, would be around $2,000. Again, 10 years ago such battery capacity would have been six times that amount (Feldman et al, 2021).

With prices falling in this way, the return-on-investment timeline for renewable energy systems is continuously shrinking. Given that these systems are also very durable (solar panels last for at least 25 years), they can be paid-off well before they become defunct. Currently, the average pay-off period for a fully installed, residential solar system in the US, taking existing subsidies into account, is between six and nine years, meaning they will provide free energy for at least another sixteen years (CSE, 2022). Yet, prices are still dropping, and could drop even more with a commonification of the solar industry, that is, a scenario where non-profits and community-centred cooperatives, with the support of municipalities, were actively engaged in solar panel production, distribution, installation, and system integration with the main grid (where needed). The result of increasing accessibility to decentralized, renewable forms of electricity in this way ultimately brings us ever closer to the realization of McLuhan's vision of decentralized empowerment – creating a more democratic, resilient, and affordable energy supply for an emerging commons-oriented movement and economy – while at the same time facilitating a significant divestment from the capital-dominated energy sector.

Still, it is important to note that the actual ups and downs of energy consumption and production makes it difficult to achieve full autonomy from the central grid, especially once we move from isolated households to larger buildings or even neighbourhoods. For instance, a recent detailed analysis of four commercial and residential communities in the Netherlands, identified as 'the state-of-the-art of decentralised renewable energy systems', showed that despite significant investments, all four locales could not be fully 'islanded', meaning they still needed to be linked to the main grid for backup in cases of shortages or oversupply (de Graaf, 2017). According to this same study, however, emerging microgrid technology could go a long way to reduce main grid, or 'macrogrid', dependency by making use of software that more effectively manages the available energy within a shared community network. AI controlled 'packetized energy management', for example, functions as an internet of energy, where the various energy demands and outputs within the microgrid can be continuously regulated to adapt to real-time current and expected future microgrid conditions.

Communities could reap several benefits from adopting such technology. Not only does a finely tuned microgrid minimize energy loss associated with transit, but it makes the most efficient use of the energy produced, which means there is less need to rely on costly external macrogrids or autonomous energy storage. Indeed, solar batteries are still not cheap, and feeding excess energy back into the grid is usually poorly compensated. Actual price dynamics within a microgrid community, however, will ultimately depend on how this grid is governed.

Currently, the most common route taken here centres on entrepreneurial initiative, where community members contributing energy to the microgrid become small-scale prosumers. An example of such an effort is Brooklyn Microgrid, which organizes the electric connections between neighbourhood producers and user/consumers, facilitating peer to peer energy trading via a blockchain-enabled platform (Sagisi, 2019). While this microgrid facilitates a more collaborative exit from big energy capital, money-based incentives are still an obvious component to the system. It is, however, also possible to envision arrangements where the governance of prices and the overall inducement for prosumers is determined along more democratic, cooperative lines – for example within the context of an intentional, commons-oriented neighbourhood or city council (Giotitsas et al, 2020). Such an approach would ultimately be more conducive to creating fully collaborative and shared means of energy production and use based on pooled resources, where energy was truly treated as a commons.

A further benefit to commons-based microgrids is that they afford the responsible community enhanced bargaining power in relation to the corporations that tend to control the macrogrid, on which some dependencies could nonetheless persist (contingent on community size). Issues to be negotiated here could include pricing, sharing infrastructure, and environmental issues related to the production and transmission of macrogrid electricity. Community-centred microgrids could even expand their market power by becoming interlinked, creating an expansive electricity provision network that actively competed with capital-based energy companies. In such a scenario, and faced with dwindling revenues, it is likely that capital would respond with increased prices, which would motivate ever more people to pursue an exit by going off-grid or linking up with a local microgrid. Ultimately, the diminished profitability of the macrogrid could make it fertile ground for some form of decapitalization.

Macrogrid dependence and the movement to democratize energy

While decentralized microgrids based on renewable energy are promising, we must nonetheless be cognizant of their potential limits, especially in terms of overall capacity. We can note here that leading research into renewable energy futures – motivated by the acknowledged environmental need to rapidly shift out of carbon-based fuels – indicates that achieving a switch to 100 per cent carbon free/neutral energy in the near future is possible, albeit with a fundamentally restructured economy that can achieve between a 40 to 65 per cent reduction in energy consumption (see Piques and Rizos, 2017). We will directly address this question of economic reorganization in the next two chapters. Yet, even with significant efficiencies in energy use (especially in the Minority World), a further fundamental question lies in weather localized electricity generation could ever be sufficient. At least in the foreseeable future, there is compelling evidence that it cannot (MacKay, 2009).

The fundamental problem, even within a larger system of interconnected microgrids, pertains to the ability of generating enough electricity in more densely populated, energy-hungry urban centres, which is where 70 per cent of the world's population is expected to live by the year 2050. We can take New York City as an example. Even if yearly electricity consumption were cut in half, from thirty to fifteen thousand gigawatts of electricity (and this is hard to imagine with a simultaneous move to electric vehicles), it would take at least eight of the largest wind or solar farms to reach such levels of production, which would require an untenable 30 or 120 square miles of land, respectively; and this is assuming that these facilities are placed in ideal settings (Feldman et al, 2021).

Given that some degree of macrogrid dependence remains unavoidable for many communities, then, the subsequent question for compeerists is how this infrastructure can best be commonified, that is, taken out of capital's hands and placed under the purview of stakeholder communities. This is precisely the aim of the growing energy democracy movement, which has linked demands for a renewable energy transition to increased citizen empowerment. To better grasp the challenges and possible ways forward in such a movement, it is helpful to view electricity infrastructure as consisting of three main components: generation, transmission, and distribution.

The first aim of compeerist-aligned energy democracy activists tends to focus on gaining community control over the last-mile of macrogrid electricity distribution. Strategies to be pursued vary here according to the underlying conditions on the ground. In the worst-case scenarios, where investor-held energy companies have monopolized electricity delivery, the most common tactic has been to strive for a cooperativization or municipalization of the energy infrastructure (Burke and Stephens, 2018).

The cooperative route is generally adopted where the underlying regulations are favourable and the population to be serviced is relatively small. Germany, for instance, has seen a significant increase in small-scale cooperatives, from less than a hundred at the turn of the millennium to close to a thousand today (DGRV, 2020). The US proves to be an outlier here, as large-scale cooperativization has also been on the table in some parts of the country, likely due to the presence of already existing large energy cooperatives that can be traced back to the electrification push of the New Deal in the 1930s. In one recent case in the state of Maine, it took a governor's veto in 2021 to block a voter referendum that would have replaced the current for-profit utility (linked to the energy conglomerate Avangrid) with a decentralized, user/consumer-owned utility (Maine, 2021).

In most instances where larger populations are involved, however, the energy democracy movement has been inclined to pursue municipalization efforts. Germany is again an exemplar of this strategy, with the city of Hamburg, for instance, ousting their corporate energy supplier, Vattenfall, as the result of a public referendum which gave the municipality full control over its grid in 2014. Notably, this transition occurred without the local support of both the dominant centre left (SPD) and centre right (CDU) parties (Provost and Kennard, 2014). In Berlin, a similar referendum, again resisted by the mainstream parties within the city council, was supported by 80 per cent of those who voted, but the measure failed because it fell one per cent shy of the 25 per cent quorum requirement (BBC, 2013). Turning to the US, while much attention has focused on Boulder's multi-year battle to break free from its corporate energy provider, Excel, a much larger municipalization effort has been unfolding in San Francisco. In the California case the beleaguered PG&E utility finds itself increasingly in the sites of the city council, which has been entertaining the idea of a municipal takeover for several years (Castle, 2020; Kukura, 2021).

Importantly, however, capital-based corporations are not always the dominant entity in electricity delivery; for example, in the US nearly half the population already receives its last-mile(s) of electricity from either a cooperative or public utility. Nonetheless, homing in on the latter first, despite tending to offer marginally better rates and greater environmental awareness than their investor-owned counterparts, these hierarchically organized public entities still generally lack options for community input and empowerment. In response to this reality, the energy democracy movement is beginning to make robust demands to address these shortcomings. Based on the Berlin case noted earlier, such demands can include the embrace of full transparency, citizen and worker participation on the board, neighbourhood advisory assemblies, and the power to force decisions through citizen petitions (Angel, 2016). The Switched On London campaign for a public utility is making similar demands (Switched On, nd). Yet, as is evidenced from the resistance to such measures from within some city governments themselves (Hamburg and Berlin are both good examples), bringing about truly commonified public utilities will be a continuing battle.

The situation is somewhat brighter when we turn to existing cooperative electricity providers, as these tend to be endowed with mechanisms aimed at facilitating community input. Furthermore, being member cooperatives that are not driven by profit – if revenues exceed the needs of the cooperative, the money is redistributed to its members – they are more amenable to member interests and wishes (Bozuwa, 2018). In the US there are hundreds of New Deal era, cooperative utilities and electricity-centred cooperative federations, which were established to distribute (and in some cases generate and transmit) electricity to the large swathes of the country that were considered too unprofitable for capitalist investments. Today, US cooperatives own and maintain 42 per cent of the distribution lines that make up the last-mile(s) of electricity supply (NRECA, 2021).

From an energy democracy perspective, having electricity cooperatives already in place on the ground is undoubtedly the most ideal starting point. To illustrate the compeerist potential here, we can take the unlikely case of the US state of Georgia, where a significant portion of the population, mostly in rural areas, receive their energy from various Electric Membership Cooperatives (EMCs). While the actual running of these membership cooperatives can be criticized for the decisions they have made, for instance a lack of investment in sustainability initiatives or barring the public from board meetings, the governance structure is still fundamentally democratic, meaning it is the members of the cooperative (anyone purchasing energy from an EMC) who are empowered to elect their respective decision-making board (Orrock, 2011).

This governance arrangement then opens up significant opportunities to 'hack' the way these cooperatives have tended to operate. Indeed, it is worth pointing out here that in the oft neglected co-op elections that are offered, candidates with the most energized base usually win (Grimley, 2020). Hence with a concerted compeerist push, greater control over a cooperative board could be used to amend operating procedures to allow for greater openness and transparency while refocusing services to be more in line with commons-based principles. Furthermore, this control could then conceivably be extended to the higher tiered cooperative federation. For example, in the case at hand, each regional EMC board is permitted to vote for their particular representative to the governing body of the state-wide Oglethorpe Power Corporation, which, beyond the last-mile, is also involved in energy production and transmission.

Decapitalizing trans-local generation and transmission

The Oglethorpe Corporation's participation in electricity generation and long-distance supply is noteworthy as municipal or cooperative involvement in this area is much scarcer, likely due to its large-scale nature, which is less conducive to community-centred governance. Indeed, looking ahead, compeerists, aligned with the energy democracy movement, are faced with the challenge of balancing their inclination for decentralization/localization with the reality of trans-local infrastructure.

The preferred approach here will ultimately be shaped by the political-economic environment in place, including the power dynamics between big (energy) capital, energy democratization movements, and government. Yet, in what will certainly be a prolonged struggle, we should note that the capital-state-societal context – where commons-based actors will seek to assert themselves – is also likely to be greatly impacted by the imperative of a future decarbonization of the economy. More specifically, a serious commitment to decarbonization will necessitate a fundamentally redesigned and rebuilt electricity infrastructure, an undertaking that will undoubtedly shake up the electricity provision status quo (Rifkin, 2013).

Consider, to start with, that the production and affordability of renewable energy potential is greatly dependent on its location. Hence, the most effective way to maximize the supply of green energy would be to make better use of the most productive energy hotspots in the world, including the high irradiation regions of the tropics and subtropics as well as the wind-rich coasts and plains (Deng et al, 2015). An argument can then be made for the need to switch the future macrogrid from alternating current (AC) to direct current (DC). Rejuvenating Edison and Tesla's 'current war' has become relevant again because many of the technologically based pitfalls associated with DC current have been resolved, meaning that DC's significant benefits could very well be worth tapping. These include the reduced cost of high-capacity, long distance DC power lines; up to 50 per cent greater transmission efficiency; enhanced grid stability; and, not least, the ability to use DC current without costly conversion to AC (Irfan, 2012). This latter point is important as our growing reliance on solar energy will be in the form of DC, which will also increasingly become the current in highest demand, from computer servers to the charging of electrical vehicle (EV) batteries

Looking at such a future, we can envision a macroscaled, highly efficient and carbon-free electricity network, comprised of interconnected, localized microgrids backed by a macrogrid based on optimal, utility-scaled renewable energy generation and transmission over longer distances (Rifkin, 2013). This energy network would be managed by a host of sophisticated AI systems capable of adjusting electricity supply and demand by being plugged into an expansive internet of things. However, in envisaging this ideal, it also becomes clear that the scale of investment and organization required would likely be impossible without governmental leadership and assistance. In this sense compeerism recognizes the state as an integral part of the long-term solution to our macrogrid energy challenges.

For most on the left, who would agree with this assessment, the obvious strategy here is to call upon the state to become actively involved as an energy provider. This option has historical precedent, as in the US state-run effort to electrify the Tennessee valley with hydro-power in the 1930s and early 1940s. Indeed, the federally owned and operated Tennessee Valley Authority (TVA) is still one of the biggest energy producers and grid owners in the US. More recently, the ideal of a nationalized, state-based energy sector has seen somewhat of a resurgence, as evidenced by the opposition English Labour Party's recent proposal to take the British electricity sector into public ownership, in the run up to the 2019 general election. While this policy gambit ultimately failed to deliver an electoral win, the fact that a major political party made energy nationalization a centrepiece of its platform is noteworthy.

Still, from a compeerist view (likely shared by many British voters), the main drawback to contemporary nationalization proposals is the lack of concrete citizen stakeholdership and power in the actual 'public' entities that are being suggested as replacements for the old ones. Promises made of 'radical decentralization ... so that local people and communities are given far greater control over their lives and prospects', ultimately prove to be insufficient due to their vagueness; nationalization still comes across as one hierarchical organization (government) replacing another (capital) (Labour, 2019, np). It would, therefore, be much more compelling if any proposed government takeover of the macrogrid were accompanied by clear, enforceable commitments to citizen oversight and buy-in, as is being increasingly demanded with energy municipalization of the last-mile, as per the Berlin case earlier.

Alternatively, then, and more in line with compeerist principles, the state could assist in the facilitation of a nationally, or even internationally, organized cooperative to take responsibility for the macroscaled aspects of electricity supply, just as the US state was involved in creating the regional electricity cooperative federations during the New Deal. In the earlier Georgia example, for instance, it was the Oglethorpe Power Corporation – currently the largest cooperative energy producer in the US – that was established to service the macrogrid needs for the hundreds of last-mile delivery EMCs scattered across the state. It is not an insignificant fact that cooperatives in the US today still account for 5 per cent of electricity generation and 12 per cent of transmission (NRECA, 2021).

In this sense, national or supra-national member cooperatives would simply entail an upscaling of what was already accomplished at a more regional level, as in Georgia. This higher tier of organization could then be made beholden to the same governance rules and commitments to members that are in place for the smaller cooperatives below. Importantly, management of higher-tiered levels of the macrogrid would again be supplied democratically from lower-tiered entities. In such an arrangement, national government would play mostly a supportive role, offering guidance and monetary assistance to bolster democratic and cooperative efforts to achieve a more community-centred and decarbonized electricity infrastructure at scale.

One area of particular complexity worth noting, however, pertains to the potential energy connections between the wealthier Minority and less-wealthy Majority World that would be called for if the most efficient use of the globe's renewable energy were to be pursued. Consider, for instance, that Africa is estimated to have nearly six times the renewable energy potential of Western Europe (Deng et al, 2015). Looking at such discrepancies, it makes sense, at face value, to find ways of harnessing the comparative advantage of regions rich in renewable energy, like Africa, in order to create win–win outcomes for both energy suppliers and receivers. Expansive, high-capacity DC power lines connecting solar farms in northern Africa to Europe is a common vision here. At the same time, such exchanges are also plagued with possible pitfalls, as evidenced by the countless examples of past and present injustices involved in Minority–Majority trade relations, especially in the energy sector.

In Chapter 6 we will return to the need and challenge of restructuring postcolonial relationships between the Minority and Majority regions of the world. What we can at least establish here, however, is that any compeerist pursuit of transnational energy trade should be made following the commons-based governance principles outlined by Ostrom, namely, that it is the resident stewards of the land who must be the primary stakeholders and beneficiaries in any such deal. The ultimate compeerist imperative from the perspective of the Minority World would thus be to engage in such a project as humble partners, in the spirit of solidarity rather than exploitation/capitalization. Yet, if such a commons-oriented arrangement is impossible to establish, the pursuit of comparative advantage would need to be put aside, with an even greater focus placed on managing demand and making the most of the less abundant local/regional energy sources available.

Commonifying the internet

The second critical material foundation of the digital revolution is the infrastructure associated with the internet, which, as with electricity, can be broken down into the distinct areas of generation, transmission, and distribution. Turning first to generation, or supply, we find that the actual digital data/content of the internet is sourced from a variety of corporate, non-profit, state, and prosumer actors. In the previous two chapters we spelled out how this digital content is contested and how it could potentially be reorganized along compeerist lines. Yet, unlike energy, which is a finite entity that needs to be continuously reproduced, digital content, once produced, just needs to be stored. This is where the infrastructural materiality of 'supply' manifests itself, usually in the form of increasingly massive data-centres packed with computer servers. Today this 'cloud' of data storage infrastructure is dominated by Microsoft, Amazon, and Alphabet, which account for approximately two thirds of all cloud space for rent (Cohen, 2021).

Next, when thinking about the actual transmission of this stored digital information, the idea of a 'series of tubes', offered by US Senator Ted Stevens in 2006 amidst much ridicule, is, in fact, not a bad analogy (Blum, 2019). Transmission infrastructure is ultimately an interconnected arrangement of networked cables and routers, tied together with internet exchange points (IXPs), forming the so-called 'tier one backbone' of the internet. In the US, the privatization of the internet in the 1990s enabled a number of large, mostly telecommunications-based corporations to dominate the tier one backbone, which soon became the norm in other capitalist economies as well. More recently, in the push to expand transoceanic broadband, it is the big tech giants such as Alphabet and Meta that have invested most heavily in both the amount and speed of these cables (Satariano, 2019).

Internet service providers (ISPs) are then responsible for linking the internet backbone to home and business computers, that is, the last-mile(s) of distribution. In addition to such direct connections, however, there is also the burgeoning and increasingly crucial realm of radio-wave based (mobile) access, established via a distinct infrastructure of cell-tower networks capable of tapping into the internet backbone with increasing speeds (4G, 5G, 6G). Both the direct and mobile connection of the last-mile(s) are also predominantly controlled by a handful of large telecommunication and cable companies. Satellite-based internet access (which is also radio-based), in turn, is primarily limited to rural settings and still makes up a relatively small part of the market (less than 10 per cent in the US) with SpaceX's Starlink arguably the most recognized and aggressive actor in this ISP sector.

A dimension to mobile internet access that deserves a bit more attention here relates to its dependency on limited radio-spectrum capacity. A problem in this is that overlapping frequency use leads to interference and compromised transmission. To deal with this problem, the US initially organized auctions to designate rights over specific frequencies in a given geographical area, quickly leading to telecommunications-based corporations monopolizing the airwaves in a bid to capitalize on another opening, to extract rents (via 'data plans') from the internet. Recently, however, the existing arrangement for allotting frequency rights has come under fire, with demands being made, for instance, to allow for the negotiated sharing of specific frequencies. Commoners active in this area, however, warn that the suggested changes are not guided by commons-based interests (O'Dwyer, 2013). In fact, beyond being motivated by the desire to expand access to for-profit digital content, a reorganized radio spectrum could be used to create 'tethered' smart devices that could only work with specific frequencies, hence opening a whole new realm of scarcity engineering (due to limited usability) and rent extraction (due to new data plans) (O'Dwyer, 2013).

The main takeaway from this brief review of the internet's underlying infrastructure is that a small number of large corporations are using this materiality within internet storage, transmission, and delivery to gain control over, and profit from, its unwieldy content. In this way, what was originally conceived as a decentralized network of co-equal computers has been transformed into a centralized, client-server system aimed at imposing rent-seeking, access scarcity. It is a development, furthermore, that has directly fostered the demise of net neutrality and a widening digital divide between those with and without access to the internet as non-profitable communities remain unserviced. Faced with these realities the populace at large ultimately has a choice: either pay the rising price to access an internet increasingly curated by capital or, as compeerism advocates, to pursue avenues of immediate and longer-term exit.

Seeking commons-based alternatives

At this point, short of refusing to use the internet altogether, there are very few ways to fully avoid the large capital actors controlling the server cloud. At the same time, it is worth noting that the decentralized, peer-to-peer roots of the internet have not completely vanished. The so-called 'dark web', for example, apart from its shady content, still works mostly along the lines of the original internet concept, with direct communication between computers/servers without a centralized middleman. P2P file sharing networks using protocols such as BitTorrent to interlink personal computers are also still very much alive, offering some guidance in how a more commons-based approach to the material management of digital storage and access could be achieved (Sandvine, 2018).

Some peer-to-peer advocates are now also seeking to overcome the client-server structure of the internet by using blockchain contracts to incentivize participants to lend out their free computing space, thus establishing capabilities based on a swarm of individual, decentralized machines as opposed to isolated, massive server farms. Currently these efforts are led by small startups, like Storj for crowdsourced online data storage or IEX and

Golem for decentralized super-computing. While these examples are still run as capital-oriented platforms, they could also quite easily be based on compeerist-inspired platform cooperatives, as exist, for instance, with other forms of resource sharing, such as for cars (eGo CarShare) or household items (Peerby). In this way, users of the internet could once again become an integral part of the infrastructure instead of being made into mere consumers. One thing that nonetheless becomes abundantly clear in such an envisioned trajectory is the need for a massive increase in the small-scale ownership of more powerful computers/servers and less reliance on mobile, cloud-based devices (Losey and Meinrath, 2016).

In line with this reasoning, yet even more far-reaching, is the idea behind the Holochain project, which aims to build a parallel, decentralized, commons-oriented internet that nonetheless offers much greater capabilities than what is possible in simple peer-to-peer connectivity. The project's primary focus is establishing a blockchain-like code that would be capable of organizing the complexity entailed in managing the endless information and transactions that make up the internet without recourse to client-server systems. In doing so, the Holochain code also seeks to overcome many of blockchain's various drawbacks, particularly the energy intensive 'proof-of-work' verification system used (via mining) and the difficulties in upscaling applications to a much larger set of transactions. This is being done by developing a biomimicry-inspired ledger that replaces anonymous, 'trustless' networks (the basis of Bitcoin) with smaller interlinked groups where trust has been established, thereby enabling greater verification speed and the ability to significantly upscale the processing of transactions (Brock, 2016).

Arthur Brock, co-founder and chief designer behind the Holochain project, explains that the foundational code works to establish a 'method and reward structure for storing and accessing data and applications between users themselves', thus creating the foundation for a people-run internet (Brock, 2021). This envisioned network would serve as the home of Holo applications, or Happs, which could then become increasingly interlinked and expansive, committed to the peer-to-peer, non-commercial nature of the network. Early examples of such Happs range from alternative social media platform initiatives, such as Junto, to energy monitoring and management systems such as RedGrid (Gerhardt, 2020).

The material autonomy that Holochain seeks to achieve is then based on the adoption of prosumer-oriented HoloPorts, which are intended to serve as the hardware that hosts the Holochain-based internet. Investing in holoport capacity is incentivized by issuing HoloFuel, a unique cryptocurrency that is used in executing transactions within Holochain-based applications, similar to how the popular cryptocurrency Ether is used to run Ethereum-based ones. All in all, given the active reworking of both blockchain and the material infrastructure of the internet as a means to exit capital, the

Holochain project is an exemplar of the abstract hacktivists' call to re-engineer and repurpose existing and emerging digital technology as a way to pursue a new social and economic paradigm.

Next, moving from storage to transmission and delivery, we must consider both long-distance interconnectivity (the internet backbone) and local access. With regard to the latter, and focusing particularly on the last-mile(s) of direct connection, there has been a surge of activity in finding alternatives to the large corporate internet service providers (ISPs), either because they show little interest in investing in broadband capability in certain areas or the services provided are considered subpar and overpriced due to monopoly-like privileges. Not surprisingly, communities are therefore turning to the same options available with regard to electricity provision: municipalization and cooperativization.

In the US there have been several examples of successful municipal interventions aimed at making broadband internet more accessible. The municipal Electric Power Board of Chattanooga in Tennessee, for instance, offers a fibre-optic network that was first in the nation to claim one gigabyte per second internet speeds for its customers (Koebler, 2016). Chattanooga's fibre-optic infrastructure is also used to establish a smart energy grid in the city, leading to significant energy efficiencies. Most of the cooperative efforts in the US, in turn, have centred on rural parts of the country (providing 30 per cent of access there), often by building on the already existing infrastructure in place for cooperative electricity provision. There are now over a hundred electricity cooperatives across the country that have diversified into offering broadband (Trostle et al, 2022).

A further critical task related to access pertains to expanding wireless connectivity. In less remote areas, one promising initiative has been through the use of mesh networks, where a large number of small-scale routing devices are shared within the network as a way to extend a direct line to the internet backbone (like a far reaching wi-fi network). Guifi.net, for example, is a community-based internet provider in the Basque region of Spain seeking to circumvent capital-oriented ISPs by establishing expansive mesh networks as a way to provide internet connectivity as a common good (Baig et al, 2015). Similarly, in Detroit, the Equitable Internet Initiative is using mesh networks to tackle 'digital redlining', which has contributed to 40 per cent of Detroit residents not having internet access (Kalischer-Coggins, 2021).

In more isolated areas, in turn, where direct broadband linkages to the internet backbone are few and far between, commons-oriented projects have focused on establishing an independent infrastructure of cellular towers for radio-based wireless connectivity. One example can be found on Native American lands, which have long been on the losing side of the digital divide. Non-profits like the Tribal Digital Village, servicing tribes in southern California, have worked to address this problem by utilizing a small band of non-licensed spectrum as a way to deliver internet access to native homes via tribally-controlled transmission towers. Yet, one of the biggest challenges in this effort pertains to limits on the publicly available radio spectrum. Thus, the push to treat spectrum truly as a commons, with much greater access allotted to localized, non-capital interests, has become a central issue to native efforts seeking not only to reap the benefits of the digital revolution, but to achieve greater autonomy and self-determination (Duarte, 2017).

In the end, however, any internet access system, whether through a direct cable connection or via some form of radio-based network, ends with a needed link to the internet backbone. This means there will always remain a certain dependence on what is ultimately a globalized infrastructure, which, as with the electricity macrogrid, raises some key questions from a compeerist perspective regarding how such a macroscaled resource should be organized. In approaching this question, it must first be acknowledged that the commons-oriented spirit associated with the original creation of the internet is still evident in its global management. To this day, the overarching governance arrangement of the internet's backbone is characterized by a collaboration involving numerous actors representing civil society, business, government, and research (Radu, 2019).

One influential organization in this management assemblage/apparatus is the well-endowed, nongovernmental Internet Society, which, among other things, aims to serve 'as a focal point for cooperative efforts to promote the Internet as a positive tool to benefit all people throughout the world' (IS, 2021, np). The commons-centric aim of the Internet Society is reflected in their promotion of open standards and protocols, the sharing of technical information, and the building of community networks. In pursuit of this latter goal, the Internet Society has been a strong advocate for increasing the numbers of internet exchange points (IXPs), especially commons-oriented ones, as these are critical in linking, smaller, lower-tiered networks to the internet backbone. Today many IXPs, including some of the largest ones, are established as non-profits with the singular drive to create a more effective and accessible internet.

From a compeerist standpoint, with an eye to fully commonifying the internet backbone, the existing commons-centred principles still evident in the oversight and management of this trans-local and unwieldy infrastructure need to be sustained and extended. In particular, more participation and input should be sought from civil society, especially from those that have still largely been left out, either due to their remote location or their lack of wealth. Compeerism here fully embraces the view (broadly adopted by the United Nations), that internet access is a human right, and hence the priority animating any governance over the macroscaled infrastructure of the internet must be to expand service (Howell and West, 2022). This need is evidenced by the fact that significant chunks of the population in the Minority World still do not have access to the internet, let alone a broadband connection, while on the global scale roughly a third of humanity remains excluded (ITU, 2021).

As these facts make evident, despite some collaborative governance arrangements, the pursuit of an expanded internet backbone to achieve high-speed access as a universal right remains fundamentally hobbled, primarily by big-capital interests that do not see adequate profit opportunities in such a development. At the same time, as with electricity, there is no alternative but to work with the existing macroscaled infrastructure and its overarching governance regime. Even a Holochain-based internet, which is primarily focused on achieving autonomy in the realm of data storage, would still need to rely on the transmission hardware currently in place. Given this scalar reality, compeerism must again acknowledge the need to engage macro-level governance actors, including, in particular, the state.

Most discussions today around how the state can best be enlisted to pursue internet access as a human right, adopt either an accommodational or confrontational approach to capital. The accommodational position sees the state coaxing and incentivizing capital in order to garner the needed investments for internet expansion and upgrades. In Japan, which is often pointed to as a model for this approach, classic incentivizations offered to key IT linked industries include subsidies, low-interest credit, and tax incentives (Atkinson et al, 2008). The confrontational approach, in turn, has primarily focused on outright nationalization. Indeed, we can point again to the British Labour Party's election platform in 2019, for which, along with electricity, the public takeover of internet provision was another key proposition.

While compeerism remains deeply sceptical of the long-term desirability of seeking synergistic relations with capital as a tactic to grow the commons, nationalization, as noted with electricity, is also considered imperfect in its current proposed forms. The compeerist concern with a government takeover of the tier one backbone again revolves around the state's hierarchical tendencies, which, in turn, are associated with excessive bureaucracy and uninventive management, largely because there are no mechanisms to allow for cross-sectional, democratic governance. Thus, following the main arguments made regarding electricity earlier, the alternative option would be the facilitation of a commons-oriented third way. While not well fleshed out, Bernie Sanders's 2020 presidential campaign platform in the US came close to such a vision in calling for 'publicly owned and democratically controlled, co-operative, or open access broadband networks' (Bernie, 2017, np). It is the focus here on establishing an internet infrastructure that is not monopolized by capital or the state, but rather is owned and governed by the people via an assemblage of democratically managed entities, that resonates with compeerist principles.

One promising option here would be the creation of so-called stakeholder cooperatives, or solidarity co-ops. More particularly, the internet's infrastructure, from long distance broadband cables and exchange points to large-scaled server capacity and cellular networks, could be placed in the hands of cooperative federations comprised of representatives from a host of commons-oriented and collaborative stakeholders. Such stakeholders could include last-mile ISP co-ops, local/regional governments, workers, and user-members. Importantly, and reflecting this organizational shift, the charter of such macro-level cooperatives could then be rewritten to focus on operating the internet infrastructure as a commons, in line with its original intent as a resource sharing peer-to-peer network and building on the commons-oriented management regimes already in place.

Looking ahead

In bringing this chapter to a close, we can see how the liberatory potential of the digital revolution is fundamentally hindered by the current, capital-oriented organization of the electricity and internet infrastructures, on which the digital relies. Nonetheless, there are a number of ongoing political initiatives and potential paths forward that could challenge capital's dominance here.

On the local level, beyond various strategies aimed at achieving greater autonomy, for instance via microgrids (electricity) and mesh networks (internet), focus has centred on the commonification of the last-mile(s) of connection, either through cooperativization or municipalization efforts. With regard to existing non-capital-based electricity/internet provision, the compeerist aspiration is to reform existing top-down, hierarchically organized utilities and ISPs to achieve, instead, ones endowed with governance regimes that prioritize transparency, accountability, and inclusivity regarding community input and decision making. In all of these efforts, the use of referendums, where they are available, have proven to be an important mechanism for pursuing the populace's commons-oriented will.

At the same time, it is also important to note that referendums can still struggle when governments themselves are opposed to them. In the Maine case mentioned earlier, for instance, the electricity cooperativization referendum was vetoed. In the Berlin example, in turn, one reason given for why the vote for municipalization fell short is that the sceptical city council offered half-hearted appeasements, which ultimately succeeded in achieving their intended purpose of derailing the grassroots effort to achieve greater energy democratization (Angel, 2016). An important takeaway from these local political initiatives, then, is that government-commons relations are impossible to fully circumvent. This realization only becomes more pronounced as we move to trans-local aspirations, such as the commonification of the electricity macrogrid and the internet's tier one backbone. As such, the pragmatic compeerist is left with little choice but to think beyond any preference for bottom-up initiatives that shun formal politics and, instead, also recognize the need to engage the state by demanding more commons-friendly attitudes, budgets, and policies around electricity/internet infrastructure.

Beyond demanding better partnerships in the facilitation of cooperativization and municipalization, in the realm of electricity provision, governments could be pressured to dismantle the many onerous barriers to going off grid, while, at the same time, incentivizing renewable energy microgrids. Regarding the internet, in turn, focus naturally falls on finding support for the establishment of mesh networks and greater access to radio-wave frequencies for commons-oriented actors. Then, looking to more macro-level interventions, compeerists could, at least in the longer term, seek to enlist the state in more far-reaching goals to decapitalize the electricity and internet infrastructures altogether, from generation/storage to transmission, preferably via a state-sponsored network of variously tiered member and stakeholder cooperatives.

The New Deal is an inspiring historical example of what can be accomplished when the state is brought on board at the highest levels. Indeed, many of the local efforts to buck capital at that time were ultimately rooted in legislation passed by the federated state and national government. In Nebraska, for instance, the decision by communities across the state to establish public utilities was made possible by the aptly titled 'Enabling Act' passed by the Nebraska state legislature, with federal support, in 1933. The Act stated that any community of a particular size could petition for the creation of a public utility if just 15 per cent of all voters in that area wanted one. It did not take long before the entire state was run by public utilities, which remains true to this day (Thomas, 2019).

Still, given the continuing solidity of the capital-state nexus, bringing about a government willing to truly challenge the corporate control of our current electricity/internet infrastructure will be a difficult and prolonged affair. It will require more than isolated political victories. Instead, a much broader consensus and mobilization must be achieved around demands for the democratization of the economy. We will return to what such a mass political movement, with all its inherent potentials and pitfalls, could look like in Chapter 9. First, however, we must work through some other key sectors of the material economy where compeerism is pursuing exits and alternatives, including in manufacturing and raw materials.

5

The Promise of 'Design Global, Manufacture Local'

In continuing our exploration of how the compeerist vision of a commons-based transition out of capitalism translates to the material economy, this chapter considers the possible commonification of manufacturing, which, as with infrastructure, is instrumental in providing the actual material hardware on which the digital revolution depends. Critically, however, manufacturing has also become increasingly dependent on the digital. Indeed, the application of digital technologies to manufacturing has brought us significantly closer to Marx's vision in *Grundrisse*, where information, rather than labour, becomes the key determinant of value creation. Yet the ability of digitized knowledge/code/data to bring about a liberated workforce while delivering greater material prosperity for all, as is compeerism's aim, will greatly depend on both who controls this digital value, a key issue in Part I, as well as how the industry that can make use of this value is organized, which is the overarching focus of this chapter.

The increasing interdependence between digital capabilities and manufacturing is worth emphasizing. To begin, product development goes through various, exhaustive stages of design, prototyping, and testing using sophisticated modelling software and computer power. The entire production process, from the logistics involved in acquiring the needed components to the actual assembly on the factory floor, is largely organized and kept on track using algorithmically driven, and increasingly blockchain-enabled, monitoring systems. Products themselves, such as cars and appliances, are becoming digital goods in their own right, outfitted with processing power, software, and internet connectivity that can significantly enhance performance. Yet, clearly, the innovation within manufacturing that entails the most far-reaching implications for human societies has been the application of industrial robots to perform manufacturing processes based on computer instructions, allowing for a large degree of automation.

Within this continuously evolving realm of digitally programmed production, the emerging technology with the most potential to disrupt the manufacturing sector is, arguably, that of 3D printing (or additive manufacturing). With the right digital design inputs, which can be changed at will, the 3D printer can produce a wide array of things within one confined location. Here, it is clearly the design code, as opposed to any actual human work on the factory floor, that becomes the main source of added value within any produced good.

More specifically, while some labour will have been involved in the production of the code, once produced it can be applied infinitely, making the initial labour quite minimal in relation to overall production capacity (we will address the raw inputs involved in the next chapter). Importantly, the variety of production that 3D printers can perform is also increasing; feedstock options have evolved to include much more than polymer plastics as essentially anything that can be powdered can be used as a printing material, including metal, rubber, and wood. Specialized 3D printers have since also been developed that are capable of executing more challenging designs, from electronic circuits to housing structures.

Looking even further into the future, the next iteration of 3D printing could encompass capabilities whose impacts are hard to fully fathom. According to Neil Gershenfeld, head of MIT's Center for Bits and Atoms, work has already begun on what he calls 3D assemblers, which will be able to manufacture items using different Lego-like blocks in nanometre, millimetre, and centimetre sizes. Like the 22 amino acids in the human body that can be combined to form all the biological machinery our body needs, these so-called 'voxels' could be combined to form a limitless array of materials and structures (Gershenfeld, 2012).

For compeerists, the potential, positive impacts that limitlessly reproducible digital value could have on commons-oriented manufacturing is immense (Mason, 2016). Indeed, if the increasingly capable knowledge/code/data involved in manufacturing were made part of the digital commons, open to collaborative use and improvement, combined with an expansion of more commons-oriented production facilities (with the help of next-generation 3D printers), the result could be a massive boon to the quantity and quality of use-value creation. In other words, we would be a big step closer to meeting all of humanity's basic material wants and needs.

At the same time, however, while it is hard to predict the impact of futuristic technologies like 3D assemblers, until now the increasing role of digital value in manufacturing has not yet led to any significant shifts – in terms of overall capacity – to commons-based forms of material production. The reason for this is twofold. For one, as we have already seen, capital has become adept at engineering and managing scarcity within the digital realm. For the other, as is becoming increasingly clear in Part II of this book, capital maintains a firm control over the material assets and resources on which the realization of any benefits linked to the digital depends.

In this way, the envisioned counter-capitalist promise of a digitally turbocharged, commons-based peer production in manufacturing brings to mind David Harvey's rebuke of 'flexible specialization'. Following Harvey, flexible specialization, which designated a 'new', decentralized form of manufacturing, was heralded in the 1980s as a post-Fordist, worker empowering development, yet in the end it was simply absorbed by capital to deal with the inefficiencies entailed in large-scale and increasingly sluggish industries, becoming a defining feature of neoliberalism (Piore and Sabel, 2000; Harvey, 2005). It is not unreasonable to ask, therefore, whether digitally empowered, collaborative manufacturing will not ultimately become similarly absorbed, bolstering capital rather than the commons.

To avoid such a scenario, and being acutely aware of capital's coopting power, compeerism understands that a concerted abstract hacktivist intervention would be needed to ensure emerging digital-production capabilities are, in fact, being employed by and for the commons in its clash with capital. As we will see, to be successful in such a clash in the realm of production would ultimately necessitate the technologically assisted leveraging of those commons-centred principles that remain largely inaccessible to capital, such as solidaristic collaboration, strategic sharing, and inclusive decision making. Compeerism holds that if these boundary-commoning-based advantages could be deepened and widely implemented, combined with a more conducive market environment provided by the state, commons-based manufacturers could offer a viable alternative to industrial capital.

To the extent that a commonification of industry along these lines has been addressed, it has primarily been through the lens of the 'design global, manufacture local' model (DG-ML) promoted by some P2P scholars (Kostakis et al, 2015; Ramos, 2017; Kostakis et al, 2018). This model is grounded on a commitment to a global commons of information and innovation sharing while the physical making of stuff is to become more localized. There are two key aims to this localization imperative. One is to develop a means of material production that is more environmentally sound, thus addressing the need for humanity to stay within the planet's ecological boundaries – something that the current industrial arrangement has been fundamentally incapable of doing. The other aim, however, is to establish a largely non-capitalist organization of production that empowers communities to participate in and significantly influence the manufacturing process. This democratization of the means of production would then be the impetus for directing local industry to produce innovative, quality, and abundant use-value oriented goods, hence enabling a far-reaching exit from capital.

This chapter thus proceeds by reviewing the DG-ML proposal, with a particular focus on the prospects of shifting to a truly localized manufacturing arrangement. We then turn to the forms of industrial organization and boundary commoning that would allow compeerist-aligned manufacturers – at the local, but also trans-local level – to successfully compete with capital by leveraging the commons-based principles of production espoused by the DG-ML model. We leave the environmental implications inherent in this approach to the next chapter, where we take up the broader question of effective, compeerist aligned environmental/resource governance.

In pursuit of 'design global, manufacture local'

The DG-ML model is, of course, the complete opposite of the existing, globalized industrial arrangement. Perhaps the present organization of manufacturing will be adjusted in the aftermath of the COVID-19 pandemic, but it is hard to imagine a truly significant deglobalization and downscaling taking place through capital's own initiative. Indeed, the current industrial model's 'efficiencies' entailed in the exploitation of globalized 'comparative advantage' (the maximum externalization of social/environmental costs) and massive economies of scale enable competitive advantages that are difficult for capitalists to forgo. These advantages are also what make it hard for the DG-ML model to get a foothold, let alone expand. Nonetheless, there are a number of ongoing initiatives and developments that point to the possible viability of DG-ML inspired forms of industrial production.

First, we can briefly address the 'design global' dimension of the model, which, being rooted in the digital commons (explored in Chapter 2), is a topic that should already be quite familiar. The overarching aim here centres on the freeing up and open-sourcing of all the digitized information and code that is increasingly involved in manufacturing. Thus, starting with actual manufacturing capabilities (tools and machines), an obvious area of relevance can be found in the open-source hardware movement. The underlying impetus for this movement is to democratize access to the means of production by making their design fully open-source, including the bill of materials, schematics, and detailed circuitry information covering all components and final assembly.

Open Source Ecology's Global Village Construction Set has already been noted as a pioneering work in progress aimed at boosting commons-based manufacturing capabilities. This is done by spearheading the development of high use-value designs that are then made available under the most lenient CC, share-alike licensing. Consequently, crowdsourced contributions and improvements, in the spirit of open research, are highly encouraged. Some designs, like the wind turbine or the induction furnace are still works in progress, while others, like the 3D printer or the pressed-earth block machine are already fully developed and ready to implement.

These efforts, furthermore, are ultimately just one aspect of a broad range of similar and mutually supportive initiatives in pursuit of the open-source hardware mission. For instance, Open Source Ecology necessitates the use of microcontrollers in order to incorporate digital capabilities within their machines. Rather than having to purchase these on the market, however, Open Source Ecology is able to tap into the collaborative work of the Arduino project, which creates accessible and fully open designs for the construction of DIY microcontrollers.

Yet, perhaps the most ambitious effort in the open-source hardware vein, and fully epitomizing the vision of achieving independence from capital in manufacturing, is the much-heralded RepRap project, which aims at crowdsourcing an open-source 3D printer that can print itself, a goal that has partially been achieved. As per one of the founders, and fully in line with compeerist principles, the primary objective of RepRap is 'to demonstrate evolution by a process analogous to selective breeding (people design improvements to the machine and distribute them on-line for others to reproduce) as well as for it to increase in number exponentially' (Bowyer and Olliver, 2016, np). If the RepRap printer were sufficiently capable (which it is not yet), it would be hard to find a more direct strategy for handing the means of production to the populace.

Beyond open-source hardware, there has also been a rapid growth of free, fully open-source designs for end-user goods. While these are currently sourced primarily from commons-oriented enterprises and the maker community more broadly, there remains significant potential for expansion if new organizational forms of production centred on the open crowdsourcing of innovations, like open-value-networks, were to become more established. The types of open designs within this growing repository run the gamut from code for the execution of specific 3D printing jobs to detailed instructions and schematics for more labour-intensive making and fabricating.

To offer just one example in the realm of architecture, the Open Building Institute and WikiHouse are both collaborative organizations offering accessible and unrestricted modular designs for buildings. WikiHouse's mission is: 'to put the tools and knowledge to design, manufacture and assemble beautiful, low-cost, low-carbon buildings into the hands of every citizen, community and business' (WikiHouse, 2022, np). To do this they use adaptable designs incorporating modular parts that can be easily fabricated in small, local production facilities. The parts, in turn, are designed so they can be easily and quickly assembled with millimetre precision.

Clearly, having access to a global repository of accessible digital designs for the making of all manner of goods, especially if managed under a peer-property regime, offers commons-oriented makers and manufacturers a significant boost to their capabilities and a possible advantage in their competition with capital. We will touch on some more examples of open-source design use and how to leverage its potential throughout the chapter. The component of the DG-ML model that is more challenging, however, pertains to its localization imperative, meant to facilitate decapitalized industrial capabilities that are democratized and community-centred.

We know that the vision offered by proponents of DG-ML is of 'a global network of microfactories/makerspaces' that are largely controlled by 'commons-oriented communities' and 'various entrepreneurial coalitions (often in the form of cooperatives)' (Kostakis et al, 2015, p 132). Still, current literature has not fully offered a concrete assessment of what moving to such a decentralized/localized system would actually entail. It makes sense, therefore, to consider next the 'manufacture local' idea in the context of current realities, first by considering maker-based initiatives utilizing makerspaces and fab labs, and then by delving deeper into the possibility of establishing more sizable, yet still small-scale, localized, commons-centred factories.

Making and fabricating

Makerspaces are generally understood as community spaces aimed at facilitating access to the means of making or repairing a wide range of things, including low-tech items such as clothing and bicycles. Fab labs, in turn, are much more specific in their denotation as they are the intentional result of a collaborative project between the Grassroots Invention Group and the Center for Bits and Atoms (CBA) at the Massachusetts Institute of Technology (MIT). In the words of Neil Gershenfeld:

> A Fab Lab today fills a room, weighs about 2 tons, and costs about $100,000. That includes 3D scanning and printing, large-format and precision machining, computer-controlled lasers and knives, surface-mount electronics production, embedded programming, and computing tools for design and collaboration. With these, it's possible to locally produce and customize products that are mass-produced today, such as consumer electronics and furniture. (In Chandler, 2016, np)

Furthermore, while both makerspaces and fab labs have a shared commitment to empowering communities to make things, certified fab labs are, in fact, obliged to be open to the public and committed to open-source design and collaboration as laid out in the fab lab charter.

There is no doubt that existing making and fabricating spaces, of which there are thousands the world over, have brought manufacturing and repair capabilities, as well as commensurate training, to countless community members who have engaged these resources to learn, invent, and build. Some even contend that these microscaled making/fabricating facilities could exponentially multiply in the near future (Thompson, 2018). Yet, from a compeerist standpoint, a key question here concerns the viability of these facilities in pursuing a commons-oriented agenda, not to mention whether they could truly serve as triggers for a transition to a DG-ML form of industrial organization.

Turning specifically to the more hi-tech fab labs, studies show that the overriding challenge facing these community-oriented production spaces is funding and finding a business model that is sustainable (Liotard, 2017). It is not surprising, therefore, due to the cost of machines and ongoing rent, that non-profit fab labs are often linked to educational institutions or municipalities. Yet, even here the openness to the public is often curtailed, either by targeting a particular clientele or through the application of fees. These limits to openness, in turn, must be recognized as being directly related to the underlying missions being pursued. While educational fab labs generally seek to facilitate the broader curricular aims of a particular learning institution, those sponsored by local governments are often focused on incubating innovations and spawning tech-savvy start-ups to boost the economy. A clear focus on the commons is generally lacking.

Barcelona is a case in point. Here, the local government has committed to establishing and supporting a digitally enabled fab lab (Ateneu de Fabricació Digital) in every district as part of a larger goal to become a 'self-sufficient' metropole. While the aim of self-sufficiency is enviable, however, the nature of this local production was never explicitly spelled out. For some, the city's efforts are seen merely as a way to foster neoliberal competitiveness by pursuing the ideals of the 'smart city', rather than being geared towards community needs. This was precisely the perception of local residents in the poorest district of Ciutat Meridiana, where the top-down establishment of Barcelona's second Ateneu was resisted as being a waste of money and space (Smith, 2015).

In order to fall more in line with compeerist aims, then, the Barcelona project, and others like it, would need to be more intentional, accessible to the public, and informed by a commons-based mission. Such a turn would mean abandoning the dominant impetus of seeing these spaces as incubators for capital-oriented entrepreneurs and rather as sites offering a form of exit from capital and markets. For example, community and municipal makerspaces and fab labs could tap into the digital design commons to manufacture electrical equipment for the local micro-grid, machines for a neighbourhood's tool library, or bicycles for the city bike-share programme. Alternatively, if enough capacity existed, they could also be offered up as a resource within intentional open-value-networks. In each case, the production site could remain true to the principle of enabling public participation in the conception, design decisions, and making of the goods being produced.

While there are not many, one good example of a truly community-oriented use of makerspaces can be found within the Nea Guinea non-profit organization in Greece, which maintains a mission of building resilience and self-sufficiency. Nea Guinea utilizes makerspaces not only for the purpose of education, but also for the production of needed goods within the community, for instance, the production of micro wind turbines for local 'solidarity projects'. Kostas Latoufis (2014, np), one of the leaders at Nea Guinea, has explained the organization's pursuit of renewable wind energy as a 'community-driven development process', where this 'community' is seen to include the 'wind empowerment' forums and designs offered via the global digital commons. Similar efforts have since been pursued for hydro and solar power. In this way, Nea Guinea has managed to create more than ten off-grid renewable energy systems for itself and the surrounding community.

Another example is Jackson Mississippi's Center for Community Production, sponsored by Cooperation Jackson, a grassroots organization committed to building a community-centred solidarity economy. The idea of community production is described as 'a campaign to turn Jackson into an innovative hub of sustainable manufacturing and fabrication that will help build and expand 'community wealth' in the city' (Akuno, 2019). The centre is run as a cooperative that also offers training and access in an effort to spawn further cooperatives. One possible project being explored is rooted in the idea of taking advantage of Mississippi's agricultural endowments and history by using open-source designs and a 3D construction printer to build affordable, yet well-designed community housing from locally sourced hempcrete (Akuno, 2019). As of this writing, however, the centre remains primarily visionary and has only engaged in relatively minor production projects.

In stepping back to evaluate the potential of maker-focused, compeerist-aligned initiatives, like those just outlined, we must acknowledge that their viability and usefulness ultimately depends on being able to deliver some form of advantage over normal market-based options. Thus, beyond any educational bonuses that may be garnered, in an economic context where everything is commoditized, this advantage quickly boils down to the ability of these makerspaces and fab labs to provide high use-value goods that are more affordable than what the market has to offer. As the successful Nea Guinea case illustrates, this is an achievable goal, but it is contingent on effectively utilizing the global digital commons and possessing an adequate level of DIY know-how within the accessible labour pool. These are two key factors that require further bolstering, support, and harnessing if larger scaled, maker-focused exits from capital are to unfold.

Still, in the end, even if made to be economically advantageous, community and municipal fab labs and makerspaces cannot singlehandedly deliver on the DG-ML promise. While potentially effective in the production of small-batch, customized goods, these maker-oriented facilities lack the specialization and scale needed to meet all the manufacturing demands maintained by modern society. As such, their purpose is mostly to deliver immediate forms of exit, and then, eventually, to play a supplementary role to a more robust and capable, yet still localized, commons-based industrial foundation.

Localizing the factory

While the prospect of a decentralized, autonomous industrial base of small-scale manufacturers has frequently been pondered, from an assortment of political approaches, more contemporary work on what a transition to such a system would involve, given our current economic and technological context, is scarce. Where this question has been taken up, however, a favourite example is that of the Emilia Romagna (ER) region of Italy. With just over 4 million people, this region boasts a vibrant and diverse manufacturing sector comprised of nearly 50,000 mostly small and medium sized manufacturing firms, employing roughly a quarter of the regions' population. The innovative, flexible, and demand-centred small-batch manufacturing system, which relies on significant inter-firm collaboration and networking, has long been an economic engine within Italy and has proven to be impressively resilient to market fluctuations.

In 2005 a team sent by the Cooperative Charitable Trust Forum scoped out the region to find a manufacturing model 'that is practical, has scale, and (is) consistent with social justice values' (P2PF Wiki, 2018, np). One of the team members documented what they found, describing, 'a fascinating web of cooperatives, small manufacturing companies, innovative social service programmes, and a complex and dynamic partnership between business, labour, and government', concluding that Emilia Romagna should be top of the list for anyone seeking an 'alternative development model' (P2PF Wiki, 2018, np). Furthermore, in seeing ER as an example that could inform a specifically non-capitalist, use-value form of production geared to meeting the needs of the community, Kevin Carson (2009b, p 5) concludes that, 'given the small scale of production and the short local supply chains, a shift to production primarily for local needs would be relatively uncomplicated'.

This optimistic assessment, however, needs a bit more unpacking, given that the ER industrial system functions primarily as a production centre for components or parts within a complex global manufacturing chain in which assembly is usually done elsewhere. The question thus arises whether assembly could similarly be localized. One possible answer to this query can be found in the emergence of microscaled factories, espoused by a handful of specialized, start-up firms whose vision it is to use digital manufacturing, and especially 3D printing, as a way to outcompete mammoth, dedicated factories. In the words of Kevin Czinger, founder of the automotive-focused Divergent Technologies:

> There needs to be an alternative to hundreds of thousands of people performing repetitive tasks in a behemoth factory centralized in the lowest cost geography – with loss of manufacturing jobs everywhere else. In our filled-up planet, we should start to re-localize and democratize production. Focus on small teams. Focus on adaptation to the local environment. Think resilience. Think adaptation. Think meaningful, human scale work. And frankly, that's how we recapture the soul of manufacturing. (Teng and Czinger, 2018, np)

Certainly, this vision of microfactory production is very much in sync with the aspirations of the DG-ML model. More critically, it points to a possible path to a compeerist entry into the manufacturing sector, due to the smaller capital requirements for startup and the competitive advantages that can still be attained despite forgoing economies of scale. To get a sense of the emerging capabilities involved here we can look at a few comparisons to big industry, with a particular focus on the automotive sector.

Beginning with product development, consider that large automobile manufacturers can take up to seven years to go from concept to production. Yet, in the case of Local Motors, an early pioneer in micro-manufacturing in the automotive sector, their commercially successful Olli vehicle (an electric, autonomous people-mover), managed to go from concept to final product in only a year (Peels and Haye, 2021). Modular, 3D enabled manufacturing also opens the possibility for a much more affordable supply chain by using simpler designs and fewer parts; the low budget, Chinese made LSEV 3D printed electric car, for example, reduced the amount of plastic components from over 2000 to 57 (Coxworth, 2018). Furthermore, Divergent Technologies, which built the first 3D printed 'supercar', claims that the dematerialization and efficiency inherent in digital manufacturing fundamentally reduces the material and energy inputs required in production (Weiss, 2015).

Looking at capacity, these microfactories also prove to be competitive. To compare, take Daimler AG's flagship Sindelfingen plant, which employs 25,000 workers in a 14 million square-foot factory to assemble up to 300,000 vehicles per year. Local Motors' microfactory, in turn, could produce up to 350 Olli vehicles annually, using 20 workers on a 10,000 square foot workspace (Rogers, 2019). When these numbers are crunched, we see the microfactory producing 17.5 cars per worker compared to Daimler's 12, and 28.6 cars per square foot compared to the 10.3 in the Sindelfingen plant.

Microfactories, which are less automated, also require less investment in relation to output capacity, making market entry much easier. Consider here that the construction of the high-tech, US based Toyota–Mazda plant that was started in 2022 is expected to cost over US$2.3 billion (Toyota, 2021). In relation to its estimated yearly car production (similar to the Sindelfingen plant), we arrive at an estimate of just over $7500 per car. According to Divergent Technologies, its small, digital manufacturing microfactory can produce up to 10,000 vehicles per year and cost roughly 20 million dollars, which comes out to be less than a third of the investment per car compared to the Toyota case (Weiss, 2015).

While the ER region and microfactories demonstrate the potential competitiveness to be achieved through smaller-scaled component production and assembly (at least with cars), it is worth noting some additional benefits to downscaling being pursued in some other industrial sectors. Growing concerns about the environmental impacts of large-scale facilities, for instance, has led to downsizing initiatives in industries that have long pursued economies of scale. Hence, the advent of the electric arc furnace has triggered a boom in the use of mini-mills capable of smaller, more targeted batch production of recycled steel; and in the chemicals industry there is growing promise in utilizing much smaller, modular, and more environmentally friendly production plants (Scherrer, 1988; Seifert et al, 2012).

We are also beginning to see a greater emphasis on downsized, more localized manufacturing to overcome the problem of uncertain and shifting demand. Deloitte, the largest professional services network in the world, reported on this trend in 2015, stating: 'The digitization of manufacturing ... has made manufacturing more repeatable and portable. Individual designers and small businesses now have the ability to produce high-quality goods locally at low cost' (Hagel et al, 2015, np). They point to the 160,000-square-foot 'Manufacture New York' facility in Brooklyn as an example. In line with the DG-ML's scalar ideals, this centre was created 'to enable more small manufacturers to subsist locally and be more responsive to local needs' (Hagel et al, 2015, np).

It is worth briefly noting here that this focus on 'local needs' could portend a broader change from a supply driven industrial system focused on throughput to a more user-driven approach emphasizing quality and durability/repairability. Importantly, such a shift could also mean placing significantly less strain on localized industrial capacity as the lifespan of goods would be significantly increased, a potential that is often neglected when considering the output limits of small-scale production. We will, however, leave the broader environmental implications involved in more demand driven, prosumer-oriented production to the next chapter.

Still, despite the growing potential of localized, small-scale manufacturing, it is nonetheless important to acknowledge that the cost-benefit analyses of pursuing such an approach will vary across industries. This means that the 'manufacture local' ideal will undoubtedly be more difficult to implement or justify in some areas. For instance, in the high-volume manufacturing of some standard items, from the spinning of thread to the injection moulding of basic tools, using fast, large scale, specialized processes will still be much more economical in terms of resource input and product output ratios than engaging in small-scale, versatile production arrangements. Ignoring this reality, as some DG-ML proponents tend to do, would be naïve. The 99 per cent reduction in the price of solar panels in the last four decades is a case in point; it is a development directly related to Swanson's law, which stipulates that a doubling of panel production leads to a 20 per cent decrease in price (Kavlac et al, 2018).

As such, in some realms of manufacturing, compeerists will be forced to contend with the overpowering logic that favours the embrace of specialization and economies of scale. This 'contending with' for compeerists here is in line with the related ruminations triggered in the realization that some components of the electricity and IT infrastructures must be allowed to function on a macroscale, as per the previous chapter, or, as we will see in the next chapter, that the production of primary goods (natural resources and agriculture) will undoubtedly remain subject to a degree of comparative advantage and hence transregional trade. While these larger scaled arrangements are undoubtedly more difficult to square with compeerist aims, they should not, however, be assumed to be irredeemably incompatible with them.

In the end, navigating the question of scale within commons-oriented industrial aspirations will be up to compeerists themselves. They must determine where, and to what degree, localized/regionalized small-scale manufacturing should be pursued. This decision will inevitably be based on a careful weighing of factors to determine the best option for achieving the goals set out by the compeerist enterprise and variously involved stakeholders. As a whole, achieving community focused production, supporting the commons, and sustaining worker and environmental welfare will be the primary driver in making production decisions. Nonetheless, achieving input-output efficiencies will still have to be factored into the overall compeerist equation, because efficiency, after all, remains a critical factor in both achieving market viability and maximizing the production of use-value goods. If the compulsion to pursue such efficiencies then leads to opting for larger scaled production, compeerists will need to ensure that they do not sacrifice the core principles that motivated this production in the first place. We turn next, therefore, to the entrepreneurial governance options available to compeerist-aligned manufacturers in successfully dealing with these various pressures and imperatives.

Commonifying industry

Today, standard governance regimes employed in large-scaled, capital-controlled industrial operations are characterized by an out-of-touch, hierarchized elite prone to issuing top-down decrees with very little understanding or consideration of on-the-ground realities, needs, and opportunities. Furthermore, when emanating from investor-owned, capitalist firms, these authoritative decrees are generally rooted in a pursuit of profit-by-any-means-necessary rationales. Consequently, the communities that are the source of their labour and buy their goods are not just ignored, but are often intentionally exploited and manipulated.

A foundational compeerist aim in the realm of manufacturing, therefore, is to replace such organizational forms with ones that are, instead, broadly committed to a number of important commons-based principles seeking generative as opposed to extractive outcomes. This includes a commitment to open-sourcing knowledge and design, collaborative production, employee and community empowerment, and boundary commoning. When considering the most effective way of establishing a viable industrial sector committed to these values, a number of options can be addressed. Importantly, while these are generally most easily executed at smaller scales, which is why the previous section on the viability of 'manufacture local' is important, they are not limited to them.

We can start by briefly addressing the compeerist credentials of benefit corporations (B Corp), which have increasingly been presented as a possible alternative to extractive, investor-owned firms. Registering as a B Corp is mostly intended to diminish the singular profit focus that shareholder-based companies are obliged to maintain, allowing them to also pursue social and environmental objectives (Alexander, 2018). While often well-intentioned, however, B Corps, which can range in size from very small to large transnational corporations, are still mostly capitalist enterprises maintaining profit as their central aim. They also lack any inherent commitment to community stakeholdership or internal democratization. As such, the B-Corp model has limited relevance for longer-term compeerist aspirations, especially if they remain linked to profit-seeking investors.

Government-owned manufacturing enterprises are another possibility. We have, for instance, already noted the prospect of municipal fab labs helping in the production of goods needed by the city. Expanding such operations to include sites geared toward a significant output of societal goods, however, is a more far-reaching, and ultimately socialist approach. Certainly, state-owned entities in the sectors of health, transportation and energy are already pursued in several market-based economies where capital is deemed to be inadequate in servicing the needs of the nation and its citizenry. Yet most state-run manufacturing today is linked to post-communist economies, where the underlying rationale is to maintain employment and prevent the implosion of domestic heavy industry. It should be noted that these government-run, large-scaled factories are nonetheless still tied to the market, and in contradistinction to commons-based peer-production ideals, they tend to be organized in a rigid, top-down manner that often results in stagnant forms of production where innovations or innovative thinking are resisted (Meissner et al, 2018).

Nevertheless, state-operated production facilities are not of necessity in conflict with compeerist ideals, especially if the economic outlook of the state were to shift in a more commons-friendly direction. A US-based example of what this could look like is the publicly owned North Dakota Mill and Elevator, which was established by the North Dakota state government over a hundred years ago when the socialist Nonpartisan League was briefly in control. Its creation was part of a broader effort to establish public enterprises to circumvent farmers' reliance on capital's exploitative control of the banking, railroad and milling businesses. We can note that North Dakota also established a state-run bank in this same period.

As a *New York Times* op-ed recently stated, 'The North Dakota Mill and Elevator Association competes with private grain elevators and mills but receives no taxpayer money to give it an unfair advantage and, like the bank, the association returns much of its annual profit to North Dakota's general fund. Isn't that socialism?' (Dykstra, 2012, np). Interestingly, the otherwise conservatively minded people of North Dakota do not seem particularly bothered by this label. Today the mill is one of the largest and most used mills in the country, offering the farmers of North Dakota fairly-priced milling services while also selling flour and grain products directly to the public. Operations like this, where the aim is directly to service the productive capacity of the community and region, while sheltering them from capital-oriented exploitation, could certainly be a component of a compeerist transition and future economy. Ideally, however, greater emphasis would still be placed on enhanced economic democratization. Thus, in the case at hand, this would mean increased farmer, worker, and community empowerment, for instance, at the very least, establishing a board of stakeholders that maintains significant power in relation to the Mill's operation.

Lastly, we can turn to what is arguably the most obvious path to commonifying manufacturing, that is, through a cooperativization of the manufacturing sector, primarily via worker cooperatives. Today, worker co-ops generally require having at minimum over 50 per cent of the enterprise owned by the workers, with significant worker voting rights in key decision making. Furthermore, accrued profits tend to be reinvested with contributions often made to a wider fund of networked worker co-ops in order to bolster the cooperative economic sector. Not least, these co-ops tend to embrace the foundational Rochdale principles for cooperatives noted earlier, which includes a focus on democratization, openness, and community outreach.

Undoubtedly, the best-known case of a contemporary manufacturing co-op is the Spanish Mondragon Corporation in the Basque region, which consists of hundreds of worker-owned businesses in numerous economic sectors, including manufacturing where it employs thousands and generates billions of dollars' worth in revenue. Given its size and reach, this 'mega-cooperative' offers an interesting case for compeerists inclined to pursue the DG-ML model. We can begin by noting that the Mondragon Corporation embraces and even goes beyond the basic principles of the International Cooperative Alliance by emphasizing worker sovereignty and a commitment to the commons, while channelling at least ten per cent of profits back into the community. The Corporation also looks beyond the local to proclaim its support for 'all those who work for economic democracy' and the objectives of 'peace, justice, and development' (Zugasti, 2019, np).

To add a more concrete, human dimension to the Mondragon example, it is worth quoting at some length the impressions of two contributors to YES! *Magazine* who wrote approvingly about it after visiting the region:

> One of the first things you notice while driving from the Bilbao Airport toward the town of Mondragon is the unspoiled beauty of the countryside—rolling green hills uninterrupted by billboards. ... The town of Mondragon, population 23,000, is solidly middle class. There were neither mansions on the hill nor poverty in the streets. We didn't see wealth but everyone had a comfortable place to live, healthy food to eat, and the comfort of modern conveniences. Equally noticeable was their convivial, even joyful sense of community. The people we met were friendly, conversational, and trusting. Mondragon is proof that a commitment to the common good ... (and) a dedication to innovation and training at all levels can bring forward the best of the community. That quality of life continues outside the workplace, multiplying the benefits for those who choose a cooperative path. (Kelly and Massena, 2009, np)

The sense of localized wellbeing that Mondragon evokes in this passage clearly overlaps with the general vision of a world uncorrupted by capital as pursued in compeerism. Yet, upon closer inspection, we also find that this picture is not as perfect as it appears.

Being a large entity committed to competing in the global market, the Mondragon Corporation finds itself under significant pressure to pursue competitively minded strategies intended to maintain market share. For one, this has expressed itself in a steady move to a greater centralization of decision making, leading to a more representative, as opposed to a direct-democratic, form of governance. While such centralization has streamlined management and, it has been argued, enabled the cooperative to weather economic storms, it has also meant a significant loss of direct and more localized power on behalf of the workers (Corcoran and Wilson, 2010).

For the other, the Mondragon Corporation has significantly departed from its local roots (70 per cent of sales come from overseas), exemplified by the problematic decision to shift much of its production to dozens of factories scattered across the world. Here, in a rather crass contradiction, the thousands of workers employed abroad are not offered co-ownership privileges. While the Mondragon coop's management insists this situation is due to the fact that these foreign locations lack the needed cooperative culture, which certainly may be a valid point, it is difficult to not also see the nationalistic undertones and the additional revenue achieved by allowing for a second-class tier of workers brought about in this way (Gibson-Graham, 2003).

Nonetheless, it should be noted that the Mondragon Corporation's failing commitment to their cooperative ideals was not due to the upscaling of their industrial capacity, per se, but rather to managerial decisions around the organization of labour – precipitated by pressures related to being a large-scale, internationally active market operator. As such, the takeaway for similarly ambitious cooperatives that nonetheless wish to escape Mondragon's fate of 'selling out' (if it was indeed inevitable) is quite straightforward. Either global markets must be fundamentally restructured to where the pressures to cut labour costs are diminished, or these cooperatives need to find untapped market advantages that lie outside of the extractive tactics used by capital. While the former is a distant aspiration, the latter could be more feasible in the near term, and we will return to it shortly. First, however, we should also consider the governance dynamics involved in significantly smaller-scaled manufacturing cooperatives that do not maintain the same global entanglements and aspirations evident in the Mondragon case.

In looking for inspiration here, it is natural to again turn to the Emilia Romagna region, where, after all, ten per cent of the total labour force works in cooperatives. Most of these, however, are so-called social co-ops, focused on various forms of service provision, not manufacturing. The flexible, often small-scaled industries that the region is known for are primarily owned by self-employed, small-scale entrepreneurs – the petite bourgeoisie. It is therefore more apt to look across the border to France where a vibrant, small-scale manufacturing cooperative economy flourishes, even if it is only a small fraction of overall economic output.

The so called Sociétés Coopératives de Production (SCOPs) are intentional co-ops committed to the same principles as those embraced by the Mondragon Corporation, except these enterprises tend to be much smaller, averaging around 20 employees per business. Currently, manufacturing is the third-largest sector within the SCOP realm, with a few hundred cooperatives employing a total of some 10,000 workers, 60 per cent of whom have opted to become co-owners (Corcoran and Wilson, 2010). SCOPs, furthermore, have proven to be resilient, popular enterprises with overall numbers climbing, year-to-year.

The reasons for SCOPs' success is multifaceted. Studies have shown that among the most important factors responsible for establishing a thriving small-scale cooperative sector are government support and solidarity within a network of cooperatives, both of which are firmly established in this case (Corcoran and Wilson, 2010; Abell, 2014). For one, SCOPs are bonded together through a larger federated organization that is supported by member dues. With the motto, 'a SCOP is never alone' this organization works to secure financing to assist and expand SCOP enterprises and to represent cooperative interests in government, hence constituting an institutionalized boundary commoning in action. For the other, the cooperative sector in France tends to fall under a nation-wide cultural embrace of the so-called 'social economy', understood as those economic endeavours that function outside of purely capitalist rationales. In the case of SCOPs, this culture has translated into supportive funding and tax breaks, as well as government assistance in helping small, privately owned enterprises transition to becoming worker-owned co-ops when the business is at risk of shutting down (Corcoran and Wilson, 2010).

It is ultimately these underlying conditions, then, that have enabled SCOPs to overcome the well-established, major obstacles facing the small cooperative sector more generally, including access to resources and funds; navigating markets and the state; and maintaining effective leadership and internal cohesion (Cheney et al, 2014). All the while these small-scaled manufacturers have been able to stay broadly in tune with their cooperative principles. Based on the SCOPs example, and given the current global economic context where extractive profit rationales are given free reign, a strong case can therefore be made that manufacturing coops have a better chance of successfully pursuing their mission if they remain smaller, mutually supportive, and more confined to a domestic market shaped by a cooperative-friendly government. Compeerists hoping to have a commons-based manufacturing sector take root and eventually thrive in their respective regions would certainly do well to take these points to heart, especially when it comes to laying the foundation for such developments.

Prospects for compeerist-aligned manufacturing

From a compeerist perspective capitalism is responsible for the unjust and destructive exploitation of labour and the environment, as well as the debilitating alienation of workers and the community from production and each other. The alternative forms of managing manufacturing entities, seen in the previous section, have compeerist potential because of their efforts to counteract these quintessentially capitalist propensities by pursuing values beyond profit. Yet, the critical question is whether they could serve as an expanding alternative to capital within a context defined by market competition. Recall that Rosa Luxemburg's answer to this question was a clear 'no', while compeerism's is a tentative 'yes'.

In simple terms, as already noted in relation to makerspaces and fab labs, market viability for compeerist-aligned manufacturers means offering something that can compete with capitalist endeavours in terms of innovation, quality, and, not least, 'efficiency' expressed in price. In a context where practically everything is reduced to market-determined price, if compeerist-oriented manufactured goods cost more than equivalent goods in the market, the justification of such production becomes questionable. For instance, if the municipality making city signs in its own fab lab or the individual purchasing a bike from a local manufacturing co-op end up losing significant purchasing power due to the higher costs associated with these items, then these purchases will be seen by many as a luxury that comes at the cost of acquiring other needed things.

Certainly, this 'luxury' can be internally reframed as a cost worth paying in order to achieve improved labour and environmental relations, not to mention a more resilient local economy. This is where the efforts on the part of commons-based producers to actively include stakeholders in operational decisions, from workers to users/consumers, can help to achieve significant goodwill and loyalty in the market, with the acceptance of somewhat higher prices. But, for the municipality, there is only so much additional cost that it can afford; and for the cooperative microfactory, as is well established, once price departs significantly from the norm, demand precipitously drops, even for values-driven consumers. In the bigger picture, then, if these compeerist-oriented forms of production cannot be market competitive, they also will not be able to supplant capital in an evolutionary way.

While rejecting exploitative labour practices (although accepting some volunteered labour), and apart from decisions related to the adoption of economies of scale (which will be resisted if possible), there are a number of strategies, already hinted at in earlier examples, that compeerist-aligned manufacturers can pursue to enhance their competitiveness. To begin, as explored with the concept of open cooperativism in Chapter 3, production costs can be cut by leveraging the savings entailed in making full use of the digital commons. Open-source hardware, for instance, is evolving to the point where commons-oriented manufacturers have the option of procuring many, if not most, of their needed machines from within the commons itself at much lower cost. Open Source Ecology, for example, claims that the building of their open-source machines leads to savings of between 50 to 90 per cent when compared to comparable hardware offered in the market (OSE, 2014). Additional cost cutting can be achieved by accessing open-source, often crowdsourced design and code for the actual making of non-branded, end-user goods, as it is estimated that 30 per cent of the price of standard market commodities is based on non-material, intellectual property (WIPO, 2017).

At the same time, however, we must also recognize that these noted opportunities are not necessarily exclusive to commoners; as we have seen, capitalist firms are also showing a growing eagerness to tap into free, commons-sourced value. Commons-oriented producers – especially those seeking to directly compete with capital in the market – are thus tasked with pursuing additional competition-boosting opportunities that are unique to them. Indeed, failure to find such alternatives, especially as competition expands to larger scales, will leave compeerists in a position exemplified by the Mondragon Corporation, compelled to adopt extractive capitalist rationales, like deciding to access cheaper, alienated labour overseas.

A first critical step, therefore, is once again for compeerist-aligned economic actors to pursue a peer-property licensing regime that would curtail capital's ability to freely access and exploit digital value produced by and for the commons. Indeed, following the precepts of the open cooperativism concept, manufacturing cooperatives, non-profits, and open-value-networks should be at the forefront of the peer-property cause given the tremendous breakthroughs that are occurring in the intersection between the digital realm and industry. As noted at the beginning of this chapter, increasingly it is the code that represents the real value in manufacturing. Clearly, then, it would be in the interest of commons-oriented manufactures to actively leverage this increasingly potent digital value to their competitive advantage, that is, collaboratively building and distributing this value among themselves while keeping it from extractive capitalists who 'don't know how to share'.

Once such an intentional and expansive peer property regime within manufacturing has been established, backed by additional resource and finance-based boundary commoning, it is possible to imagine how this cooperation and mutual support could then be expanded to other sectors. Along the lines of open-value-networks, which connect the various aspects of production into one collaborative effort, mutual supportive agreements and assistance could be established within a pool of commons-oriented entities. This could include actors involved in raw materials, input production, assembly, logistics, marketing, and retail. These could come together to form a large, commons-based, boundary commoning 'in group' that comes with significant competitive perks, including unfettered access to peer propertied digital value and special pricing on goods and services.

As noted in Chapter 2, some have compared such organized boundary commoning with the formation of medieval guilds, which served as powerful solidaristic organizations pursuing the interests of their members in the face of the economic and political challenges of their time (Bauwens et al, 2019). While guilds were not centred on the cause of the commons, the comparison is instructive, especially in terms of how these organizations were also used to mobilize political pressure to influence economic governance. Translating economic clout into political power in this way is important because, despite the efficiencies and solidarity that a united commons sector could achieve internally, much of its competitive potential will still hinge on the outcomes of the never-ending political debate and struggle over the socio-economic principles and goals to be embraced, operationalized, and pursued within society more broadly.

As such, it then also behoves commoners to utilize their boundary commoning connections politically to influence public opinion and the political realm with the intent to significantly enhance the market viability of commons-oriented production. The broad embrace of the 'social economy' in France, which is a critical factor in the national government's support of the country's cooperative economy, is a prime example. If such a culture of support for the commons and commoning could be broadened and amplified – finding expression in government-sponsored financial assistance, preferred vendor contracts, and a regulatory context that hinders big-capital's ability to externalize social and environmental costs – the conditions would be much more favourable for the ability of small-scaled, cooperative manufacturers to thrive and multiply.

6

Contending With the Limits of Our Natural World

Every economy, no matter how sophisticated or diversified, is ultimately tied to the limitations and boundaries of the material world on which it depends for food, energy, raw materials, and stable ecological systems. Thus, while commonifying infrastructure and the industrial means of production is necessary for a compeerist transition, it is not sufficient. In this chapter, therefore, we consider efforts and ideas for fundamentally reshaping, along compeerist lines, the management and use of our natural resources and systems (the primary sector of the economy). More particularly this means pursuing more fair, democratic, collaborative, and ecologically sound governance arrangements when it comes to our earth-given endowments.

The importance of the ecological dimension, rooted in the ultimate limitations imposed by the physical laws of our natural world, cannot be overstated. Over and beyond its goal of commonifying the economy, compeerism is thus confronted with an imperative that is as straightforward as it is challenging, namely, to divert us from our current path towards planetary ecocide and guide us, instead, on an arc that ensures the establishment of long-term, environmentally (and socially) resilient communities and societies. It is a recognition that points to the necessary overlap between compeerism as an alternative organization of our social relations and, at the same time, a materially embodied alternative to our current relationship with the planet.

The ecological concept of resilience is useful here as it describes the ability of a system to achieve the long-term conditions needed to maintain wellbeing by effectively contending with various stresses; it is an outlook and understanding of the world that maintains significant synergies with compeerism. To achieve social and environmental resilience, for instance, non-market-based assets, such as social capital, diversity, and ecosystem services are seen as integral (Lewis and Conaty, 2012). For compeerists, in turn, creating an economy primed for equitable and democratic use-value production is intended precisely to create the conditions in which such non-market factors can fully develop and be harnessed; furthermore, this economy is itself dependent on processes like cooperation and solidarity that also lie outside exchange-valuation measures.

Fostering and applying knowledge/data to maximize positive outcomes is also a critical component of both resilience and compeerist frameworks, the latter of which pursues this aim by supporting the creation and collaborative use of an expansive data commons. Not least, compeerists also embrace the importance of modularity and redundancy that is often emphasized in resilience theory. This is evident in the compeerist preference to decentralize/localize, which serves as a form of modularizing economic and political processes intended to facilitate greater commoning and subsequent capacities to adapt. In doing so, the risk of large-scale systemic failures are diminished.

Taking these various points together, we can see a clear connection between the compeerist pursuit of a robust and intentional commons and commoning, on the one hand, and the ability to establish resilient communities that maintain more functional and harmonious social and environmental relationships on the other. The question for compeerists, particularly in terms of the pressing ecological challenges we are already facing, is how these two sides can effectively come together to contend with and ultimately replace the current mismanagement of the world's foundational resources and natural systems. Taking our cue from Ostrom, we can start to address this mandate by once again recognizing that effective commons governance is rooted in the clear bounding of a commons resource and the establishment of an internally and externally acknowledged agreement on how, and by whom, this resource is to be managed. Within this scheme, there are clearly designated management responsibilities, rules to ensure enforcement, and processes for mediating disputes (Ostrom, 2015). Yet, achieving these governance ideals on a large scale is a multifaceted challenge.

For one, commons-oriented actors often lack access/control over a given resource, thus leaving its management, in most cases, to capital. For the other, even when they have control, commoners must still agree to a stewardship and use of the commons resource that is not only ecologically sound, but also economically and socially viable within the broader political-economic context. In addressing these challenges as they pertain to the primary sector, it is helpful to employ the classic bifurcation of non-renewable and renewable resources. We can address these in turn, beginning with the non-renewable sector, with a particular focus on non-energy resources, before turning to agriculture as one critical and exemplary case within the renewable resources realm.

Non-renewable resources and circularity

In the last chapter we covered the 'design global, manufacture local' (DG-ML) model, which aims to establish an alternative, commons-based organization of industry. A critical component of this model's purpose, as per its P2P proponents, is to create a more sustainable manufacturing sector, which is particularly entwined with our demand for non-renewable resources. In assessing this aim, we can begin by noting DG-ML's most straightforward environmental implications.

Shipping, for instance, which accounts for seven per cent of global greenhouse gas emissions, could be significantly reduced in a more localized industrial arrangement (ITF, 2015). It is also clear, following from what we know about threshold dynamics within localized ecosystems, that smaller, dispersed environmental impacts are generally more tolerable than ones that are large and concentrated. Additionally, greater community control and/or input over local production processes can be expected to lead to higher environmental standards, especially as they relate to localized impacts. One factor that deserves more research in these considerations, however, is whether energy efficiency per unit of output would significantly decrease through downscaling production.

Arguably, the biggest environmental potential that the DG-ML model holds, however, pertains to the foundational challenge of excessive 'material throughput', which includes the extraction and processing of raw materials, and then the usually swift disposal of the goods produced (Schor, 2010). In focusing on the non-renewable resources involved here, we must keep in mind that it is not only a question of the environmental burdens linked to this material throughput, but also one of limited supply. As it turns out, both of these challenges have the same solution, that is, finding a way to use our finite resources efficiently, and, when possible, re-using them into perpetuity. It is a demand that can only truly be met by establishing some form of circular economy, where non-renewable resources would mostly remain within the cycle of production and consumption. In such a system, waste would be massively curtailed due to well-organized and supported assemblages/apparatuses ensuring the widespread adoption of durability, repairability, upcycling and recycling.

Given the potential overall resource savings entailed in a functioning circular economy, it is not surprising that the idea has received increasing attention within academia, government, and business. Yet, most of the analyses and recommendations resulting from this focus still place the aims of such circular economies within the confines of existing capitalist rationales and frameworks. As such, the ability to actually achieve true circularity has been convincingly questioned by pointing to the incompatibility between a circular economy and the undisputed dominance of the growth (profit) imperative that lies at the heart of contemporary economic thinking (Jackson, 2017; Daly, 2019; Bauwens, 2021).

More precisely, today's manufacturing is characterized by the drive to maximize sales, hence fostering a deeply rooted materialist, throwaway culture in which perceived and in-built obsolescence, as well as the many barriers to easy repair and reuse, are hardly questioned (Schor, 1998). Governments, in turn, remain fundamentally averse to seriously challenging the amount of throughput needed to feed growth demands. We should add that the idea that technology could offer a straightforward way out of this predicament is highly doubtful. This is because, given the current assemblages/apparatuses in place, the social response to environmentally beneficial efficiencies in production is to simply consume more, a phenomenon known as the Jevons paradox (Foster et al, 2010).

It is in relation to these shortcomings, and the need to achieve a truly closed-loop material economy, that the DG-ML proposal must ultimately position itself (Piques and Rizos, 2017; Kostakis et al, 2018). More specifically, the promise of a collaborative and democratic DG-ML arrangement lies in its capacity to switch from a supply-based to a demand-based production, that is, one that replaces the dominance of distant capital, and its top-down emphasis on quantity, with localized production capabilities that are collaborative and focused on quality (Chapman, 2015). Such a switch is critical in reining in our unending buy-and-discard mentality, and it is the first and most critical step in achieving circularity.

In practice, on the manufacturing side, the DG-ML model ultimately fosters an economy in which prosumers are able to become involved in localized production, demanding tailored goods that are less likely to end up unwanted. Furthermore, if community-oriented makerspaces and fab labs were made easily accessible, it would allow for the continuous remixing, reuse, and repair of our increasingly modularized stuff, meaning that very little would ever be deemed unusable or broken. Importantly, creating such a resource conscious form of production/consumption would not only be a boon to the environment, but also a meaningful exit from capital in the form of significantly diminished consumption.

Indicators of a potential shift in the relation people have with their goods can already be discerned, as for instance in the burgeoning interest and enthusiasm around the issue of repairability as a way to foster economic democracy and environmental resilience (Graziano and Trogal, 2019). Also notable is the simultaneous surge in virtual sites assisting in DIY making and product hacking, repair, and even 'waste hacking'. A good example is the iFixit website, which declares a mission to 'defend your right to fix' and offers free, open-source manuals while encouraging the public and government to get involved in making repairability a public prerogative.

Turning to design, the potential benefit of a vast, open-source repository of collaboratively perfected designs, blueprints, and schematics that reflect the demand for circularity is immense. As an example, consider the Dutch company Fairphone, which maintains a commitment to open design as part of its support of the prosumer and even offers the option of utilizing a fully open-source phone operating system. Fairphone declares its aim as 'fighting against a market trend where the average phone is replaced every 24 months', hence designing and manufacturing phones with repair in mind (Fairphone, 2021, np). As such, the Fairphone 3 has seven modules, allowing easy replacement of the screen, camera, speaker, and motherboard.

In one of its heralded 'teardowns' of the Fairphone 3, iFixit revealed an extremely easy process of not only taking apart the modules but also of removing and replacing some key components within them. The main critique iFixit offered was that the modules were not yet interchangeable between Fairphone models. It is worth noting that iFixit and Fairphone have since agreed to collaborate in their efforts for giving end-users more control over the products they own. In contradistinction, it is also telling that the Apple corporation has responded to iFixit's tutorials on Apple products by taking the aggressive move of banning the iFixit app from its AppStore (Wiens, 2015).

In sum, then, DG-ML offers a model of a restructured economy in which a global, collaboratively produced digital commons of design can be readily tapped into to enable the local, democratized production of goods centred on maximized use-value, meaning they are tailored, durable, modular, repairable and user friendly. As such, it offers a valuable framework for achieving circularity by massively reducing the amount of throughput in the system.

In pursuit of the urban waste mine and its limits

Even with the use of new material highly curtailed, as just described, some recapture and reuse associated with the latter stages of the circular economy will, nonetheless, still be needed. The processes involved here ultimately go beyond the immediate purview of the DG-ML model, yet the overall mission of creating an economy where 'whatever is heavy is local' still remains relevant (Kostakis et al, 2015, p 128). Indeed, the reliance on distant raw materials, which invariably are also dominated by large-scale, extractive capitalist actors, clearly flies in the face of the compeerist ideal. Hence, in seeking to stay true to the preference for local, democratic economies, it becomes imperative to focus on the 'urban waste mine' as a raw material commons from which to source our non-renewable resource needs (Krook and Baas, 2013).

Most experts concede that almost full waste recapture and reuse is technically possible with the right infrastructure, logistical organization, and product design (hence pointing again to the promise of a global design commons) (Piques and Rizos, 2017). To achieve such a feat, manufacturers, households, retailers, and recyclers would need to be tied into a cohesive system of incentives and enforceable mandates, that is, a macro-level governance system overseeing the urban waste commons that is in line with

Ostrom's principles. Currently, however, such macro-level assemblages/apparatuses are largely lacking in most of the world, where recycling is characterized by haphazard coordination, limited buy-in from key actors, and the dominance of exchange-value rationales responding to the fluctuating market price of recyclables. Thus, even if the amount of recycled raw materials used in manufacturing has significantly increased, it is still far from supplying most of the non-renewable resources being used. In some cases, furthermore, as with the many rare-earth minerals on which our expanding range of electronic devices depend, there is no recycling done at all, leading to an almost complete dependence on just a few, distant sources.

In the short term, compeerists are left with no choice but to navigate this imperfect environment, using boundary commoning between commons-based actors to engage in the recovery and reuse of critical materials where possible (Gutberlet, 2019). Still, such localized or regional efforts remain isolated and largely insignificant as they find themselves swimming against the current of broader market and big-capital dynamics. More specifically, linear, cradle-to-grave product pathways remain not only cheaper than circular ones, but they also ensure the continued need for the profitable production of more raw materials and products. This is why the promise by the plastics industry to finally make plastics recycling effective on a large scale is highly doubtful, since a truly functioning recycling system for plastic would spell the end to their industry.

As in other sectors, the results-oriented compeerist committed to the *longue durée* is therefore compelled to supplement on-the-ground initiatives with more macro-level efforts aimed at the state. In the pursuit of a truly circular economy, governments, for instance, could be pressured to issue mandates requiring designs that follow certain modularity and recyclability requirements. The state, at various scales, would also be the natural entity to spearhead efforts at reaching 100 per cent capture, reuse, and recycling of all waste via a multi-stakeholder system, driven by decrees and supporting funds for the required infrastructure.

An important component to these efforts would most likely be the imposition of 'extended producer responsibility' (EPR), where manufacturers are made responsible for organizing the recycling of the products they produce, as is being increasingly explored and implemented in Europe (Marques and da Cruz, 2018). Recycling requirements, furthermore, would need to be extended to all materials involved, including vital rare-earth minerals. Critically, the implementation of such top-down reforms would not need to be done by state-run entities; instead, much of it would likely fall to compeerist-aligned actors, as cooperatives and non-profits are already significantly involved in, and adapted to the recycling/reuse economy. Indeed, with a serious government commitment to circularity, compeerists would naturally pursue commons-centred control over the management, processing, and reuse of the recaptured raw materials of the various urban waste mines.

Managing to get the state engaged on such a level undoubtedly hinges on the ability to foster and tap into the environmental awareness and commitments within the populace more broadly. On this front, at least, there are some encouraging signs. For instance, in a massive UN poll of over one million people across 50 countries, two thirds of respondents considered climate change a global emergency (Flynn and Yamasumi, 2021). There is also evidence people are becoming more intentional in their own actions. For instance, in the US, which is by no means at the forefront on such matters, over 50 million households participate in kerbside recycling without monetary benefit or punitive threat, which represents about a 70 per cent participation rate where such services are available (Mouw, 2020).

One development that could boost this growing environmental consciousness even more, while simultaneously empowering users/consumers to vote with their pocketbooks, would be the establishment of much greater transparency and communication regarding the details of a product's environmental impact and credentials. Compeerists could here make the mandated documentation of blockchain-enabled product sourcing and other qualities a key demand on government, including visible certifications of a product's ecological footprint and, as is being pioneered in France, its overall repairability (Gerhardt, 2020; Stone, 2021). Offering clear product evaluations to users/consumers in this way can again significantly assist the competitiveness of compeerist-oriented enterprises that would do well in such assessments. Market research, for instance, has shown not only a growing demand for environmentally friendly products, but also a willingness to pay more for them. One study by McKinsey found that 70 per cent of Europeans and Americans are willing to accept a five per cent price increase for environmentally sourced goods, and roughly 50 per cent are willing to pay 15 per cent more (Miremadi et al, 2018).

Still, even with a significant, state-supported shift to localized, commons-oriented waste mines, where the circular resource loop comes full circle, it is nonetheless important to also acknowledge that full autonomy from distant non-renewable resources will take time. The technology of indefinitely recyclable plastic, for example, still has a long way to go before it can become the standard in all applications. Furthermore, in some cases the amount of already extracted material is insufficient for the needs of the economy of the future. For example, there is currently nowhere near enough lithium in circulation for the massive expansion of renewable energy storage required to transition out of carbon-based fuels (IEA, 2022).

From a compeerist perspective, then, to the extent that mines, quarries, and wells are still needed, they should be subjected to commons-based governance regimes. Importantly, this does not mean state nationalization in the name of the people. Government-run mineral and carbon-based extraction is not uncommon, but it tends to be large-scaled, hierarchically organized, and market-oriented. If there is one key takeaway from Ostrom's research, and borne out in the countless instances of social and environmental injustice throughout the world, it is that any approach to resource management that does not involve the people where these resources are found is a recipe for mismanagement and abuse.

When it comes to non-renewable resources available for local/regional consumption, therefore, member cooperatives are the most obvious option. The Ohio based Energy Cooperative is a good example. While starting as a regional electricity member co-op, it made the move to secure local natural-gas reserves by purchasing the private company that owned their leases (NGO, 2022). In this way, The Energy Cooperative was able to expand its member services to home gas provision as well. As noted in the prior chapter, such cooperatives still necessitate significantly increased member-driven, commons-oriented input to steer them in a more compeerist direction, but the example is illustrative of how community control of critical local resources could be executed.

In most cases, however, due to the uneven and concentrated nature of their geographical distribution, non-renewable resources are extracted to service distant demands (as is the case with many renewable resources as well). In such instances, where trade is a primary motivator, commons-based governance is especially critical, yet still extremely rare. Taking mining as an example, the compeerist ideal would be the application of less invasive but efficient technology within an operational regime characterized by significant worker and community buy in (Batterham, 2017; Alves et al, 2019). Such an arrangement is by no means an impossibility, yet given the large capital investments and specialized expertise needed to run competitive mining operations, these generally tend to be controlled by large, centralized corporations or states pursuing maximally extractive rationales.

Only in the poorer and lower-tech Majority World can we find some isolated exceptions, such as in Bolivia, where significant mining concessions are offered to local, mostly small-scale operators organized as worker cooperatives (Salman et al, 2015). These examples are noteworthy in that they highlight the compeerist potential inherent in the relationship between government and the mining sector. For instance, it becomes possible to imagine how the US's efforts to create a cooperative friendly environment for electricity during the New Deal could similarly be pursued regarding raw material extraction. The difference, however, is that the state, in the US and most other contexts, would be required to take an even more aggressive tack by actually decapitalizing (and then commonifying) the extractive mining industry that is already in place (in the case of rural electrification, capital-based actors were not yet present).

We should nonetheless also add that apart from the state-cooperative alliance that characterizes the existing mining co-ops in the Majority World, these offer little else in terms of inspiration for compeerists; their community empowerment efforts, worker conditions, and environmental practices all leave much to be desired. More to the point, the long-term viability of these largely artisanal operations, and their ability to deliver real development, remains questionable at best. This is because there are much more rooted, postcolonial assemblages/apparatuses in place that stand in the way of allowing local peoples to truly benefit from the resources on the lands that they inhabit. We will return to this predicament later in the chapter; first, however, we must consider the compeerist potential and challenges within the renewable resources sector, and especially agriculture, where, incidentally, many of the same postcolonial dynamics are in play.

Agriculture as a renewable resource

Any serious consideration of transitioning to a sustainable, post-capitalist world will necessarily need to address the realm of renewable resources. Not only are such resources (food and fibre) the foundation of any civilization's wellbeing, they are also the most obvious component of our relationship with the environment. This is because the health of our living resources is intricately bound to the strength and resilience of the ecosystems in which they are embedded. Effectively managing these resources is thus not only about establishing fair and sustainable use but ensuring that a balance is maintained with the various planetary and ecological systems on which these living raw materials depend. Only in this way can these be continuously replenished.

In this section we will limit ourselves to what is undoubtedly the most critical amalgamation of renewable resources: agriculture. Today agricultural systems, especially in the Minority World but increasingly in the Majority World as well, are firmly in the grip of profit-oriented big-capital in pursuit of ever-greater efficiencies, that is, the drive to achieve the biggest bang for your buck. In practical terms this equates to the industrialization of agriculture, where economies of scale are pursued to create ever-larger, more mechanized farms with an emphasis on expansive monocrops and concentrated animal feeding operations. It is these strategies that also lead to the unsustainable, damaging impacts on the undergirding ecosystems due to the heavy and often indiscriminate reliance on limited ground water, fossil fuels, artificial fertilizers, pesticides/herbicides, and genetically modified organisms (GMOs).

An alternative, compeerist-aligned form of agriculture, therefore, has two interrelated aims. One is to achieve a more equitable, community-centred, and, ultimately, use-value oriented governance arrangement for our agricultural means of production. The other, and seen as a direct consequence of the former, is the establishment of a more generative (and hence symbiotic) relationship to the land and its natural systems (Piques and Rizos, 2017; Giotitsas, 2019). Relevant techniques employed to achieve this second imperative include the use of organic fertilizer, integrated pest management, limited soil tillage, intercropping, and concerted soil maintenance and recovery. As such it is a form of agriculture that participates in the circular economies in nature via the nutrient, energy, and water cycles already in place. At the same time, and supplementing the focus on localized commons governance and stewardship, there remains an emphasis on the power of the digitized general intellect to assist in the execution of such agriculture. Given the obvious similarities here with the basic impetus of the DG-ML model, then, we can denote this approach 'design global, farm local' (DG-FL).

Feeding the world

The first issue to be resolved in the pursuit of a DG-FL arrangement is whether it could actually provide enough food to meet the needs of a global population expected to reach over 10 billion people in this century. The biggest focus when considering this question tends to fall on analyses of yields and productivity. Those in support of the current industrial agricultural system argue that it produces the highest possible yields with ever-diminishing labour needs; any shift from these gains, it is argued, would cause a serious reduction in food supply, rising prices, and hence hunger. The pushback to such arguments, however, emphasizes the fact that smallholder, non-industrialized agriculture is, in fact, a major source of our current food supply and that there remains much still untapped potential in this more sustainable farming approach.

Homing in on the question of potential, the first point to be made here is that feeding humanity is not just about yields, but about creating broad socio-economic arrangements that support and foster much more efficient agricultural production and consumption, measured in terms of overall resource and ecosystem use and impact. A widely circulated and esteemed study by the Research Institute of Organic Agriculture, for instance, found that organic forms of food production, which are often performed at smaller scales, could meet the needs of the world with the caveat that food waste, meat consumption, and non-food crop commitments would need to be significantly reduced (Muller et al, 2017). In essence, existing agricultural land needs to be reorganized to achieve use-value, that is, the aim should be feeding people, not animals or combustion engines (via bio-fuels).

A DG-FL approach to agriculture could go a long way in bringing about such a needed shift. Most obviously, growing food within a reasonable distance to where it is consumed would significantly help in reducing food waste, most of which is linked to getting agricultural goods to distant users/consumers. Indeed, it is estimated that about a third of the world's produced food ends up as waste, representing a massive squandering of energy and land (Hawken, 2021). Additionally, a localization and democratization of agriculture could re-establish a connection between farmer/farm and user (challenging deeply entrenched alienation), which, in turn, could foster a greater demand for more resilient and humane forms of production and consumption, even if they are more labour intensive, and hence pricier. Relatedly, rediscovering the rewards of local food, such as eating fruits and vegetables that actually taste like something, could boost overall supply through the expansion of personal and prosumer food production in yards, rooftops, and community gardens.

Turning to yields, there is ample research indicating that organic agriculture is not only more productive than assumed, but that it could still significantly increase its productive capacity with the right technologically enabled interventions (Badgley et al, 2007; Rodale 2018). It is here that the design global component of the DG-FL model also becomes relevant, as a vibrant digital commons could become an invaluable source of agriculturally focused knowledge/data/design/code that could boost sustainable production while reducing labour demands. We will consider this potential in more detail shortly when we delve into the directly related challenge of making commons-oriented farms more economically viable. Yet before moving on, we must briefly also address what is undoubtedly the most controversial of all yield boosting technologies: GMOs.

To begin, it is important to note that a 100 per cent adoption of organic or even small-scale production is not always required within a generative, compeerist-aligned farming arrangement. In some cases, as in the production of grains, non-organic inputs and monocropping may be justified if these are holistically monitored and supplemented with restorative techniques to ensure any affected ecological systems are not overly stressed. The same logic then applies to the use of genetically modified organisms, which are generally rejected in organic production. While there is much disagreement on the risks associated with this technology, there is mounting evidence that GMOs could significantly boost the yields of smaller farms engaging in otherwise generative agricultural methods (Rotman, 2020).

The fundamental constraint on this potential today is that GMO technology is primarily controlled by capital, which has focused on the development of seeds intended to play a particular function within a broader industrial agricultural system geared towards profit. As such, plants are designed for their compatibility with synthetic inputs, their ability to be transported long distances, their outer appearance, and their infertility (a classic case of imposed scarcity that makes the purchase of seeds necessary). However, in the spirit of abstract hacktivism, GMO research could very well be turned towards other aims instead, for instance making plants more resilient, productive, and nutritious without the need of additional, non-organic inputs. Importantly, many of these benefits can be achieved without using genetic material from non-related species, that is, cisgenic as opposed to transgenic modification, thus posing a much smaller chance of unwanted mutations and other risks.

Proponents of cisgenic GMOs argue, therefore, that less regulation in this form of modification is called for. In their view, a loosening of government restrictions could boost a much broader range of collaborative, commons-based research, leading to much bigger yields in regions currently suffering from paltry agricultural production (Benkler, 2006b; Rotman, 2020). Further bolstering this potential is the development of gene editing techniques, such as CRISPR, that are becoming more precise, easy to use, and cheap. Still, despite the latent promise here, compeerism refrains from prescribing the degree to which any technology should be adopted. In the end, compeerists pursuing a post-capitalist path to food security will need to weigh the pros and cons of GMOs for themselves, based on their respective contexts and priorities.

Irrespective of the specific approach taken, however, in looking ahead to pursuing the implementation of a compeerist-aligned DG-FL approach to agriculture, we are again confronted with the familiar intertwined challenges found in the previous two chapters, that is, accessing the needed means of production and then, subsequently, finding market viability/competitiveness. We can address these in turn.

Accessing land

In agriculture, the most fundamental means required to produce food is land, and the question of who should control this land is highly contested, accompanied by a long and often brutal history around its acquisition and use. Currently there are numerous land-governance regimes, each with different insinuations for a compeerist trajectory in agriculture. We can start with 'public land', owned and controlled by the state. In the US, for example, nearly 40 per cent of all land is in the hands of government entities, pointing to the immense potential the state possesses in influencing land use. This land is often set aside for preservation or recreational use, but a significant portion is also utilized for economic purposes. This generally takes the form of leases or permissions, which most often are given out to larger-scaled, capital-oriented actors for the purposes of mining, harvesting timber, or grazing for cattle.

For compeerists, this top-down land management arrangement is problematic as it falls significantly short of the aspired-to commons-based governance principles outlined by Ostrom. A preferable approach, therefore, would entail significant stakeholder input in how the land in a given region is to be used with the intent of supporting more community-centred, sustainable operations. Even though public land suitable for agriculture is limited, it is not negligible. Hence, if the US, for instance, were to adopt Germany's commitment to reach 20 per cent organic farmland by 2030, it could strive to attain this goal by making certain federal lands available to local, organic farmers through a host of bottom-up, community partnerships (EC, 2019). Establishing such a commitment from government regarding its public land, however, would require a significant change to the capital-state nexus currently in place. As such, in the short term, activism is likely to bear more fruit within lower tiered governmental jurisdictions, for instance in the form of establishing municipally leased commons-oriented farms and gardens.

Privately held agricultural land, in turn, which is the norm in Minority World economies, is firmly plugged into the corporate food-based commodity chains controlled by 'Big Ag'. To confront this reality, one compeerist-aligned effort has been the legal pursuit of a transvestment of land from private to community hands by establishing land trusts and easements. Currently, conservation is the main goal here, in which a particular plot of land is protected from development in perpetuity, even with a transfer of land title. The US has seen a boom in such trust efforts over the last few decades, with conservation-based trusts making up nearly three per cent of all US territory, exceeding the size of the entire United Kingdom (LTA, 2022).

Some land trusts, however, are focused specifically on maintaining agricultural land. The US government's Purchase of Agricultural Conservation Easement programme (PACE), for instance, has worked with private landowners to protect over three million acres of farmland. Private agricultural land trusts, in turn, make up roughly the same amount; combined with PACE the total size of agriculturally focused land trusts in the US equals the approximate area of Albania (AFT, 2021). While the PACE programme offers significant potential for the government to implement further land-use conditionalities, it is mostly in the private trusts where the aim for more intentional agriculture has been pursued. The US based Agrarian Trust, for example, purchases land and then manages it in line with commons-based principles in an effort to protect 'farmland for sustainable agriculture' while preserving 'its affordability for new and disadvantaged farmers' (Agrarian Trust, 2021). The Trust currently presides over 11 agrarian commons across the country, consisting of up to 12 farms each.

At the same time, while land trusts offer an ideal option for pursuing commons-centred agriculture, it is important to note that Ostrom was not singularly focused on land ownership when considering the principles of sound commons governance. What matters, instead, are the mechanisms in place that allow for bottom-up input and power in determining the status of the land, that is, who has access to it, and how it can and cannot be used (Fennell, 2011). As such, given that trusts/easements still make up a relatively small portion of total land, arguably the most likely scenario for an expansion of compeerist-aligned, DG-FL practices would be for privately-owned small and medium-sized farms to voluntarily embrace community-oriented production and governance principles.

Such governance can be pursued in a number of ways. One popular option has been the establishment of specific community-sponsored agricultural (CSA) purchasing agreements – in the US over 12,000 farms sell directly to users/consumers using CSAs (NAL, 2021). While such agreements generally include specifications on what and how to farm, they also often embody much more, including monetary and labour investments by CSA members in the farm and its operations. In this way, these commons-centric community-farmer collaborations offer an enticing alternative for local farmers to the outright control that the massive transnational food industry currently exerts over the management of both small and large farming operations.

Additional community-based purchasing arrangements with local farmers could come from municipalities, for example via increasingly popular farm-to-school programmes, as well as from retail cooperatives, which have a long history in pursuing specific standards for their members. Grocery member co-ops, for instance, were pioneers in demanding the disclosure of ingredients and nutritional information, as well as for introducing organic food. Today such co-ops still have significant market share in Europe and could again become more active in their purchasing standards if their members demanded it. Importantly, this could include forging cooperative relationships with local farmers with the intent to push for more humane, local, and sustainable agriculture.

A final example of pursuing commons-oriented governance over farmland can be found in the food sovereignty movement, which takes aim, among several other targets, at the distant governmental regulations placed on local agriculture (Edelman et al, 2014). The goal here is generally to achieve bottom-up forms of governance in the pursuit of a more viable community-oriented agricultural sector. In practice this can mean that a community decides to exclude their local, community-serving farms from specific rules and restrictions that are clearly meant for large, industrial operators, and place undue burdens on small-scale producers. For instance, communities adopting food sovereignty measures may allow local farmers to sell certain products that are officially not permitted according to federal law, such as unpasteurized milk or food that was not processed in an industrial, federally regulated facility. Importantly, in this way, a community exerting more control over the rules and regulations related to proximate food production then also enables it to exert more say in how local agricultural land is used.

Contending with capital-oriented markets

The efforts to establish CSAs and food sovereignty, just noted, highlight the second major and interconnected challenge to a DG-FL model, that is, making commons-oriented agricultural production economically viable once land has been secured. Indeed, it is only through the competitiveness of alternative, compeerist-oriented farms that the envisioned DG-FL transition could begin to take hold. As we will see, the answer to the question of viability, as in previous sectors we have explored, once again hinges on making the most of available commons-based resources (especially in the digital realm); pursuing boundary-commoning initiatives; and collaboratively working to create a more supportive political-economic environment for compeerist food production.

Turning first to the digital commons, noted earlier as a promising factor for expanding yields within more generative forms of agriculture, we can begin by pointing to the tremendous potential in simply opening up global channels for the exchange of farming know-how. Studies have shown the tremendous impact that knowledge exchange can have on small farmers' success and the important role information technology can play in facilitating this process (Zhang et al, 2016). Such exchanges, furthermore, are particularly valuable in more generative forms of farming, which is especially knowledge intensive due to the numerous geographically specific ecosystem interactions that must be taken into account. The need for cutting-edge academic research to be made available within an open access, global digital repository, as noted in Chapter 2, also becomes apparent here.

Beyond information/knowledge sharing, however, the digital commons also offer significant openings for tapping into more affordable production-boosting tools and machines (Giotitsas, 2019). Along similar lines to the Open Source Ecology project noted in prior chapters, the Farm Hack initiative sees itself as 'a community of users and organizations joining together to build a collaborative platform for developing and sharing tools of all kinds, in the name of open knowledge sharing and resilient agricultural systems' (Farm Hack, 2016, np). Farm Hack maintains an extensive tool design inventory that anyone can contribute to, use, alter, and distribute. Examples of tools include a bicycle-powered fanning mill, a solar-powered off-grid pasture-monitoring system, and an online software platform to assist in planning and managing a farm.

The management dimension just noted is worth emphasizing, since so much of what makes a local farm successful lies beyond production, from effective operational administration to establishing the many linkages needed to find buyers. Regarding this latter point, it is important to recognize that there is a great deal of networking involved, for instance, in assembling all the right actors for a successful CSA initiative or farmers market. Consequently, there are several commons-based digital solutions being pursued on this front. One good example is that of Open Food Network, a globally linked group of commoners committed to fostering 'a sustainable and resilient food system' by establishing a free, open-source software platform that links intentional farmers to various types of buyers through online networks and markets (OFN, 2022, np).

A further area of research and design that is especially hard to come by in the digital commons pertains to GMO technology. For compeerists interested in pursuing this potential within more generative forms of agriculture, a primary aim is to create a collaborative, open-source effort in which the process and product of such efforts are made available to the digital commons. Important initiatives along these lines are already being explored, as with the Australia-based Centre for the Application of Molecular Biology to International Agriculture (CAMBIA). CAMBIA's biological open-source project is centred on fostering a network of participants (including private, governmental, and civil-society actors) interested in developing collaborative technological innovations along free open-source software principles (Benkler, 2006). Particular attention here is paid to the need to bridge the gaps in technological access – often maintained by big-capital's proprietary patents – that block lower-budgeted, local farmers from the many innovations in molecular biology.

In considering the value of these various digital resources in the pursuit of a DG-FL transition, however, we must return to what we have seen to be a central component in compeerism's tactical outlook in contending with capital, namely the establishment of peer-property licensing regimes. While some of the examples of agriculturally relevant digital value just covered would be of limited use to Big Ag operators, others clearly could have broader market implications. By pursuing protections in this latter realm, compeerists can strive to gain a broader foothold in the agricultural sector of the economy. Targeted peer-property licenses could be applied, for instance, to ensure that a commons-sourced GMO seed that is particularly adept at thriving in dry conditions, or cutting-edge software for real-time soil analysis, is intentionally managed, with free access made conditional on either being a subsistence farmer or having embraced certain commons-based principles. In this way, if such peer-licensed resources significantly expanded, compeerist-aligned farmers would maintain privileged access to tools that both increased their yields and decreased their operating costs, giving them an important market advantage in relation to their capital-oriented counterparts.

Yet, the compeerist-aligned farmers' boundary-commoning options are not just limited to the digital, there are many more solidaristic endeavours that could be instrumental in securing viability, including the collaborative arrangement of low-interest loans and the pooling of physical resources, such as the local sharing of land and expensive machinery. To help in such efforts, formal compeerist-aligned cooperatives could be formed. These could then also be employed to better control input and product prices, as well as make unified political demands. Agricutural cooperatives are, of course, already a well-established institution, but in the Minority World these generally represent large-scale, capital-oriented farmers pursuing the expansion of market share within a particular sector (such as Land O'Lakes and Sunkist in the US). In the Majority World, however, there are a number of examples where such cooperatives are employed to empower the oft-exploited small-scale farmer. The Indian Amul milk cooperative is a case in point; co-owned by over 3.5 million dairy producers, this massive co-op shows that it is indeed possible to productively organize an immense number of small-scaled farmers to great effect (Somjee and Somjee, 1978).

Importantly, the desirability of choosing a commons-oriented approach to farming increases as the benefits of boundary commoning expand. Currently, many farmers engaged in corporately controlled, industrial agriculture are not in a particularly happy place. The control exerted from higher up the Big Ag complex, and the demand for continuous and often risky investments, are resented by many farmers who feel they have no alternative but to comply. Relatedly, more and more farmers are frustrated by their diminishing self-sufficiency, which is a deep-seated value in farming communities.

The reason for this loss can be linked to the ever-expanding role of intellectual property, applied to everything from seeds to the software running the farming equipment (Rotz et al, 2019). Indeed, farmers can increasingly be added to the hacking community as they collectively resist the corporate repair monopoly by finding ways around the proprietary protections placed on the digital innards of their tractors and other machines. In light of these conditions, it is therefore conceivable that farmers could be tempted by a viable commons-oriented alternative (Kuipers, 2021).

As with digital value production and manufacturing, however, in agriculture we must also acknowledge that extensive boundary-commoning efforts are unlikely to be sufficient in achieving thriving compeerist-aligned economies. In the Minority World, in particular, food production is characterized by a state-sponsored context that explicitly favours extractive, profit-seeking, industrial farms. As such, a reorientation of government priorities is critically needed. Keeping our focus on the Minority World, there are many policies that could be pushed for in this effort.

First, the subsidization of agriculture, which is already broadly established, would need to be restructured so that support did not overwhelmingly and unjustly favour the largest and most industrial operations (Gordon, 2021). Then, and more proactively, extra monetary incentives could be directed to the production and consumption of sustainably farmed goods, while targeted regulations and fees could be imposed to ensure any environmental externalities involved in food production are reflected in the final price. The ability to engage in small and microscale, community-focused farming, in turn, could also be facilitated by offering concrete resources, like targeted, low-interest loans, preferred access to affordable leases on viable government land, and high quality and well-endowed extension services. Relatedly, demands could be made that agricultural research within government funded institutions focus more on sustainable, open-source agriculture that is aimed at serving community needs, not just global trade. More education and outreach on commons-based agriculture would also be beneficial, especially if accompanied by trusted certification and labelling programmes – administered at no cost to the farmers – that informed users/consumers about the sourcing of their food, with a particular focus on environmental and humane practices.

A final move that could be immensely beneficial to the compeerist agricultural cause is abandoning one-size-fits-all regulations on the production, processing, and selling of food, which is often drafted by corporate interests in a way to burden small-scale competitors (Carson, 2009a). Instead, more nuanced arrangements could be pursued in which localized, small-scale agricultural producers maintain their own, distinct guidelines. In this way – following the food sovereignty movement's demands – rules and regulations targeting small-scale community-oriented farmers could be largely decentralized, allowing leeway for local communities and even farmer-buyer relationships to play a bigger role in determining a farmer's restrictions and responsibilities.

Locality limits and the challenge of Minority–Majority World relations

Even with significant inter-commons and state-centred initiatives to boost the pursuit of a DG-FL model, we cannot ignore the reality that inherent limitations to the localization ideal persist, as they do with the other material economies explored thus far. Climate realities, in particular, are difficult to overcome as there are always limits to what can be grown in any given region. Yet it is hard to imagine that the Minority World would be willing to give up on bananas, cocoa, or coffee; or, for that matter, for the Majority World to forgo its acquired taste for northern grains. It follows that some continuation of the pursuit of natural comparative advantage in agriculture, with the aim to trade, even at significant distances, is likely. The same predicament, it should be noted, pertains to non-renewable resources and even, to some extent, manufactured goods (where economies of scale are adopted), for which the following discussion is equally relevant.

While trade is economically rational and has the potential to establish significant win-win relationships, it is a process that nevertheless also complicates the localization ideal in the DG-ML/DG-FL models and brings to light numerous additional challenges for the compeerist. In addressing these, we will limit ourselves to a compeerist vantage point from within the Minority World. We can here distinguish between export- and import-based issues. Turning first to export, the primary producer's relationship with the community immediately becomes more difficult as the benefits, for instance by exporting the land's harvest or mineral wealth, do not necessarily trickle down to the local community. In other words, it is not a symbiotic relationship in the way it is when the primary producer, like the local farmer, services local demand.

In a trade-based scenario, then, a commons-oriented governance arrangement would, ideally, entail a community say in the decision to produce for export, where consent could be linked to a number of conditions, like sharing in any earned revenue. On the most basic level, efforts could be made to establish farms that, as with manufacturing cooperatives, adopted governance procedures where decision making was significantly democratized to include meaningful input from workers and the stakeholder community. To further concretize such relations, an additional step could be to amend property rights to where 'ownership' was actually made conditional. This could mean, for instance, that the use and profit from a piece of land was tied to legally binding usufruct requirements, like the adoption of commons-based governance protocols that ensured a certain level of community empowerment.

Yet, seeing that such a far-reaching democratization of the land would require a significant, compeerist-aligned societal and political transformation, immediate goals would likely focus on more limited policy aims. This would include, as outlined in the previous section, pursuing the support of locally oriented, cooperative production arrangements, while holding non-cooperative ones to account when it comes to the most pressing interests of the community, for example by imposing redistributive taxes and establishing regulations around issues of labour and the environment. We will, however, revisit what an alternative property regime could look like in a fully developed compeerist society in Chapter 10.

Turning then to the import side of trade we are confronted with distant production systems, both with renewable and non-renewable resources, that are generally managed by actors far removed from one's locality. As such, it is not difficult to step away from any sense of implication or responsibility for what happens there. Compeerism nonetheless recognizes that many of the hurdles to a more just and sustainable future are geographically complex, entailing what Doreen Massey (1996) termed 'power geometries', which describe how any particular locale is intricately entwined with many distant ones via uneven power relations.

Critically, this relationality between places does not only pertain to the present, for instance how purchasing distant commodities ends up supporting the economic, political, and environmental processes involved in their production; it also includes past unequal relations and interactions that are largely responsible for how and why these processes have been adopted. These power geometries thus also clearly come into play on the export side, with issues pertaining to how any specific export arrangement with a distant place, and the price dynamics involved, have come to be established. In this sense, compeerism's understanding of trade inevitably gives way to questions related to the complex power geometries involved, or, in other words, it becomes an issue of international relations and the global world order more broadly. As such, we are confronted with the question of compeerism's trans-local and ultimately global outlook, especially with regard to Minority–Majority World relations. It is a topic that deserves some fleshing out.

We can begin by establishing that compeerism considers the power geometries of greatest concern to be those that link the Minority World to the most dire forms of economic and political stagnation/dysfunction in ex-colonial, Majority World societies in the south. This is why the term 'postcolonial' is helpful, as it points to how these societies have been, and still are, fundamentally impacted by a global political-economic (and cultural) arrangement that favours the wealthy Minority World in the north. It is a condition that is well documented and presented within a range of critical theoretical 'schools' dealing with the issue of 'development', from the earlier, economically focused 'world systems theory' and 'dependency theory' to the more recent and culturally centred work on postcoloniality.

Minority World compeerists in the north, then, who find themselves looking south to trading partners in the Majority World, see variegated but often deeply contested economies, particularly in the primary sector. In agriculture this plays out as an ongoing struggle over land use, that is, whether to prioritize productivity and export crops in a bid to modernize and access valuable foreign currency, or whether the land should remain, or be reverted to, small-holder plots focused on broad subsistence capabilities and basic food security. As with the Majority World's efforts to benefit from their mining sector, however, neither of the noted land use options offers a path for bringing about real prosperity as long as the involved societies remain fundamentally hobbled by their historically rooted, economically compromised position in the world.

Given this underlying context, some in the Minority World have pursued interventions that would allow Majority World societies at least a partial exit from their constrictions, especially when it comes to trade. An initial model can be found in the Fairtrade movement, which aims to guarantee a minimum price for key cash crops to participating farmers, thus creating greater economic stability for these communities. The use of certifications and labelling is again important here. It should nonetheless be noted that

Fairtrade and other similar initiatives are still reflective of postcolonial relationships and a capital-dominant economy. More specifically, Fairtrade arrangements are largely shaped by for-profit companies committed to maintaining an unequal division of labour, where production of mostly non-lucrative raw materials is left to the Majority World while profitable added value is claimed by the Minority World in the north.

In light of these shortcomings, a more far-reaching framework and strategy worth noting here is that of 'cosmo-localism' promoted by some P2P theorists. Similar to the DG-ML model, the cosmo-local idea focuses on the global digital commons as a means to localized empowerment and development, yet now with a particular focus on the Majority World. As such, it represents a type of commons-based, and digitally mediated technology transfer intended to bolster not just the traditional primary sector, but also manufacturing and services. In this sense, the aim is more far reaching than Fairtrade as the actual subservient trading position of the Majority World is being addressed. One of the first attempted enactments of the cosmo-localism model was the Free Libre Open Knowledge (FLOK) project launched by Michel Bauwens via the P2P Foundation in 2013. The FLOK project, in quasi-coordination with the Ecuadoran government, was aimed at rethinking the country's economy along digitally enabled, peer production lines as a way to remove it from its still heavy dependence on colonial-style extraction (Commons Transition, 2014).

As Bauwens later acknowledged, however, significant power interests linked to the existing extractive economy were still entrenched in the government, thus fundamentally limiting the project's potential (Bauwens and Gerhardt, 2020). Consequentially, Bauwens ultimately concluded that it was not, in fact, possible to 'hack a country' with the intent of bringing about a new, commons-based economy, without the concomitant 'political will' and 'social basis' for such a transition (P2PF Wiki, 2021, np). While this is certainly a valid insight, compeerism nonetheless sees the challenges involved here as being more deeply rooted.

To begin, despite some bright spots, the digital commons/commoning on which the cosmo-local idea hinges is still too limited in its capabilities to offer a viable path out of the chronic disadvantages the Majority World faces. This is because the general intellect that is to be captured and shared in the digital commons has not yet been adequately liberated, primarily due to capital's continued command over the apparatus of capture. Furthermore, as we have seen, even with a vibrant and rich digital commons, there still needs to be a material foundation with which to access and make use of this digital value, and here much of the Majority World is in woefully short supply, especially when it comes to domestically owned assets. As such, the Majority World remains stuck in its efforts to break free from its postcolonial disadvantages, unable to escape its dependence on foreign, capital-sourced investments, which remain primarily focused on exploiting and extracting distant labour and resources.

Of utmost importance in all of this, however, is that global capital's predatory arrangement with the Majority World continues to be abetted by the most powerful Minority World states. The reason for this synergy, furthermore, ultimately lies in a deeply embedded 'us versus them', win-lose rationality that can be traced back to these states' colonial histories. In applying this rationality to their respective postcolonial, geopolitical/geoeconomic gazes, these states see a natural alliance between themselves and the globally active capital that is headquartered within their borders. Consequently, these states continue to do this capital's bidding when it comes to their outward looking strategies, with very little effort made to actually reform the global order in a more equitable direction.

In sum, then, there truly is no hacktivist, back-door path to rapid economic and human development in postcolonial societies. This does not mean that bolstering the global digital commons or supporting local commoning efforts within the Majority World are futile. With time, they can still play an important role in helping these societies achieve greater wellbeing and resilience. Arguably, however, the most direct route to improve the outlook of the Majority World would be by fundamentally breaking the capital-state nexus in the Minority World, especially as it pertains to foreign relations. Only in this way could the problematic power geometries linking the Minority and Majority World, and their concomitant trade relations, be redressed and equalized.

More specifically, this would entail powerful nation-states rethinking the rationale behind their current geoeconomic/geopolitical outlooks, where the imperative of competitively amassing wealth in a world seen only through the lens of scarcity is replaced by one of cooperatively pursuing universal wellbeing and peace. Such a shift would be expressed in a concerted mission to actively liberate, expand, and make accessible the world's general intellect and pursuing commons-based, just, and sustainable governance regimes for the global material commons. Getting there, however, will ultimately entail a rejection of the foundational capitalist assumption that exchange-value, mediated through markets and quantified through money, should be the ultimate measure of all worth in the world, and hence the basis of humanity's *raison d'être*. The next part of this book is dedicated to how this deeply embedded and institutionalized assumption can be contended with and ultimately challenged.

PART III

Money and Value

7

Coping With Money's Monopoly on Value

In considering the interconnected realms of the digital and material commons/commoning in prior chapters, one clear underlying theme has been the continuous tension between compeerist-aligned forms of economic activity and a still dominant capitalist mode of production. Recall that a mode of production consists of the self-reinforcing economic and social arrangements that determine how the production and consumption of goods and services takes place. These assemblages/apparatuses, in turn, are agglomerations of animate and inanimate forces, meaning that we are not only dealing with the materialities of physical and social (re)production, but also with the realm of affect, state of mind, and mental frameworks.

Some mental frameworks are so ingrained and pervasive that they are barely acknowledged. We can call these hegemonic, as their taken-for-granted validity have become foundational in the scaffolding of our entire worldview, keeping us locked into a particular mode of thinking and operation. There is an apt story that captures this inability to see past our taken for granted way of perceiving the world. It goes something like this: two fish swimming in the river encounter an older fish swimming towards them. The older fish asks, "How's the water?" The two fish swim on until one finally turns to the other and says, "What the hell is water?"

One immensely important hegemonic frame through which we see the world is our currently dominant conceptualization of value, which is well captured in the words of the ancient Latin thinker Publilius Syrus who is credited with saying, 'everything is worth what its purchaser will pay for it'. It is a view that has become so firmly entrenched under capitalism that it is embraced as dogma by economists and as 'common sense' by everyone else. It has become the water that we swim in. Here the obfuscated working of the market – the invisible hand – is unconsciously accepted as a kind of omnipotent God, or supercomputer, 'cranking out the current value of everything in the form of price' (Gerhardt, 2020). It is a world described by the concept of commodity fetishism, in which we cannot help but see the world through an exchange-value lens. Any thought of intrinsic or derived value in natural or humanly crafted things never comes to mind.

Yet, this sterile market approach to value is actually quite recent. Historians and anthropologists would point out that prior to the advent of capitalism, valuation was always linked to broader cultural outlooks and values, even when markets and money were involved (Graber, 2011). It is only when money shifted from being a mere token of value to becoming value itself that everything changed. This is well captured in Marx's central understanding of capitalism as hinging on a central shift in which production for the sake of commodity exchange facilitated by money (C-M-C) changes to using commodities as a means to gain more money (M-C-M). In short, money becomes synonymous with all the tangible value in the world. It is an outlook that compeerism recognizes to be intentionally incomplete and broadly destructive as it alienates us to value outside of the market, facilitates the exploitation of people and the environment, and reduces human life to something that must be earned through labour, captured in the taken-for-granted sentiment of having to 'earn a living'.

As we noted in Chapter 1, many Marxist thinkers view the commodity fetishist, exchange-value lens as a predetermined and inescapable condition linked to market-oriented production. Compeerism, however, while acknowledging its source in the three-headed apparatus of capture, contends that commodity fetishism is also a mental construct, albeit one that has largely become hegemonic. Nevertheless, as a construct, it is ultimately something that can be questioned, the source uncovered, challenged and changed. Finding a way out of exchange-value's grip on our thinking and doing, however, is far from easy, especially if the answer to change is seen as necessitating a working through, and partially even a maintaining of, the very assemblages/apparatuses (like markets and money) that serve as the underlying source of the condition from which an exit is pursued.

We must keep in mind here that compeerism rejects a communist solution; at least one in which the state replaces the market and exchange-value by becoming the provider of all goods and services. Indeed, as argued with respect to various economic sectors in earlier chapters, even far-reaching socialist economies are viewed sceptically. It is in this light that compeerism looks to expand the operationalization of values, rationales, and outlooks inherent in the commons and commoning – a third force apart from the state and capital – as the potential spark and motor of a socio-economic-political transition that can tame commodity fetishism and harken a post-capitalist future.

As it turns out, despite the deeply entrenched commodification of the world, the commons have managed to hold on. They function in the interstitial spaces where work and consumption are governed by different logics and affects. It is precisely the potential of such commons-based spaces and endeavours to thrive and challenge capitalism that we have explored thus far in this book. Indeed, the commoner consciousness and acts of commoning depicted in these chapters are a display that commodity fetishism is not unassailable. There are openings for alternative valuation frameworks, even within economic arrangements in which money and market exchange still exist.

It is helpful here to consider the commons and commoning as a type of subeconomy, like the economic version of a subculture. This alternate, nascent subeconomy is multifaceted, entailing dimensions that are both prefigurative, spontaneous, and informal as well as ones that are more institutional and expansive in their aims. Both the informal and formal commons-based subeconomies are committed to valuation frameworks that support and foster the universal and sustainable access to basic needs and wants. Yet they ultimately diverge in how to pursue this valuation within a mode of production where exchange-value thinking is still hegemonic. One seeks immediate exit strategies and non-market-based support, while the other engages markets and property regimes in an attempt to directly challenge capital on its own turf. This divide is in line with P2P theorists' distinction between purely commons-based activity (the informal) and the commons-oriented entrepreneurial actors (the formal) that add value 'on top of the commons' by engaging the market (Bauwens et al, 2019, p 18).

In the rest of this chapter, we review the promise, limitations, and barriers involved in the methods employed by both the informal and formal iterations of the commons subeconomy in dealing with a context where value is reduced to money. We begin by considering the various options – exit, gifting, markets – that commons-oriented initiatives and actors have available to them in contending with their dependence on money, before exploring possible, alternative channels of financial support via commons-centred credit and savings institutions. In the subsequent chapter, then, we turn to options for fundamentally de-monopolizing exchange-value altogether. Such a coup would entail the dismantlement and rebuilding, or even the complete replacement, of the current organization of money in our society. The final aim of such an effort would be the creation of an alternative money regime that could foster intentional forms of production, motivated by the pursuit of use-value rather than solely exchange-value.

Dealing with capital through exit, gifting, and markets

The informal side of the commons-based subeconomy is often considered the quintessential core of the commons; it is predicated on mutual aid and sees itself as fundamentally antithetical to the market and the money that defines it. As Bollier and Conaty argue, rather than being exclusionary, as money tends to be, the commons are based on social reciprocity. In their words, 'An individual's contribution is not linked with a direct exchange of value with another, but rather on fair-share contributions to the larger collective that provide less quantifiable (and often unmeasurable) benefits over longer periods of time and to the community' (Bollier and Conaty, 2016, p 40). From this perspective, then, the ideal commons-based answer to dealing with markets and capital is to disengage and prefiguratively establish an alternative.

An important dimension to such exit tactics is the general shift from user/consumer to obtainer/provider identities. We have already touched on several instances of such efforts, including the creation of free digital resources, going off grid, establishing microgrids and mesh networks, and engaging in DIY making. Also included here are actions inspired by the spirit of barter and collaborative consumption, including carpools, childcare swaps, community gardens, libraries of things, and various forms of labour/asset sharing and exchanges.

Yet, while non-market forms of consumption are important in achieving a certain level of divestment from capital, we must nonetheless acknowledge their limitations. For instance, social-solidarity efforts rooted in the sincerest, non-market commitment to mutual aid, like offering free lunches at a community soup kitchen, remain viable only as long as someone, somewhere can be made to pay for it. Resilience efforts, in turn, like going off-grid or engaging in collaborative consumption arrangements, remain mostly small-scale, localized token exits, given that most of the people involved still primarily consume and work within normal markets controlled by capital. Alternatively, efforts to play outside the rules of capital, for example through pirating, hacking, or squatting, are difficult to sustain as they are generally met with state-based punishment and violence.

A case can certainly be made that some exit strategies, especially in the realm of collaborative consumption, have the potential to be significantly expanded with the help of digital technologies, hence overcoming some of their initial limitations. A good example here is Netherlands-based Peerby, a platform that manages a country-wide network for the mutual borrowing of people's household items. It is estimated that Peerby hosts shareable goods in the Netherlands alone worth up to US$1 billion (WEC, 2016). Another example is Seva Exchange, a benefit corporation and subsidiary of the non-profit TimeBanks USA, which is currently working to facilitate and incentivize the egalitarian trading of work between individuals, where one hour of work equals one credit. Seva Exchange is thus committed to developing an app that applies blockchain-based ledgers and AI algorithms to ensure security, trust, and incentivizations in order to significantly expand the timebanking network (SevaExchange, 2021).

The upscaling and expansion of collaborative consumption efforts in line with the examples just noted could, indeed, help participating commoners achieve much greater autonomy from markets and money and should be an integral part of the compeerist aim to boost the commons subeconomy. Yet, it is also critical to remember, as covered in Chapter 3, when considering platform cooperatives, that doing so ultimately results in a return to the position of needing additional resources to pay for the organization involved. As the original Couchsurfing platform exemplified, upscaled collaborative-consumption operations struggle to thrive on localized, volunteer labour alone. It is therefore not surprising that Peerby and Seva Exchange are both run as revenue-earning enterprises, although, as opposed to Couchsurfing's current form, a strong case can be made that they still remain true to their commons-oriented inspiration. Nonetheless, the line demarking the informal commons-based subeconomy has been crossed.

The takeaway, then, is that while various forms of exit from markets/money can play an important role in pursuing a commons-based transition out of capitalism, trying to seek a complete exodus based on non-monetary economic and social relations remains untenable. This is because there is generally insufficient scale in such efforts to enable a complete substitution of market-based goods and services, and where upscaling efforts are pursued, they too succumb to the need for external resources tied to the market. Thus, in considering Thomas Mehwald's definition of commoning as 'a process of imagining and creating shared resources ... funding people to enable them to common', the imperative question remains how precisely are these resources for commoning, including space, labour, and other inputs to be acquired (quoted in Bollier and Conaty, 2016, p 40)? In an economic context still monopolized by exchange-value, the answer will always fall back on the need for money.

Gifting

For actors committed to the informal commons-based subeconomy's preference for avoiding market-based engagements, yet where the need for money is openly acknowledged, the solution is usually the embrace of gift-economy rationales. There are two options here. One is to pursue endogenous gifting, meaning contributions sourced from within the community and civil society more broadly. The other possibility is gifting from exogenous state or capital actors. Both of these are the bread and butter of NGOs, which, while not inherently compeerist in nature, represent a large portion of non-market based economic activity, much of which has a solidaristic or commons-oriented component to it.

Turning first to endogenous gifting, preferred by many compeerist-aligned actors due to the lack of strings attached, we find significant potential for fundraising. In the US, for example, 70 per cent of all charitable donations are sourced by individuals (IUPUI, 2018). Certainly, a large portion of this is explicitly local and often religiously linked (giving to your local church), but significant amounts of funds also flow to national and globally active non-governmental organizations. More recently, the importance of individual, small donations have also become evident in funding political movements. For instance, Bernie Sanders's run for president in the US as a self-proclaimed democratic-socialist boasted one of the best funded primary campaigns in 2018, with nearly 80 per cent of those funds coming from small donors (US PIRG, 2019).

Beyond the critical need to find a compelling message, which we will return to in Chapter 9, a key challenge for compeerists in tapping into the giving disposition of like-minded people comes down to finding the right medium. While local networks and face-to-face outreach will certainly remain an integral part of fundraising, the real potential for growth undoubtedly lies in utilizing digital technologies to crowdfund. Commoners here will try to avoid commoditized tools and strive to establish their own fundraising platforms when possible, or, if dealing with smaller projects, resort to a growing number of commons-based services. A good example of the latter is the Spanish open-sourced, non-profit Goteo platform, which focuses specifically on commons-centred crowdfunding. The platform's success is based on its ease of use and the clear transparency demands placed on fund seekers. As a result, Goteo, which has funded over a thousand projects worth over US$2 million, boasts a success rate of nearly 70 per cent in reaching an applicant's fundraising goals, significantly higher than their commercially oriented counterparts (Bollier and Conaty, 2016).

Next, in looking to exogenous gifting opportunities, the primary funding sources are state-based grants/subsidies and capital-based philanthropic/charitable donations. To get a sense of the potential wealth to be tapped here, consider that the assets held by philanthropic foundations in the US amounts to nearly $1 trillion, or roughly the size of Turkey's GDP (Di Mento, 2019). Or, on the government side, consider that about a third of NGOs' garnered funds in the US comes from various government grants and contracts (the latter of which lands in the grey space between the informal and formal economic realms) (NCN, 2019). Yet, at the same time, exogenous funds also come with a number of shortcomings and pitfalls.

First and foremost, we must acknowledge that the most outspoken entities in pursuit of a commons-based future rarely qualify for exogenous monies as they contradict the accepted norm that non-profit work is intended to improve (or simply make tolerable) the status quo, not change it. For those that do qualify, furthermore, there are a number of potential conflicts that must be navigated. Recall, for a moment, the various forms of contributions to the commons covered in previous chapters, such as the establishment of a 'community' fab lab that is really intended to incubate tech-sector startups, or IBM paying to support commons-based means-of-production code. As noted then, such 'gifts' do not prove a sustainable synergy between exogenous actors and the intentional commons pursued by compeerists. In many cases, these external actors are strategically funding the commons to pursue their own agendas.

Faced with these realities, compeerist actors are left with difficult assessments to make. For example, is the acceptance of a government grant to a poverty alleviation NGO part of a broader strategy of cutting back much-needed government spending on social services? Or, is the donation of a large tract of virgin forest from a global energy corporation worth the potential greenwashing campaign that underlies this gift? In the end, there are no easy, one-size-fits-all answers to such questions. Given compeerism's general embrace of a pragmatic, *longue-durée* approach to systemic change, each opportunity linked to capital or government giving will, therefore, require careful assessments of both short- and longer-term costs and benefits.

A final critical point that cannot be missed when considering gifting, however, is that it is, in most cases, not really an effort to exit capital at all. This is because the commons entities that rely on gifting to circumvent exchange-value rationales are nonetheless dependent on actors whose gifted wealth is generally the result of this very form of thinking and operating in the market. In this sense there is a danger of gifting providing a false sense of purity for recipient, commons-based entities, while offering an easy but ultimately fake redemption to capitalist actors.

Hence, while gifting in this way may still represent a certain transference of wealth from capital to the commons, and while the recipients may be doing valuable work to foster the commons and commoning, as long as these gift-dependent entities do not seek to challenge the market share of capitalists they remain relatively tame and unthreatening background actors. Furthermore, as noted in Chapter 2, even in those cases where non-profits like Wikipedia do manage to outcompete capital (for instance in the encyclopedia business), the dependence on volunteered labour still largely leaves the apparatus of capture – which forces most labour into the hands of capital – unchallenged. In short, gifting (as with exit) is incapable, on its own, of delivering a compeerist transition out of capitalism.

Engaging markets without corruption

It is in light of the shortcomings entailed in the tactics of exit and gifting that the need to engage markets becomes apparent. John Restakis, approaching this issue from the perspective of cooperatives, argues: 'To cut off a collective, whether a commons, co-operative or the wider social economy, from the world of markets and money is self-delusional and ineffective, it undermines the purpose of these organizations, which is to socialize and democratize the economy' (quoted in Bollier and Conaty, 2016, p 11). Building on this line of thinking, the compeerist framework holds that market engagement by formal commons-oriented actors makes up a critical source of wealth that is needed to expand the commons and ultimately challenge capital, especially since the feasibility of a revolutionary, forced commonification is rejected.

The fundamental proposition here is that compeerist-aligned organizations and enterprises, with the support of tailored emerging technologies and an increasingly commons-centric socio-economic political environment, could usurp the current mode of production by outcompeting capital within the market itself. Despite having market generated revenue, these entities would still be part of the commons realm because of the non-capitalist values they embrace and operate by. We have seen these values play out, for instance, in the way profit is made subservient to the pursuit of the commons and commoning, the focus on worker empowerment and fair remuneration; and the efforts made to include the community as a stakeholder with legitimate claims to economic democracy and revenue sharing. Following from this, the earnings generated should not be understood as 'profit' in the traditional sense, but rather as a transvestment of wealth from capital to the commons. Furthermore, and in distinction to gifting, the market engagement that is the source of this transvestment is simultaneously seeking to displace capital in the market of goods, services, and labour, hence offering a fully-fledged alternative to the organization of our productive capacities.

The major question begged in this proposal, however, is whether such a compeerist form of production could ever truly thrive to achieve significant scale. On the one hand, following Rosa Luxemburg (2011), there is the issue of non-capitalist economic endeavours failing to achieve critical mass as they refuse to take advantage of extractive/exploitative operational tactics. On the other hand, the obverse corollary of this point (often emphasized by anarchists and autonomists) is that if scale actually is achieved through market engagement, it generally comes at the cost of the motivating values being espoused. The increasingly profit-oriented attitudes and actions of large cooperatives, like the Mondragon Corporation, are here often referenced as a case in point.

Nonetheless, the previous chapters have attempted to show that a commons-based trajectory out of capital's dominance in various economic sectors is conceivable, but it would by no means be given or easy; the inability to match capital's market-capturing tactics, or becoming corrupted in the process of trying, are both immense challenges. In response to the former, compeerists are tasked with finding non-extractive/exploitative sources of market competitiveness that can match those of capitalists. As we have seen, the focus in such a pursuit has generally fallen on the imperative to leverage boundary-commoning advantages, like peer-property regimes, while additionally seeking government-sourced policies/interventions to establish more commons-friendly market conditions. The critical need to bring about alternative financial/monetary arrangements in such efforts, in turn, is a key focus in this chapter and in the next.

Yet the latter challenge identified, pertaining to the corruption of compeerist ideals, has not yet been fully addressed, especially in those instances where it cannot simply be traced back to market exigencies. Indeed, in the case of the Mondragon Corporation covered in Chapter 5, it is, in the end, difficult to assess the degree to which market pressures forced the mega-cooperative to abandon its worker co-op commitments when shifting manufacturing overseas. Given its market positions and overall revenue, it could be argued that such a capitulation to exchange-value driven rationales was not necessary, and hence that this move can be traced to an internal loss of direction. We can, hence, briefly review a number of compeerist-aligned business practices and strategies that can ultimately be adopted to avoid such potential internal digressions, which pose a legitimate threat to the compeerist vision of achieving a post-capitalist future via market engagement.

A first critical step here would be for compeerist-aligned enterprises to establish a public mission, vision, and values statement as well as intentionally formulated and legally binding bylaws regulating operational procedures. These foundational documents would include norms against abetting extractive capital actors while supporting the aim of inclusive, boundary commoning. Also, in line with Ostrom's insights concerning effective commons governance, they would reflect a commitment to openness, inclusion, and democracy both in terms of internal operations and stakeholder relations. Indeed, exclusionary or discriminatory practices, which can also be found in commons production, are not only viewed by true compeerists as inherent 'bads' that vitiate the vision of a better, commons-based future, they are also recognized as being antithetical to the overarching strategy of expanding and hence fortifying the commons (Stavrides, 2016; 2019; Pentzold, 2021). In other words, it is only through an intentional openness that the commons can be expected to gain supporters, grow, and hence ever achieve a release from exchange-value's monopoly on economic organization.

In applying this philosophy to stakeholdership relations more broadly, we find there is significant room to expand inclusion within existing cooperative arrangements. Hence, while commons-based worker cooperatives and open-value-networks are well placed to look after the interests of their workers, preferably, they would also recognize the community and end-users linked to this production as 'invested parties' with rights to participate. Similarly, non-profits, member-cooperatives, and municipalities engaged in commons-oriented service provisions should ensure that their members and constituents, as well as the workers themselves, have a say in how these services are generated and delivered. An important consequence of broadening democratization in these ways is that it helps prevent a corruption of values, ensuring that the relevant entities remain focused on serving the community.

While establishing an expansive formal commons-based subeconomy operating according to the ideals noted here will undoubtedly take time, the logistical execution of such governance regimes is becoming ever more feasible. For instance, the Loomio app developed by the New Zealand based Enspiral collaborative is designed to help organizations achieve buy-in and manage decision making using various functionalities like proposal-making tools, poll taking, feedback forums, and secure voting (Loomio, nd). As discussed in Chapter 2 when considering the potential of such technology for open-value-networks, it is likely that we will soon see even more capabilities to control operational procedures via the use of decentralized autonomous organizations (DAOs), where the rules and procedures of an economic entity are coded directly into its internal decision-making mechanisms.

In sum, then, if compeerists can pursue both the right external and internal tactics to gain market competitiveness without becoming corrupted, then the market engagement response to the monopoly of exchange-value with which we started the chapter, represents a further strategic route to be pursued beyond that of exit and gifting. Yet, the advantage here is that market involvement offers commons-oriented actors both an option to access the resources they need while also directly challenging capital's grip on consumers and labour; this makes it the lynchpin of compeerism's overall evolutionary approach to achieving a post-capitalist mode of production.

The contemporary credit system and the pursuit of alternatives

The compeerist-aligned tactics of exit, gifting, and market engagement just covered are all centred on the commons-based subeconomy's need to deal with its dependence on money. Yet a further undergirding factor that must be considered in this constant struggle, is the commons-based subeconomies' relation to the financial/monetary arrangements currently in place more broadly. This is because these arrangements, rooted in the power that banks have to actually create money by issuing interest-bearing loans, are responsible for impeding access to funds for commons-oriented endeavours as these are funnelled, instead, to extractive/exploitative production and debt-fuelled consumption. It is an agglomeration of forces and relations, which we can call the monetary-banking apparatus, that proves to be a massive win for the banks at the cost of most everyone else.

In the US, for example, a quarter of low-income households waste 40 per cent of their income on debt service (Hoskins, 2011). Household debt as a percentage of GDP is also steadily climbing the world over, more than doubling in the biggest ten economies between 1980 and today, from 34 to 72 per cent (IMF, 2021). Globally this ratio for advanced economies has doubled since 1990. Corporate debt, in turn, most of which takes the form of bank loans, is also on the rise, reaching all-time highs globally as a percentage of GDP, hence raising fears of an impending bubble. Yet, the impact of this mounting corporate debt also comes back to bite the populace, in the form of increased prices. In Germany, for instance, Margrit Kennedy's research estimated that 50 per cent of the ticket price of essential goods is based on passing along the cost of servicing the private sector's mounting debt to the consumer (Kennedy and Kennedy, 1995).

Beyond these direct burdens and costs placed on the populace for the sake of boosting the financial sector's profits, a further impact to note from a compeerist perspective is the role that this financial situation plays in enhancing the apparatus of capture, as the imperative to meet the demands of debt repayment only compounds the need to sell one's labour to capital. Not least, from an even broader perspective, the credit that is essentially created from nothing by banks greatly intensifies the demand for never-ending, unsustainable economic growth. We will return to ways of directly challenging the apparatus of capture and the exponential growth imperative in the next chapter. For now, however, we can focus on more immediate compeerist options in dealing with the entrenched financial arrangements in place, keeping in mind that compeerists also have credit needs as well as savings that must be placed somewhere.

Hence, in the here and now, compeerists are faced with the challenge of circumventing capital-based credit by establishing their own commons-based arrangements around finance. One of the most basic forms of internalized, commons-based banking is 'cooperative accumulation'. Such cooperative financing efforts were established, for instance, in the 18th-century British and Irish 'terminating building societies', which would pool money to make low-cost credit available to help members purchase critical assets for their household or business. Today the Swedish JAK banks are replicating this model, with 30 local branches accumulating the savings of members to offer interest-free loans for everything from mortgages to community projects. Loans average US$23,000 but reach up to $1 million and the default rate is only 0.05 per cent (Bollier and Conaty, 2016).

Other, more targeted forms of cooperative accumulation include the pooling of funds to save a particular community asset such as a pub or soccer club, or to expand community-oriented capacities, for example by supporting investments in local renewable energy or agriculture. A good example is the Slow Money Movement, a non-profit focused on organizing zero-per-cent interest loans intended to support farmers and initiatives committed to sustainable, community-centred food production. In this way dozens of local groups have formed since its start in 2010, mobilizing more than $79 million in loans to hundreds of local food system initiatives (Slow Money, 2017).

Digital technology has also been harnessed to facilitate much broader lending pools via P2P lending or crowdlending. This platform-based system functions essentially the same way as crowdfunding, with the expectation that funds are repaid. While a circumvention of established banking institutions is a significant draw here, the most established P2P lending sites such as

Prosper and Zopa are generally still controlled by capital-based middlemen, and participation by lenders is mostly done with a considerable focus on returns. More commons-oriented approaches to P2P lending, however, can also be found. Kiva, for instance, is a non-profit that links funds offered by the public to micro-loans to specific projects in the Majority World. Once the loans are paid off, the returned money can be committed to another project or reclaimed by the lender. Since its inception in 2005, Kiva has granted more than 2.1 million loans, totalling over US$1.72 billion (Kiva, 2016). In 2011 Kiva began offering US based P2P loan mediation with zero-per-cent interest, offering what is essentially a more expansive, online based version of the Swedish JAK banks.

Boundary-commoning approaches to addressing credit needs between commons-based entrepreneurs can also be found, as noted in a number of cases covered in previous chapters. Along the lines of cooperative accumulation, many of the early member co-ops often worked together to combine extra revenue from their operations to form a cooperative bank, which, over time, would administer an ever-growing equity fund to service the needs and expansion of the cooperative economy. While there has been a waning in the intentionality and mutual support within some cooperative sectors, the tightly-knit cooperative alliances evident in France and northern Italy still participate in such arrangements.

More recently, finance-based boundary-commoning initiatives are also being employed in open-value networks or similar forms of digitally networked production. The New Zealand-based, commons-oriented Enspiral network, for instance, responsible for the Loomio app noted earlier, maintains a financial entity within its collaboration-focused production organization that actively diverts a chunk of earned revenues (averaging around 20 per cent) to be managed and utilized internally in the pursuit of its mission to facilitate a transition to a 'post-capitalist, sustainable economy' (Enspiral, 2021, np). The banking entity overseeing this task, named 'my.enspiral', oversees the collection and allocation of these funds, hence overcoming any need for external banking. The setup is explained as 'a bank for a "microcosm economy" protected from the outside world by the walled garden of a limited liability corporation' (quoted in Bollier and Conaty, 2016, p 32). Importantly, allocations of funds, while overseen by my.enspiral, are based on a democratic process, enabled by the Loomio app, where the voting power of a member is proportional to the contributions that have been made to the network.

Larger scaled alternatives to banking

Until the bottom-up financial initiatives just covered are significantly expanded, however, the capacity to mediate between commons-oriented savers and borrowers remains constricted. It is also unclear if these relatively confined and targeted forms of finance would be sufficient in supporting large-scale projects with high initial capital requirements. Given the general aim of finding a way out of the regular capital-oriented circulation of money, compeerists are, therefore, also committed to pursuing additional, more formal commons-oriented banking alternatives.

One option is that of government-run public banks. The German public banking sector is often pointed to as a potential model, consisting of a network of savings and development banks with the mission to service the financial needs of the local/regional citizenry and business sector. It should be noted that the Sparkasse savings banks at the heart of this network maintain significant clout, overseeing close to 15 per cent of Germany's banking assets, and serving as one of the three main pillars of the German banking system (Choulet, 2016). Another more isolated but noteworthy example is the Bank of North Dakota (BND) in the US, which was formed as a state government-run bank in 1919 together with the North Dakota Mill and Elevator. The BND offers credit for farmer and small-business startups as well as student loans with very low interest rates.

From a compeerist perspective, public banks have the potential to boost credit availability to commons-based projects, although doing so is ultimately contingent on the mission and visions of such banks. This is where the obvious limitations to such institutions lie. Given the capital-state nexus, public banks act primarily as support to regional, capital-oriented development. Furthermore, while public banks may not have the same profit drive as commercial banks, they are still usually mandated to achieve revenue. It should not be neglected, for instance, that the Bank of North Dakota has greatly benefitted from and abetted the profit-driven and unsustainable oil shale boom in the region (Dawson, 2014). Not least, public banks tend to embrace the power to lend money with limited or no reserves, known as fractional reserve banking, which is an integral component of the monetary-banking apparatus and is seen by many monetary reform advocates as being implicated in the numerous ills plaguing capitalist monetary systems and economies. These advocates have therefore also strongly criticized the proposed establishment of new public banks if their charter retains a commitment to such forms of lending (Bongiovanni and Switzer, 2021).

Another approach to more structured and large-scale commons-oriented banking can be found in cooperative and 'ethical' banks. Cooperative banks, which include credit unions, are chartered to service the needs of their members and community; they also generally include an obligation to maintain a one-person-one-vote governance system, giving members a say, at the very least, over the institution's board of directors. It is worth noting that credit union membership has steadily been rising in the US, even before the counter-capitalist campaign that encouraged angry Americans to divest their money accounts from the big corporate banks implicated in the Great Recession of 2007/8. As such, American credit unions currently have more than $1 trillion in savings and can claim more than a third of the US population as members (CUToday, 2019).

'Ethical banks', in turn, follow the same principles as B-corporations by lending money in line with values rooted in social and environmental sustainability. The European Federation of Ethical and Alternative Banks and Financiers, for instance, is a coalition of over 20 alternative banks across 15 countries seeking more transparency, intentionality, and democracy in the banking process. The pursuit of partnerships, as opposed to standard creditor/debtor dynamics, is seen here as a critical component of ethical banks and is pointed to as a reason why their default rates tend to be significantly lower than in commercial banks (Koivusalo and Mansour, 2018).

Still, while it is certainly promising to find banking arrangements committed to facilitating less profit-driven and more democratically informed investments focused on members, the community, and intentional projects, there are also aspects to these that conflict with broader compeerist aims. For example, as with public banks, there remains a general embrace of fractional reserve banking. It can also not be ignored that cooperative banks (credit unions) have become increasingly consolidated as they struggle in a market that continues to favour big banks (CUNA, 2021). Thus, without a more intentional mission, credit unions quickly succumb to an ever-greater focus on returns. Even in the more intentional ethical banks, we must acknowledge that the primary aim, as with existing public banking, is to assist communities in managing to thrive within the given parameters of capitalism. As such, many of the more explicitly non- or counter-capitalist projects emerging from the commons are still mostly excluded from being accepted as eligible 'partners'.

In this sense, the more formal 'alternative' banking arrangements available today still demonstrate some significant limitations from a compeerist point of view. To unleash their full potential would require moving them even further away from their revenue-generating focus, essentially making them more akin to upscaled forms of the cooperative accumulation covered earlier, as in the Swedish JAK banks. To achieve such upscaling, however, also requires more access to savings, meaning commoners of all stripes must themselves rise to the occasion and pursue an exit from their own investment mentality. In other words, a mass divestment is required from the capital-controlled financial institutions peddling returns sourced from extractive/exploitative activities, with savings funnelled, instead, into more solidaristic, boundary-commoning initiatives that offer low or no monetary growth. Only in this way would it be possible to establish a more robust and expansive, commons-oriented circulation of money, at least within the standard dynamics of our current monetary/financial arrangements.

Alternative forms of money

The just noted 'standard dynamics' referenced in relation to our current organization of money highlights the potential of finding additional, non-conventional ways with which to grease the wheels of the commons and commoning, particularly through alternative forms of tender. The use of currencies that exist alongside official, state-based money has long been a tool used to stimulate economic exchange, mobilize resources, and incentivize certain activities. In some instances, where such currencies are widely adopted, they can also bestow a significant level of financial power to the issuing entity and establish a degree of protection from any negative developments within the broader economy.

The most heralded, affirming case of the economic potential of a complementary currency can be found in the experimental issuing of so called 'freigeld' (free money) during the Great Depression by the mayor of the small Bavarian town of Wörgl (after which the currency was named). As is often the case with freigeld, the Wörgl was linked to a demurrage function, meaning that the money had a built-in expiration to prevent hoarding and encourage circulation. As a result of the Wörgl's introduction the town was able to sustain robust economic growth and employment while the rest of the country was experiencing deep decline.

A more recent, pioneering example of a complimentary currency, focused particularly on boosting commoning and not just economic activity, is the Toreke currency issued by the city of Ghent. Toreke money can be earned by contributing labour to various service projects in the impoverished Rabot neighbourhood. The value of the currency, in turn, which incentivizes such labour, is rooted in the fact that it can be used to rent coveted, municipally owned gardening space in the neighbourhood (Telalbasic, 2017).

With the advent of blockchain-enabled cryptocurrencies, there is now a growing interest in how the commoning potential of alternate forms of money can be expanded and deepened. Some of the most ambitious efforts have even set their sights on offering a commons-based money that could provide a viable alternative to state-based tender, that is, one that can function as a widely-adopted means of exchange and currency of account (for the actual buying and selling of goods and services within a broader economy). We will consider the steep uphill climb facing such initiatives in the next chapter, which deals with the more far-reaching aim of actually replacing the existing monetary-banking apparatus with a commons-friendly substitute. Most commons-based cryptocurrency efforts, however, are more limited in scope, but also more immediately achievable. Their potential and the challenges they face are worth considering.

The Toreke concept, for instance, has been embraced and furthered in a number of cities with the help of blockchain-based ledgers. One example is the English city of Hull, where certain community-centred volunteer work is paid in HullCoin, which can then be redeemed at participating retailers (Sylvester-Bradley, 2019). Blockchain capabilities here work to maintain a record of rewarded activities and currency issuance and use, thus allowing for user-friendliness, transparency, and security within a commons crediting system that is significantly more complex than the Ghent example. We can note that the reliance on participating retailers in this case, however, ultimately makes this currency dependent on a form of capital-linked gifting.

A further locality-focused currency is that of city-cryptos, where the issued crypto coins can be used to pay for specifically designed digital processes and smart-contracts, as Ether is used to run Ethereum-based 'DApps'. Yet, being a cryptocurrency that depends on proof-of-work 'mining', as Bitcoin is, some of the earnings of this mining activity are shared with the sponsoring city. As such, while city cryptos are generally capital owned and initiated projects, they still maintain a promising B-Corp component to them due to their commitment to the municipality.

MiamiCoin, established in the summer of 2021, was the first large scale city-crypto implemented, with 30 per cent of mining revenue (issued in tradable MiamiCoin) going directly to the municipal government (Volpecelli, 2022). In this way the city of Miami garnered over $7 million in just the first few months, and while MiamiCoin's value has plunged since its inception, there are many who still believe the promise of such city cryptos is just beginning (Brown, 2021; Volpecelli, 2022). Still, from a compeerist perspective, to truly work in support of commons-based aims, city-cryptos would preferably be organized along cooperative or non-profit lines, where there would be direct buy-in from the municipality and civil society, and where most revenue was earmarked to support the urban commons. While certainly conceivable, however, such a commons-based city-crypto has yet to be executed.

Another crypto-based initiative pursued by compeerists is the creation of an alternative form of money that can help generate funds and incentivize behaviour to achieve a specific, usually trans-local aim. Arthur Brock (2018), mentioned in Chapter 4 as the co-founder of the Holochain project, has argued there is room for a large number of such crypto-based currencies; the key to their viability, however, is that they actually denote something of value.

Consider, for instance, the Fishcoin project which seeks to incentivize fisherfolk in Southeast Asia to record essential data from their catch for the purposes of sustainable resource management. The fisherfolk are awarded Fishcoin crypto tokens for providing the data and uploading it to a database. The data itself, which is of interest to a wide range of stakeholders, including environmental NGOs, governments, and users/consumers, can only be bought with Fishcoin, which provides its foundational value (Gerhardt, 2020). Due to this value the currency maintains a certain level of worth in exchange markets, which is also why the fisherfolk view it as an adequate reward for participating. Not least, by being linked to an actual value-generating endeavour (and hence representing more than just crowd-based speculation), Fishcoin was able to generate significant funds from the get-go through an 'initial coin offering', hence garnering critical capital for its early stages.

In the absence of any foundational, undergirding value, however, incentive-oriented cryptocurrencies remain mostly speculative with little prospect for growth. SolarCoin, for instance, seeks to incentivize solar investments by awarding anyone producing solar energy with their crypto token. Yet, these tokens maintain limited appeal as there is very little of value they can be used for. Thus, to significantly improve the prospects of SolarCoin, the issuers could, hypothetically, follow Fishcoin's example by selling energy data collected from project participants, where SolarCoin would be required for the purchase. Alternatively, the currency could seek to become an accepted form of payment within participating electricity cooperatives. Unlike the gifting noted in the HullCoin example earlier, in this case the gift would not be directly dependent on capital, but rather it would come from a commons-oriented enterprise offering an alternative mode of operation. Boundary commoning synergies such as this will likely be critical if cryptocurrencies are to play a significant role in boosting commoning incentivizations.

Based on the various examples just offered, we can see how commons-oriented, crypto-monies have the potential, if well-designed, to help fund and foster the commons and commoning with very little initial capital. Yet there are also noteworthy challenges. Apart from issues related to finding willing partners to build the value of a commons-based cryptocurrency, not to mention the volatility and speculation associated with crypto markets, we should lastly also emphasize the inherent challenge of working with blockchain technology. This code, which was born out of and designed for the libertarian principles of independence and a lack of trust, is not conducive to the types of money compeerists seek to create. As such, alternative currency projects are tasked with not only hacking blockchain's intended application, but also, especially in the longer term, with fundamentally redesigning, repurposing, and re-governing its underlying code to ensure that the compeerist-aligned functions being pursued can be effectively performed.

While no easy task, we have, nonetheless, already seen some promising executions of such abstract hacktivist thinking, for instance how Holochain has completely reworked the fundamental structure of blockchain to create a more expansive digital ledger optimized for collaborative, commons-oriented transactions. In terms of governance, furthermore, where many cryptocurrencies such as Bitcoin are characterized by top-down, opaque, and highly guarded decision-making structures, commons-based efforts have pursued an intentional balance between an emphasis on technical skill, on the one hand, and open, inclusive decision making, on the other. A good illustration of this is the ambitious, means-of-exchange FairCoin cryptocurrency (covered in more detail in the next chapter); while FairCoin is maintained by a limited number of code administrators, the overall intentions and strategies associated with the project are determined democratically in a 'general assembly' of stakeholders (König et al, 2018).

In the end, however, and looking back to the entirety of efforts reviewed in this chapter that seek to address the commons' fraught dependency on money, we would do well to remember that these are all essentially coping strategies. They are intended to help commons-oriented actors find the means to swim in the taken-for-granted water of exchange-value monopolization. Yet compeerism is critically aware of this assumption and has begun to actively question it, just as the mature tadpole begins to see the possibilities that lie beyond the water's embrace. More precisely, compeerism acknowledges that the *longue-durée* goal is not simply creating better conditions for the commons to contend with the dominant monetary-banking apparatus in place, rather it is to fully usurp and replace it. Only in this way can the compeerist vision of a world beyond capitalism have any chance of coming to fruition.

8

Reinventing Money's Role in the Economy

Compeerism recognizes that the dominance of exchange-value driven thinking expounded at the outset of the last chapter is ultimately rooted in the three-headed apparatus of capture, which combines the governance of property, labour, and money in the service of capital. Each of these reinforces the other, making it difficult, at least from within the limited commons realm, to overcome just one on its own. Most of this book has thus far been focused primarily on the potential for exit and replacement within the two 'heads' of property and labour governance, yet it is clear that the third component, money, must also be addressed.

It is money, after all, that enables exchange-value monopolization and the subsequent commodification of everything (property and labour), hence degrading the perceived worth attributed to the non-commodifiable commons and commoning. This underlying function of money as the third 'head' is honed and guided via its current iteration: the monetary-banking apparatus. This apparatus governs money's creation and distribution in the form of debt issuance, which, being focused solely on making more money, is a purely exchange-value driven process. Thus, if compeerists could succeed in shifting how money is organized and managed, essentially removing it from capital's control, then the commons-oriented modes of organizing property and labour could be allowed to function within a much more conducive environment. More to the point, however, if all three components of the apparatus of capture could be replaced with synergized, commons-based alternatives, then capitalism as we know it would cease to exist.

Following from this, then, a fundamental, long-term aim on the part of compeerists must be the reinvention of money as a technology and tool that is designed to bolster the commons and commoning. Yet, achieving such a breakthrough means overcoming the currently dominant monetary-banking apparatus introduced in the previous chapter. There are essentially two options to meeting this challenge. One is a bottom-up effort from within the commons subeconomy itself aimed at a wholesale exit from the state-based monetary system. The other is a top-down approach that seeks to compel a monetary restructuring through a commons-friendly state. We can start with the latter.

The state and its reluctant potential

The potential of a state-based, top-down dismantling of the monetary-banking apparatus is best understood in relation to the challenge of contending with the mounting socio-economic-political instabilities linked to capitalism more broadly, which are threatening to explode into a deep and punishing civilizational crisis. Compeerists are here tasked with prodding the state into the realization that a band-aid approach of merely addressing symptoms will not suffice. Instead, the apparatus of capture as a whole must be undone and replaced by something more humane and sustainable.

For the state, if it were to agree in this assessment, the most natural target for intervention would be the apparatus of capture's monetary component, as the state maintains significant power in this realm, for instance by playing a key role in establishing money's broad acceptance as a means of exchange – largely by demanding taxes denominated in this money. Homing in on the monetary-banking apparatus also makes sense because it has come to play a particularly important part in exacerbating the inherent 'unsustainabilities' linked to capitalism, primarily by turbocharging the growth imperative. On top of this, however, by giving banks the primary power over the issuance of money, the apparatus also forces states into a position of fiscal paralysis when it comes to actually dealing with the problems that these unsustainabilities give rise to. Before considering how the monetary-banking apparatus could be replaced, however, the noted motivation to do so in the first place deserves a bit more unpacking.

The state's paralysis in the face of crisis

Today, it is increasingly accepted, as evidenced by a recent official paper by the Bank of England, that fractional reserve banking is the basis of the money creation process in contemporary capitalist economies (Werner, 2014). In other words, most money in circulation is generated by commercial banks that conjure it out of nothing in the form of interest-bearing loans, a key characteristic of the monetary-banking apparatus. Furthermore, in most cases this conjured money must be understood to be a 'fiat' form of tender, since, going back to 1971 when the US moved to cancel the gold standard, it is backed by nothing more than the state's decree designating it to be the official instrument for mediating exchange.

An important consequence of this monetary shift has been an exacerbation of the capitalist growth imperative. This is because, even if banks annul their lent-out money once it is paid back, there nonetheless remains an interest income that stays within the system, which represents a subsequently needed increase in exchange-value based goods and services. Indeed, it should not be hard to fathom – if massive devaluations or inflation are to be avoided – that the continuous demand for more money being returned to the bank than was taken out must be accompanied by a concomitant expansion in commodities.

More pertinently, this expansion, based on the issuing of interest-bearing loans, is now hardwired to increase in percentile increments, meaning it must be exponential. For instance, even with a modest growth imperative of only two per cent, the US economy, which had a GDP of roughly $20 trillion in 2021, would need to double in size in the next 35 years. This never-ending demand for growth has led to a feedback loop of ever-increasing debt reliance across the economic spectrum, a reality that is evidenced by the steadily climbing total debt to GDP ratio, which currently stands at nearly three-to-one globally, a 150 per cent increase since 1970 (Gaspar et al, 2022). In short, more debt requires more growth, which in turn brings about more debt.

It is ultimately this economic growth imperative, aggressively stoked by the monetary-banking apparatus, that comprises a critical source of problems for the economic and social order in the medium to long run (Harvey, 2015). In other words, the monetary arrangement within capitalism today is not just a facilitator in exchange-value's hegemony, it is an active participant in pushing the commodification machine to function at ever-greater speeds. The negative consequences of this acceleration have been myriad.

For one, as covered in the prior chapter, there has been a burgeoning dependence on interest-bearing loans to keep up with the growth imperative, ultimately bogging down the budgets of households, enterprises, and, indeed, governments – not only in the form of interest-payment burdens, but through higher prices for everyone (the cost of sustaining astronomical profits for rentier capitalists who do not actually produce anything of value). Furthermore, as laid out in Chapter 1, the need to meet continuously accelerating growth expectations has also led to the expansion of imposed, forced scarcity and ever-deepening financialization, linked, in turn, to the periodic formation of asset bubbles and concomitant, socially painful recessions. Lastly, and arguably most problematic of all, the demand for exponential growth has gone hand in hand with the need to increase material throughput, giving rise to the subsequent deterioration of our supportive, natural planetary systems.

Yet, when confronted with the monetary-banking apparatus's deep implication in these developments, the state has limited itself to superficial tweaks aimed at only preventing the most egregious forms of abuse by the banking/financial sector, such as limited curtailments on financial speculation and/or predatory lending. There is no sign of seriously questioning the unsustainable and ultimately dangerous assumption that the economy's market value must double in 35 years, and quadruple in 70. As such, the state has generally opted to focus on addressing the symptoms of the many problems that, quite predictably, are mounting in synch with the escalating growth expectations. As it turns out, however, the monetary-banking apparatus also prevents the state from executing this band-aid approach effectively. This is because in the current setup, it is banks that are bestowed with the power to create money and hence control credit/investment, while the state is forced to raise its funds through the limited means of taxation and debt, thereby imposing debilitating fiscal restraints.

To place this predicament into more concrete terms, we can consider some specific challenges that the state will imminently have to contend with. One is the impending environmental meltdown that is bound to transpire as global climate change begins to trigger a host of ecological tipping points across the world. In response, and taking the US state as an example, one ambitious policy that has been proposed is that of a 'Green New Deal', aimed at fundamentally restructuring the capitalist economy in a way that will drastically cut back on carbon emissions while ensuring increased human welfare.

The average cost of such an ambitious investment is estimated to lead to a roughly 100 per cent increase in the overall budget, which would be a 375 per cent increase of discretionary spending (Holtz-Eakin et al, 2021). Yet, when President Biden tried to get a drastically reduced semblance of the bill through Congress in 2021, which was estimated to cost less than five per cent of the Green New Deal proposal, it was considered too expensive and failed to pass. One group that stood in the way of the bill's success were the 'deficit hawks', who could point to projections showing that interest payments on debt are due to sharply rise in the US as its debt continues to mount, reaching up to 26 per cent of its entire budget by 2050 (CBO, 2020).

Another example where the state's fiscal limitations may prove to be particularly costly pertains to the increasingly plausible development in which a growing portion of the populace faces un- and underemployment. Given the accelerating evolution and affordability of AI and robotics, and the continued jostling for limited market share that spurns the adoption of these technologies, the possibility of escalating labour redundancy in the not-too-distant future is considerable. This includes technological breakthroughs such as autonomous, self-driving vehicles and fully automated kitchens replacing low-income workers, while natural language, deep learning AIs replace technicians, lawyers, and consultants. Several observers have pointed out that the COVID-19 pandemic has already shifted momentum in the robots' favour (Korinek and Stiglitz, 2021).

We can note that several iconic economic thinkers have pondered what the dawn of such hyperproductivity could entail. Apart from the already noted early Marx of *Grundrisse*, John Maynard Keynes is another notable example. Keynes (1973) offered the year 2030 for when most work would become automated, at which point people would see a welcomed boost in free time and a fundamental shift in social relations. For instance, Keynes (1973, p 329) suggested that when we do finally manage to achieve a world of largely automated, massive production capabilities, we would come to recognize our past love of money as a 'semi-criminal, semi-pathological' propensity. The problem, however, is that this envisioned liberating potential of technology, shared by the early Marx, is far from given.

Even before the pandemic, Stanford's otherwise non-alarmist *One Hundred Year Study on Artificial Intelligence* warned: 'As labour becomes a less important factor in production as compared to owning intellectual capital, a majority of citizens may find the value of their labour insufficient to pay for a socially acceptable standard of living' (Stone et al, 2016, p 39). Such a condition, deeply rooted in the commodification of everything brought about by the apparatus of capture, would certainly pose substantial problems for capitalism, not only because of potential social destabilizations, but due to the difficulty of maintaining economic growth in the context of significantly depreciated consumer demand, an oft noted, fundamental contradiction within capitalism (Harvey, 2015). The paradox here, that increased production capacity, under current conditions, is likely to create greater precarity than prosperity, exemplifies the compeerist case that capitalism is becoming increasingly absurd.

It is in this light that the introduction of a universal basic income (UBI) presents itself as the most obvious solution by loosening the tethering of labour with money, which remain inextricably linked within the apparatus of capture. While still not mainstream, the UBI proposition is gaining ground and has become an established discourse in political and policy circles from Europe to the United States. It is worth noting that even President Nixon briefly considered implementing an unconditional UBI in the US before he became convinced by misconstrued analyses that it would induce laziness (Bregman, 2016). Today, however, a true, no-strings-attached UBI has regained credibility with several studies showing that people who gain access to regular 'free' money tend to invest this windfall into various activities aimed at improving their, and their children's, economic standing more broadly (Lowrey, 2018).

At the same time, as the UBI idea begins to find traction, a host of counter-capitalist scholars have come to the fore critiquing it. Some see it as a last-ditch effort to save capitalism, while others highlight the libertarian sentiments in some UBI proposals. Even more doctrinaire rejections argue that a UBI would do nothing to overcome the exchange-value mindset that lies at the centre of capitalism, which can only be achieved by getting rid of money altogether (Pitts, 2018b).

In juxtaposition to these aspersions, however, Compeerism is naturally drawn to the promise of a UBI. While in no way interested in throwing capitalism a lifeline or privatizing basic needs, a UBI is recognized as presenting an enormous opportunity in overcoming the apparatus of capture's hold on labour, and its intertwined labour–money governance more broadly, which keeps this labour from participating in commoning and commons expansion (an issue repeatedly noted in past chapters) (Orsi, 2009). In this sense, a guaranteed income is seen as a freeing up of labour and money that can then be hacked and put to use in the service of the commons, with the more far-reaching potential of eating away at the internal bonds holding the apparatus of capture together.

Yet, before getting lost in such promise, we are again confronted with the difficult fiscal demands that such a programme would place on governments. Providing a UBI, depending on the amount of income given, would translate to a 50 to 100 per cent gross increase in government expenditures, although the actual net cost, which hinges on the particular tax code, could be significantly lower (Widerquist, 2017). Still, even with just a 15 per cent increase in yearly government spending, as per more optimistic calculations, the prospect of the state being able to execute a UBI appears unlikely given the state's existing fiscal constraints, not to mention the powerful interests in place that stand opposed to dealing with such limitations via higher taxes. This incapacity is noteworthy considering that a UBI offers a clear, rational path to eradicating poverty and dealing with the social debilitations, and even dangers, linked to a hyperproductivity that lies just on the horizon.

In sum, then, as the difficulty of pursuing a Green New Deal and a UBI demonstrate, the state has become fundamentally incapable of offering more than lacklustre, superficial, and, in the end, ineffective responses to the growing, internally derived challenges associated with capitalism's continuing evolution. This impotence is due to the fact that the state fails/refuses to question its underlying commitment to staying within the bounds of the existing assemblages/apparatuses within the three-headed apparatus of capture, and hence contemporary capitalism more broadly. Yet, as dysfunctions begin to mount, as with growing precarity and ecological collapse, the state, and perhaps more importantly its citizenry, will become increasingly inclined to recognize the need to think outside the box of the current economic dogma, especially as it pertains to the governance of money. More specifically, the state could actively pursue the dismantling of the monetary-banking apparatus by reclaiming control over money creation. In doing so, the state would have the power to significantly diminish the existing imperative for endless, exponential growth while simultaneously recapturing the ability to command investment priorities.

While this would be a first step in the right direction for compeerists, it is critical to note that the state must simultaneously be convinced to approach these deep restructurings from within a commons-oriented framework. This would mean that the power unleashed by reclaiming the control over money should not be used by the state to massively inflate its direct participation in productive activities, as per socialism, but rather to empower civil society to become engaged in the expansion and deepening of the commons-based (sub)economy. If such a shift were to be achieved at a deep, institutional level, it would signal a monumental step closer to realizing the long-term compeerist vision of a post-capitalist future.

Reclaiming money

The contemporary capitalist state's refusal to play a more integral role in the governance of money has not always been a given and continues to be questioned by some unorthodox economists. Probably the most obvious exception to the complete submission to the monetary-banking apparatus is the use of the state's central bank as a source of free loans to the government. Essentially the central bank can here be used to create money, buy up government bonds, and then, because the bank is beholden to the state, repatriate the interests on the bonds back to the state, in essence providing interest-free lending. This practice has become increasingly relied on in recent times to deal with significant financial crises, for example via so-called 'quantitative easing' meant to inject liquidity into the economy by buying government bonds with money created with a few taps on a keyboard.

Some economists and monetary activists, however, are making the case that such 'interest-free' lending could be made use of more actively to help governments expand their budgets and be less on the hook for interest payments to various, and increasingly foreign, creditors. Canada is often pointed to as an example where the central bank was actively involved in funding the government from the 1930s up to the 1970s, at which point a growing, neoliberal consensus – along with monetarist views on the cause of inflation – led to a disavowal of internal government funding sources. In response, a concerted movement has emerged to rejuvenate the Bank of Canada's role in supplying internal credit for public programmes and projects, hence releasing the government from its dependency on usurious debt (Ryan, 2018).

Beyond the Canadian case, however, there has recently been a significant increase in the development and embrace of a number of even more 'radical' heterodox economic theories. In essence, these suggest a monetary rearrangement is possible that would give states direct control over the money supply, thereby circumventing the need for loan intermediaries altogether. In such an instance, the state can create and then release money into the economy directly in pursuit of its policy goals.

One popular theory in this vein is that of modern monetary theory (MMT), which puts the state, as opposed to the central bank, in charge of pursuing full employment (Kelton, 2021). Here, in times of high unemployment, the state can use internally created fiat money to generate the stimulus needed for the economy to recover. In other words, the state is empowered to unilaterally spend money into existence, thus establishing a 'sovereign money' regime. In this arrangement, taxes and bonds are viewed as mere tools to be used to control the quantity of money; and this, according to MMT, becomes an issue only after full employment has been reached.

We should note here that MMT still leaves private banks and debt-based lending in place because, according to its reasoning, these banks would now be primarily at the mercy of state spending, which would become the driver of monetary expansion. It is this unwillingness to challenge fractional reserve banking, however, that has led some to seek even more far-reaching monetary reforms (Zarlenga, 2002; Huber, 2014; 2017). In these proposals, and in line with the thinking of Irving Fisher and the Chicago Plan of 1933, a demand is made that banks can only loan out what they have in their account, thus drastically reducing the growth of the overall money supply. State-issued money, in turn, can be released in various ways, including so-called 'helicopter money' made accessible directly to the public, as well as targeted loans and government spending on specific programmes (opening up the compeerist-aligned option, for instance, of funnelling investment towards the pursuit of use-value rather than exchange-value). In such a monetary context, generating funds via the state to address society's most critical needs, while also overcoming the debt-driven, runaway, and unsustainable growth imperative, suddenly appears like a real possibility. We will consider one specific, albeit hypothetical application of such a sovereign money regime in Chapter 10.

Yet, it should also not come as a surprise that most contemporary, mainstream economists tend to scoff at such heterodox positions. When any such notions cross their path, it does not take long before references to Weimarian wheelbarrows full of useless money enters the discussion. The ultimate fear here is a scenario where money is used to demand much more from the economy than the economy can deliver, leading to crippling inflation and ultimately a complete loss of confidence in the currency and the ability to conduct exchanges. While such inflation concerns cannot be dismissed, they must nonetheless also be put into perspective. In the end, there is a complex array of factors, particularly with regard to consumption and production, that come into play in determining inflation. For instance, a society that is highly dependent on a critical commodity that is inelastic in responding to demand, like oil, will be much more susceptible to inflationary pressures. Yet, when supply has the capacity to be more reactive to consumption, any increase in money supply tends to lead to increased economic activity, hence neutralizing inflationary pressures (within obvious limits).

Following from this, then, it is also possible to see that the use of sovereign money on 'non-productive', use-value focused investments, such as ecosystem service restoration or a universal basic income, can still be monetarily viable. While such initiatives do not appear to add immediate, additional market value (needed to prevent inflation), the money added to the system and used to pay for supplies and labour can still lead to an overall increase in such value over time as this money works its way through the economy – especially if newly unleashed demand is not heavily focused on inelastic goods. Furthermore, in the case of investments aimed at improving apparently non-commodifiable endowments, an increase in market-based value often also ensues with time; for example, replenished ecosystems can lead to all around higher production and the creation of new economic activity, ranging from agriculture on reclaimed land to a boost in (eco)tourism.

In short, we should recognize the malleability and longer-term dimensions of economies when worrying about 'non-productive' money entering the system. We would, in fact, do well to keep in mind here the millions of so-called 'bullshit jobs' within capitalism – identified by David Graeber (2019) to include work in unneeded bureaucracy, advertising, lobbying, and ego stroking – that also fail to directly contribute to an increase in exchange-value based goods and services. Indeed, our current economy has been more than capable of absorbing this superfluousness for decades, with no one harping about possible inflationary pressures. In a similar way, then, a state in possession of sovereign money should be able to pursue significant (use-value) investments considered to be 'gratuitous' without automatically triggering the collapse of this money's worth.

Still, we would also be imprudent if we completely ignored the impact that the money supply can have on prices. It is therefore incumbent on any state that has embraced a sovereign tender to establish a sound monetary policy that ensures currency issuance is in line with the actual supply of goods and services it denominates. Most fundamentally, and particularly given that economic growth rates are to be significantly reduced, this means states must also find ways to reabsorb much of the money that has been released, thereby taking it out of circulation.

To begin, one advantage for the state controlling its own currency is that it has become the primary lender of credit, meaning that any interest collected would essentially entail a decrease as opposed to an increase of the money supply. Next, where additional shrinkage is necessary, along the lines of MMT, a state can resort to targeted taxation/fees and the sale of state-derived goods and services as ways of taking liquidity out of the system. Lastly, and most critically, if any emerging inflationary pressures were detected, the state presiding over a sovereign currency could respond directly by curtailing monetary outflow, which is significantly less tortuous than the predominant reliance today on steadily increasing interest rates.

A more radical option worth noting here would be to place a demurrage function on the sovereign currency. Due to its built-in devaluation, the state would hence be absolved from having to retrieve money from the economy. Such a currency would serve primarily as a tool to facilitate exchange and would no longer function as a useful store of value. Yet the challenges in such a move for the state are significant. The subsequent hoarding of certain goods as a way to pursue savings, for instance, would have to be addressed. International trade could also be significantly impacted, as the value of a demurrage currency would likely be quite low due to its fleeting worth. We will return to how a demurrage currency could potentially be adopted by a partner state within a post-capitalist context in Chapter 10, but its viability in the near term is doubtful.

Even with sound monetary policies, however, sovereign currencies will likely still face inflationary pressures from time to time just as bank-issued currencies do today. As such, any budgetary 'belt tightening' on the part of a state would need to proceed carefully to ensure that the most critical economic interactions remain active. One particularly powerful economic stabilizer in this regard would be a guaranteed income, which, due to the maintenance of basic consumption that it enables, would prevent a precipitous economic retraction in the most critical areas of the economy.

The role of a vibrant commons-based sector in helping to weather difficult economic adjustments is also worth noting here. For instance, if the state's curtailment of money circulation led to a squeeze in household budgets, any ensuing difficulties could be minimized by leaning on the commons, which, if having been fostered and allowed to flourish, would have found some autonomy from the formal economy and its money system. In this way, a family dealing with an income reduced to the UBI could use the commons to access free, cheaper, or bartered goods and services that they previously acquired in the private sector. This household could then re-engage the market economy when the opportunity arises, or, as the optimistic compeerist would argue, the experience may lead them to stay and commit to the commons-based economy for good.

Given the emphasis on sound monetary management, a final concern that needs to be acknowledged pertains to the ability of the state, which is viewed by many with great suspicion, to effectively execute such responsible stewardship. Critics here point to our deeply imperfect political systems and humanity's well-established corruptibility. In short, politicians will be tempted to abuse their power over monetary management, pursuing short-term wishful thinking or selfish desires rather than decision making based on objective, detailed analyses and long-term planning.

Monetary reformers are cognizant of these concerns, which is why they generally suggest that monetary governance should be left to an independent body of persons committed to act in an informed and nonpartisan way. Most proposals emphasize public input and transparency as well as clear barriers between monetary managers, who determine the money supply, and the executive and legislative branches of government, who then decide on fiscal priorities, that is, how this money should be used. The National Emergency Employment Defense (NEED) Act, a US House bill, is often pointed to here as an example of actual (although dormant) legislation that would establish sovereign money (Kucinich, 2011). In this proposal, the independent body charged with monetary policy would consist of nine members serving six-year terms, where each member would be appointed by the President and approved by the Senate, but no more than four members could be of the same political party. While such an arrangement could undoubtedly be made even more apolitical and bound by oversight, it is, at least, not a bad starting point.

Nonetheless, even if such an independent and accountable monetary governance authority were established, there would remain ample room for internal clashes of opinion regarding policy, which is inevitable when dealing with extremely complex systems entailing many unknowns. This is where emerging technologies could be of significant assistance. As Paul Mason (2016) has argued, it is high time that the incredible capacity to model complexity that we already have at our disposal be actively applied to the realm of economics, which has thus far largely avoided such tools. Indeed, if this modelling potential were to be fully tapped, especially in light of its growing power via the use of big data crunching AI systems, it could be possible to establish a relatively clear picture of the current and future impact of any specific release of money, for instance in the form of a UBI or as larger, targeted investments.

Given a broadly accepted, transparent, and effective modelling system, like that for projecting hurricane trajectories within meteorology, debate over monetary and fiscal policy could mostly avoid disagreements over the reality of certain processes and outcomes, as these would now be largely understood and acknowledged. Focus could, instead, turn to the imperative question of what we want the economy to do for us, as opposed to the current, obverse emphasis on what we can do for the economy. Importantly, any such data analysis and modelling should also be released to the digital commons, allowing for greater oversight and informed input from civil society and the populace. This is where the onus would fall on compeerists to demand comprehensive and deep analyses that are not limited to using only exchange-value as an assessment metric. Indeed, compeerists are of the conviction that any well-rounded, long-term modelling based on big-data and effective AI processing would ultimately validate and bolster their policy positions.

Challenging the monetary-banking apparatus without the state

There is no doubt that a move to sovereign money by the state would be a monumental shift with enormous implications for the capitalist mode of production, while at the same time opening up significant opportunities for commons expansion. Still, given the uncertainty of whether or when states would be prepared to trigger such serious monetary reforms, we must also consider efforts for finding a wholesale exit from, and replacement of, the monetary-banking apparatus that could be pursued via bottom-up mobilizations.

One of the things that has characterized past complementary currencies and alternative trading networks is their focus on a relatively limited economic space. This was partly due to an ideological focus on localism, but it was also the result of limited technological means to expand such efforts. Yet, in the previous chapter, we saw how cryptocurrencies have enabled much more expansive transactions, for instance to incentivize compeerist-aligned behaviours. Now a growing number of projects, albeit many still conceptual, are also using cryptographic and blockchain technology to pursue entirely new means-of-exchange money that can help facilitate and support a growing and more delinked commons economy (Fritsch et al, 2021). In other words, these currencies strive to become units of account used in actual transactions, as opposed to simply a store of value that is mostly held as a speculative investment, as most cryptocurrencies still are.

The enticement of a non-state means-of-exchange tender from a compeerist perspective is that it could potentially endow the issuer with similar advantages to that of a state managing its own sovereign currency. This is, however, assuming the currency allows for some form of intentional control, which is difficult to achieve in blockchain based cryptocurrencies due to the intentional decentralization of their validation and issuance procedures, as with Bitcoin. Still, even if an alternative design could be developed along abstract hacktivist principles, hence allowing the currency to be used more intentionally, managing to successfully launch and then reap the benefits of such an alternative money is still fraught with sizable hurdles.

Undoubtedly the greatest challenge is that of creating enough buy-in to make the currency viable. Cryptocurrencies are known to be particularly vulnerable to speculation and subsequent valuation swings based on herd-like movements within the volatile world of cryptocurrency exchanges. Such instabilities are particularly untenable for means-of-exchange tender as it makes it difficult to price goods and services, hence significantly damaging such currency's appeal. While much of this instability could be remedied if the intended unit of account actually denoted a sizable economy of things to be bought and sold, the big question is how to get to that point when this money starts off as unstable, unwieldy, and impractical. We should add that if such a currency were, in fact, to ever achieve viability, the utmost care would then need to be taken to not over-issue it, as this could quickly lead to devaluation and abandonment, with very few means to remedy the problem.

Currently there are still no instances where an expansive, non-state-based currency of account has effectively been implemented. Paradoxically, the closest example is Bitcoin. Although treated primarily as a speculative store of value today, Bitcoin was originally intended to be a means-of-exchange money that could compete with state-based tender, hence the much-told story of the first pizza bought with Bitcoin shortly after its launch (the amount paid for two pizzas at that time is worth about US$150 million as of this writing). Since then, Bitcoin has, in fact, steadily been making inroads as a legitimate unit of account, with a growing number of big vendors accepting Bitcoin payment and the prospect of more Majority World countries – following El Salvador's example – adopting the cryptocurrency as legal tender (Bernstein, 2021).

While Bitcoin is not a sovereign currency (due to its in-built decentralization), if a sovereign, means-of-exchange crypto token/coin were to actually reach Bitcoin's overall valuation, the concomitant economic power bestowed on the issuer would be significant (Fama et al, 2019). Bitcoin may currently only be the equivalent of 0.1 per cent of the world's overall accessible money supply (known as broad money), yet this still signifies a third of the money supply of Kenya (US$10 billion) and ten times that of the Seychelles. Indeed, a sovereign, alternative currency that denominated $10 billion worth of value within a commons-based subeconomy could be leveraged in various ways to boost the commons and commoning.

There are currently several nascent efforts pursuing such a goal, usually adopting one of two main strategies. The first is an exit-centred effort in which crypto tokens are issued with the aim of achieving a viable commons-based network of exchange that could support a guaranteed basic income. The second is a more radical project where an alternative money form is created to denominate what is to become an expanding commons-based economic realm that can compete with (and perhaps even replace) the dominant capitalist economy and its adopted state-based currency of account. We can start with the former.

In basic-income type cryptocurrencies, such as SwiftDemand, Mannabase, and Circles, the aim is to establish a means-of-exchange money that is accepted by enough people to enable its incremental release as a form of free income. Focusing on just one example, Circles, which runs on Ethereum's blockchain-based xDai sidechain, is pursuing a guaranteed income currency by creating relatively closed, trust-based networks comprised of individuals and businesses who agree to accept each other's Circles tokens as tender to be used for any goods and services they bring to the network (Circles, 2020). A key challenge facing such basic-income cryptocurrencies, however, is that many may be interested in free money, but few will be thrilled about denominating their assets in such a currency if there is little expectation that doing so will be reciprocated. In Circles this issue is decentralized, leaving it up to the various trust networks to establish systems of accepted reciprocity; only if you are invited into the network can you receive your steady stream of Circles currency. While this may lead to a slow start, it also creates more confidence and security in the currency. With time, then, the aim is to have the trust-based networks begin to interlink, expanding them from very small complementary economies to ever more expansive and diversified ones.

The expansion of Circles networks also means that the inflationary pressure of a continuous issuance of guaranteed income money can be partly offset. At the same time, inflation is also not fully shunned in the Circles project, which strives to maintain a set level of seven per cent yearly inflation to dissuade its use as a store of value. In the Circles whitepaper, the currency is clearly envisioned as a currency of account that is meant to be used for economic interactions. Thus, the pursued level of inflation serves as an intended demurrage, ensuring that the Circles money stays in circulation as a means of exchange (Circles, 2020). Yet, while inflation poses an ongoing challenge to be managed, the Circles currency also comes with the benefit of avoiding sudden and unpredictable fluctuations in its value. This is because the Circles currency is not set up for external trading; it is an internalized system where each Circles participant is given their own individualized crypto tokens to be used in a closed, mutually agreed upon network or group of networks. In such an arrangement, there is no easy way, even for an individual, to sell their Circles money outside of the network.

Importantly, while the individualized approach to Circles money issuance prevents any entity from gaining a singular sovereign control over the currency, the Circles monetary arrangement can still be leveraged to achieve commons-based, use-value centred ends. In other words, the currency's power is devolved to the Circles communities themselves who can decide on what can be denominated in Circles tokens and hence what counts as 'valuable'. In this way, these networks can use the Circles system to foster intentional economies that are not driven by purely exchange-value determinations. In the longer term, then, if the Circles networks were to significantly grow and interconnect, these economies could offer ever more options to exit capital and, as per their main aim, find a significant reprieve from the apparatus of capture via a guaranteed income.

The second approach to pursuing a more expansive, commons-based currency of account centres on establishing a money form that can be used by the issuing entity to directly subsidize a commons-based subeconomy. The aim in such a project is ultimately to assist in the compeerist goal of a transvestment of capital-controlled wealth to the commons by engaging state-based money. In other words, such a currency strives to be more than simply complementary. In the most ideal scenario, then, a highly competitive commons-based subeconomy using its own sovereign currency could establish current account (trade) surpluses with market-based economies. The resulting boost in access to state-based currencies could then be used to acquire critical assets held by capital, including land, infrastructure, and means of production.

While there are not many, one example of a project that roughly adopts such a vision is the anarchist-inspired FairCoop and their FairCoin currency. The aim of this project is to create a FairCoin denominated marketplace that would ultimately confer quasi-sovereign currency privileges to FairCoop (König et al, 2018). More specifically, FairCoop has here taken control over a significant chunk of initially created FairCoin (estimated to be about 20 per cent of the total) while the rest of the currency was either gifted to other actors or was created as part of the cryptocurrency's decentralized, proof-of-cooperation mining process. Yet, with the FairCoin that were internally held, FairCoop has pursued various commoning efforts, such as the funding of Freedom Coop, which offers legal and banking services to self-employed individuals looking to make a living outside the exploitative grip of capital or the state.

Importantly, with a cryptocurrency that is designed to engage other forms of money in the open market, the challenges that emerge are distinct from those faced by basic-income crypto projects, like Circles. To begin, we should note that FairCoin, at least, is not burdened with the need to continuously release its currency, hence dampening inflationary pressures. Instead, the issuing of currency can be more intentional and limited with the aim of controlling its overall value. In line with this reasoning, after an initial airdrop (free distribution) of coins and a limited period of mining, FairCoin put a cap on currency creation. Such a cap makes sense given that a decay of FairCoin value would undermine the likelihood of its adoption as well as the wealth position that FairCoop has created for itself. Nonetheless, if the currency's value significantly increased, a fork in the blockchain could be instigated to allow for further money issuance, an option that has not been ruled out (König et al, 2018).

A much more far-reaching and complex problem, however – one that the Circles currency manages to circumvent – pertains to the danger of succumbing to speculation, hoarding, and value fluctuations, as FairCoin is not shielded from being treated primarily as a store-of-value asset. This issue comes especially into play because FairCoop has not achieved a big enough economic realm denominated in FairCoin to establish an autonomous, externally backed pool of market value. In response to FairCoin's wild fluctuations, and in an effort to ensure the currency can function as an effective means of exchange, a minority of FairCoop stakeholders have proposed pegging FairCoin to a more stable, state-based currency (Barinaga and Ocampo, 2019).

Achieving such a fixed exchange rate, however, is not tenable if FairCoin is to remain a tradable, means-of-exchange form of money, as this would require costly currency market interventions to maintain the targeted currency value. More specifically, such interventions require large sums of valuable state-based tender that are generally not available. The dominant view within FairCoop, therefore, is to continue allowing the market to determine FairCoin's price. Supporters of this line of thinking argue that swings in value must be accepted as an inevitable component of the strategy they have adopted (FairCoin, 2018).

In fact, the market-oriented strategy adopted by FairCoin entails a recognition that value fluctuations can cut both ways, and thus have the potential to be exploited. As such, we can see that an underlying, initial aspiration within the FairCoin project was to essentially hack the unstable cryptocurrency markets by playing the store-of-value game, even if the eventual goal was to become an expansive currency of account (not unlike Bitcoin's potential trajectory). Initially this appeared to be a promising strategy. In 2017, riding a wave of Bitcoin fuelled upward speculation, FairCoop was able to garner a significant amount of state-based reserve currencies for its FairCoin holdings as the coin's value reached €1.2. In the end, however, there was ultimately nothing FairCoop could do when the bubble popped and FairCoin's price came crashing back to earth, demonstrating the extreme difficulty in replicating Bitcoin's route to widespread adoption based on its acceptance as a store of value. After hitting rock bottom, the FairCoin project has begun picking up the pieces in a bid to re-establish its worth. As of this writing FairCoin's exchange rate stands between €0.05 and €0.08 euro cents.

At this juncture, arguably the only way FairCoin could truly alleviate the challenges it faces is if it could significantly broaden the microeconomy it denotes. How big is big enough remains an open question, but it would be wrong to assume outright that a commons-based economic realm could not reach the needed scale. Take the example of the Seychelles again, which maintains the smallest economy to employ a free-floating independent currency. This economy maintains a GDP between US$1 and $2 billion per year and has managed a remarkably stable currency over time. Then, consider that the total sales of the Mondragon mega-cooperative is well over $10 billion. Clearly, there could be commons-aligned economies that are big enough.

Following from this, then, rather than trying to build up a commons-based currency from the bottom, with dreams of hacking the cryptocurrency market, as with FairCoin, a more promising approach would likely be one that was more orchestrated and started big. This would mean launching a means-of-exchange currency with the backing of an already well-established pool of market value. Such an initiative could be spearheaded by a massive cooperative like the Mondragon Corporation, or through a broad alliance of cooperatives, non-profits, and open-value networks, which could account for an even larger economy to be denoted by the new currency. Of critical importance here, however, is that the currency is launched with all of this backed value from the outset.

The organizational effort and far-sighted intentionality required to launch such a large-scale, commons-based cryptocurrency would, without a doubt, be considerable. The odds of success, furthermore, would be greatly dependent on the broader monetary context. This context, of course, is primarily controlled by the state. Lest we forget, it is the state that maintains ultimate authority over the legal status and allowances afforded any alternative currencies.

Presently, in the most liberalized capitalist economies, cryptocurrencies are legal and increasingly subject to codification and control. Somewhat paradoxically, the more states seek to restrict cryptocurrencies via regulations and limiting laws, the more they seem to gain recognition and stability as a viable asset. How far these states are willing to allow cryptocurrencies to function as actual means-of-exchange tender is another matter, however. While Bitcoin's impact on national economies and their money system is understood to be mostly negligible for the time being, there is no saying that this would continue to be the case if cryptocurrency adoption and use, especially as a unit of account, were to significantly increase. A basic concern here is that the state's monetary and fiscal tools to shape the economy could become fundamentally hampered (Claeys et al, 2018).

Undoubtedly the biggest possible potential threat in this regard is that posed by big corporations, who could also benefit from establishing some form of centralized means-of-exchange tender for themselves. We can point here to the big US airlines' rewards programmes as a precursor to such currencies, where the points that can be redeemed for air travel have become a financialized micro-economy in their own right, becoming a leading source of revenue for these companies (Genter, 2022). Currently, large tech firms are exploring similar possibilities with the help of crypto-based technologies; while Meta (Facebook) has thus far been stymied by regulators in pursuing their vision of the 'Diem' currency, Amazon is forging ahead with a more careful exploration of their internally used Amazon Coin. If regulatory limits were removed, it is not difficult to imagine how the massive amount of value that is funnelled through such corporations could quite easily be leveraged to launch an immediately sizable, sovereign cryptocurrency.

Once established, corporations could then use such currencies as units of account for their goods/services and as the de facto money used for intra-company transactions, possibly including the payment of wages (depending on laws). Additionally, massive initial (and subsequent) coin offerings could be initiated to access state-based tender. Importantly, the significant state-based currency reserves controlled by these large companies would also enable them to engage in currency market interventions to partially control their own currencies' value. Not least, if the corporation's private tender were to become broadly adopted, it could even garner seigniorage privileges, meaning that the issued money could be used to purchase goods and services without it returning to make claims on the corporation's assets.

The fate of commons-based sovereign cryptocurrencies, then, which are unlikely to match the power of those linked to big corporations (at least in the near term), will likely depend on how states respond to such monetary developments. A state largely in the grasp of capital-oriented interests could theoretically be persuaded to cede even more of its monetary power to corporate actors, opening up a complex monetary environment characterized by a multitude of interacting and competing state, corporate, and possibly some minor commons-based currencies. At the same time, a nationalist turn could lead to the outright banning of all non-state-based monies as the state seeks to re-establish its own power over the monetary realm; China, for example, along with a handful of other countries, has already adopted this approach by outlawing the use of Bitcoin. From a compeerist perspective, therefore, the most favourable scenario would be one in which the state significantly restricted the development of expansive means-of-exchange tender controlled by profit-seeking capital, while leaving commons-oriented crypto projects largely untouched. Yet such a policy adoption would, naturally, depend on the state finding common cause with commoners.

Indeed, in the final analysis, and in taking the top-down (sovereign) and endogenous, bottom-up (crypto) approaches to exiting the monetary-banking apparatus together, the likelihood of success for either hinges, as with so many other compeerist initiatives, on the continuously evolving relation and power dynamics between the state, capital, and the commons. It is the charge of compeerists to greatly increase the power of the commons in this dynamic if the envisioned transition out of capitalism is to ever transpire. To succeed in such a task will ultimately necessitate a widespread socio, cultural, and political upheaval demanding that the rationality and practice of the commons and commoning be embraced as a political-economic alternative to capital. The question of how such an upheaval could come about, and what it could result in, is the focus of the final part of this book.

PART IV

In Pursuit of a Post-Capitalist Future

9

Compeerists of the World Unite!

The previous chapters have pointed to concrete, compeerist-oriented efforts centred on values that are fundamentally at odds with those of capital, offering contours of what a compeerist transition out of capitalism could look like within various sectors of the economy. In all of these explorations the need for an expansion, deepening, and synergizing of such actions on the prefigurative, institutional and, ultimately, government-based level, was emphasized. In other words, an economic trajectory out of capitalism can only succeed if all of the various initiatives noted in the prior chapters are not just intensified but pursued simultaneously, with each pulling more or less in the same direction. Yet this, for many, is seen as the hardest part.

As Peter Kropotkin (1975) astutely observed nearly 150 years ago, 'New ideas germinate everywhere, seeking to force their way into the light, to find an application in life; everywhere they are opposed by the inertia of those whose interest it is to maintain the old order'. In this chapter we thus turn to the political mobilization needed to overcome this inertia by enabling the prefigurative lines of flights explored in the past chapters to intentionally consolidate and break free from the existing 'old order'. However, it is important to note that compeerism does not offer a dogmatic answer as to what the exact outcome of such a mobilization would entail. Indeed, there are multiple forms that a compeerist-aligned organization of the political economy can take. In Chapter 10, therefore, we move on to consider just one possibility of what a fully evolved compeerist mode of production could look like, emphasizing, in particular, the organization and governance of production, consumption, investment, and environmental stewardship. But first we must address the question of getting there.

Building a compeerist movement

As explained at the outset of this book, the compeerist outlook is best understood as an amalgamation and sharpening of existing thought. Hence, while it embraces the P2P position that commons-centred, collaborative production has the potential to outcompete and ultimately replace our current mode of production, such a process is also seen, in line with most autonomous Marxists, as far from easy or straightforward given that capital currently infiltrates almost every aspect of our socio-economic reality. In thus seeking to answer how an evolutionary turn from capital to the commons could unfold, we can start by revisiting the insightful work of autonomists Massimo De Angelis and John Holloway.

For Holloway, our reality within capitalism is seen as dominated by abstract labour, understood as work that is stripped of all meaning for the worker beyond its value as a commodity, what we have posited in this book as a consequence of the apparatus of capture (Holloway, 2010; 2012). Holloway goes on to point out that abstract labour, which has far-reaching material and psychological consequences, is largely inescapable as long as capitalist social relations dominate. For De Angelis, in turn, who broadly accepts Holloway's starting point, alienated labour makes up an integral component of the broad 'middle class', defined as a 'stratified field of subjectivity' that is fundamentally formed by, and complicit in, capital's 'disciplinary markets, enclosures, governance and … profit seeking enterprises' (De Angelis, 2010, p 960). Also naturally included in such a subjectivity, we should add, is the acceptance of 'consumerism as a way of life that contains its own self-reproducing end values' (Carroll, 2010, p 190). In other words, De Angelis's specific understanding of the middle class encompasses the majority of the populace living by the dictates of capitalism.

Given how entwined we are in capitalism's logics and mechanisms, the imperative to have an 'outside' space (both mental and physical) from where resistance can be envisioned and pursued, takes centre stage. For both scholars such an 'outside' is hard to come by but not impossible. Importantly, for Holloway, it is not to be found by positioning ourselves in relation to socially constructed, reified 'things', like money, capital, or the state, as these simply lead us to become 'entrapped within an organizational and conceptual prison that effectively strangles any aspirations for revolutionary change' (Holloway, 2010, p 917). Instead, Holloway's answer, which resonates with many other anarchist and autonomist approaches to the commons, is that the outside to capital is essentially achieved through a continuous, prefigurative act of often local or site-based 'doing', where work is reclaimed for the purpose of creating use-value.

De Angelis similarly points to the need for Holloway's 'doing', which he calls instantiations of 'commoning'. Importantly, for De Angelis and many others, 'commoning' must here not be conflated with simply engaging in collective work organized from the top down. It is only in the pursuit of a commons that is democratically conceived and governed according to community-established values, such as fairness, charity, and sustainability, that actual 'commoning' is being conducted (Caffentzis and Federici, 2014; Dyer-Witheford, 2015; De Angelis, 2017b).

De Angelis and Holloway, however, also recognize that such genuine, counter-capitalist efforts of 'doing' and commoning must achieve some form of critical mass to effect larger, systemic change, but details here are scarce. Holloway (2010; 2012) posits how the many acts of 'doing' must be multiplied to form the 'millions of cracks' needed to overcome capitalist domination. The accumulation of these prefigurative cracks, which align quite well with our lines of flight, is ultimately to be achieved via a 'chaotic and fragmented ... movement of movements' (Holloway, 2010, p 918). Yet, beyond referencing the cracks that would comprise such a movement, there is little that Holloway is willing to say regarding its emergence, coalescing, and ultimate dynamics.

De Angelis, in turn, offers a somewhat more specific proposal by suggesting the need to figuratively explode the 'middle class' mental framework to create a consciousness that can think beyond taken-for-granted capitalist assumptions (De Angelis, 2010). In his view, such rogue consciousness would entail the mental internalization of some key insights that are actively repressed by current middle class subjectivity. These include:

1. recognizing the increasing irrationality of our collective work in the service of capital (leading, for instance, to artificial scarcity and environmental meltdown);
2. understanding that this service to capital is leading to stagnant and even slipping wealth and wellbeing for most; and
3. realizing that the threatening 'other' we have been made to blame for our growing insecurity/unhappiness is, in fact, a myth spawned by the ulterior motivations of vested, powerful actors.

De Angelis further explains that a full 'explosion' of the middle class would express itself in a 'proper movement', describing it as a 'socio-cultural shockwave' (De Angelis, 2010, p 968). At the same time, however, he also honestly concedes to not knowing how such an explosion would actually be triggered and sustained.

Commoner consciousness and compeerism's post-ideology

In line with De Angelis and Holloway, compeerism embraces the possibility of an outside to capital while acknowledging that this exterior is always contested and vulnerable. Compeerism also views the emergence of a different consciousness – the explosion of De Angelis's middle class – as a necessary component of this 'outside'. We can call this self-reflective, commons-oriented form of seeing and thinking 'commoner consciousness', which will find different sources and iterations depending on a person's particular experiences and mental processes in their engagement with the capitalist mode of production. Yet, in an effort to avoid the overt vagueness for which some autonomist approaches have been critiqued, we can nonetheless attempt to offer a bit more specificity regarding what a commoner consciousness would entail, and, even more critically, the role of such a consciousness in the creation of a broader political mobilization.

To begin, and in line with Holloway and De Angelis, compeerism does not see the essence of being a 'commoner' as rooted in some form of intellectual illumination; it is rather through acts of non- and counter-capitalist 'doing' and 'commoning' that commoner consciousness is brought about and sustained. Such doing could involve, for instance, volunteering at a soup kitchen or refugee centre; helping to organize a community maker/repair space; or building and contributing to the open-source designs of an off-grid tiny house that is intended to facilitate an exit from the demands of a never-ceasing earn-and-spend culture. As such, commoner consciousness is also not contingent on a conscious 'class position', but rather on the establishment of common interests and subsequent common organization in the face of capital's exploitative/extractive nature more broadly (Hardt and Negri, 2005; De Angelis, 2010; Wright, 2021).

Importantly, and following from this focus on doing, for commoner consciousness to be truly active it can never rest idle; commoning must continuously and intentionally be reengaged and reinvented to not be coopted. In other words, static and unreflective 'anti-system' positions, for instance choosing to be vegan, will not suffice; capital will simply respond with the McVegan burger at McDonalds and a vegan section at the local Walmart. Yet a key question that must be answered here is how the intentionality and depth needed to continuously challenge capital can be brought about, which would also go a long way to explain how a lasting and impactful counter-capitalist movement of movements can be galvanized and sustained.

Regarding such political mobilization, we can point out that many autonomists and anarchists, especially those falling in line with the thinking of Hardt and Negri (2017), would here refer to the spontaneous, decentralized, and intentionally amorphous multitude as the needed motor to propel any large-scale anti-capitalist activity and organization. The view here is that nothing can match the power of an anarchic swarm, leading to the ideal of the 'headless' movement, as exemplified in the Occupy Wall Street protests. Yet, it is precisely this thinking around the multitude that has also been dismissed as overly nebulous, and hence ineffective in explaining, let alone bringing about, progressive systemic change (De Angelis, 2007; Mouffe, 2009; Rancière, 2016). Indeed, with the Occupy movement increasingly in the rear-view mirror, it is not unfair to conclude that there were few lasting gains or concessions achieved. All the while capitalism marches on.

The compeerist position, therefore, loosely shared by a smaller cohort of autonomists who are more critical of Hardt and Negri's approach, is that greater unity and strategic intentionality is needed in the disparate and latently powerful forms of counter-capitalist consciousness already emerging (De Angelis, 2010; 2012; 2017a; Dyer-Witheford, 2015; Toupin, 2021). In compeerism, specifically, achieving this political cohesion is seen as ultimately depending on commoner consciousness embracing a malleable, but still broadly shared, morally informed political-economic outlook. This is decidedly not a vanguardist proposal for a grand and dogmatic ideology or a prescriptive agenda of specific actions that must be taken; indeed, the hierarchical power arrangements inherent in vanguardism are fundamentally counter to the compeerist preference for decentralized and egalitarian crowdsourcing. Rather, it is a call for a flexible yet cohering outlook and state of mind, which is seen as already being innate in most commoning-type doing, that can help commoners coalesce their efforts to actually achieve real systemic change (Bauwens and Ramos, 2018; Bollier and Helfrich, 2019; Kioupkiolis, 2020a; Ramos, 2020).

Hence, in terms of its foundational, ethical core, the commoner consciousness espoused by compeerism is rooted in the broad value of human equality. As such, any form of oppression is rejected and resisted, including, for example, the use of identity-based bias and discrimination to exploit commons-based labour or to block or restrict access to the commons and commoning (Federici, 2012; 2019). Furthermore, the compeerist aspired-to commoner consciousness entails an embrace of justice and solidarity, rooted in a rejection of an ontologically posited, autonomous and individual subject. Instead, our social/psychological reality is better conceived as fundamentally inter-subjective and interdependent, giving rise to values such as openness, sharing, and collaboration (Bauwens 2005; Hyde, 2012; Bollier and Helfrich, 2015). It is this same inter-subjective outlook that lies behind the recognition of humanity's geographical and hence ethical interconnectedness across distance and time, as emphasized in Chapter 6 with regard to the concept of power geometries (Massey, 1996). It follows, therefore, that the pursuit of an expansive and non-discriminatory commons is embraced as a global effort, requiring transnational mutual aid and camaraderie (Esposito, 2013; Dardot and Laval, 2014; Schismenos et al, 2020).

At the same time, while the ethical and strategic embrace of inclusivity is seen as foundational, a well-honed and intentional commoner consciousness will also recognize that inclusivity cannot be infinite. Following Ostrom (2015), boundaries and regulations are still required for effective commons governance, especially when it comes to more physically limited, and hence rivalrous resources. Thus, the complex and contested nature of the commons reminds us of the quarrelsome politics that will always be a part of their governance. It is in light of the inevitability of politics, and indeed contestation, where the importance of more particular commons-centred dispositions come to the fore. It is these dispositions, which would ideally also be shared across commoner consciousness more broadly, that are needed to ensure the commons can, in fact, become the basis of a more just and sustainable prospering for everyone.

Details of what an execution of such a mentality would entail are well expounded in the work associated with the Heteropolitics project initiated by Alexandros Kioupkiolis (2017). Here, political theory and commons practices are combined to articulate an 'alternative' politics that would be needed to intentionally align the management of the commons with the ideals of egalitarianism, fairness, and resilience. The result is ultimately an 'agonistic' form of commons-oriented politics that, in the words of Kioupkiolis (2020b, p 73), is rooted in 'openness, diversity, elasticity, inclusivity, grassroots autonomy, participation, assemblies, process, horizontality, prefiguration, work in everyday reality, networking and action over fixed ideologies and closed identities'. These intentionally non-vanguardist, yet also purpose-driven governance principles align well with the ideals compeerism adopts in its approach to commoning. However, compeerism is not just concerned with prefiguring or envisioning the commons, it is also, critically, about overcoming capitalism.

This is where compeerism sees the value in commoner consciousness also maintaining a broadly shared, more macro-oriented political-economic outlook, which could function to tie commoners together within a powerful movement of movements. In terms of what the substance of such an outlook would entail, compeerism's starting point aligns well with Michael Hardt's (2010, p 353) basic premise, traced to the early Marx, that the ultimate aim of societal struggle is the 'autonomous human production of subjectivity'. In other words, it is a broad and flexible embrace of the inherent value of pursuing, on our own terms, our self-determination as individuals and communities. Clearly, such a never-ending process of self-determination will vary over time and between people(s). Yet, from the compeerism perspective, a unifying ground to be found here is in the shared desirability to expand and wisely govern the material and digital commons needed to pursue our own and collective self-determination, and hence, thriving.

As such, and keeping in mind the 'middle class' outlook that is to be 'exploded', a commoner consciousness would preferably evolve to entail a shared acknowledgement of the unsustainable, unjust, and squandering nature of our current organization of labour and resources. Further building on this insight, then, would be the conviction, given our technological endowments, that the principles of cooperation, collaboration, and mutual assistance are much more sensible principles for organizing our societies than those of cut-throat competition and targeted exclusion. Compeerism ultimately addresses these overarching internalizations by pursuing a replacement of capital by commonifying the means of production. Yet, at the same time, there is an intentional openness as to how these processes must unfold.

For instance, private and/or state property are not presented as inherent evils needing absolute dismantlement. Instead, the degree to which these forms of property should be maintained, within the larger context of pursuing a vibrant and accessible commons, must be determined primarily by and for the people that are most impacted. It is in this light that we can also understand compeerism's commitment to greater economic and political decentralization as a deliberate facilitation of localized self-determination, albeit within the confines of respecting the interests and concerns of legitimate external stakeholders (Bollier, 2017). This opening up to socio-economic-political diversity, in essence, is what is meant by a post-ideological ideology, or post-ideology. It is an acceptance that communities may pursue divergent prioritizations, and find different answers to the same problem, while still being bounded within a set of overarching aims and principles.

A compeerist (and not fascist) movement of movements

Compeerists seeking a large-scaled political movement of movements to help drive a systemic commons transition will naturally seek to spawn, solidify and tie together a commoner consciousness as outlined in the previous section. Yet, as was also made clear, such a consciousness, despite its idealized presentation, is far from monolithic. Instead, it will exist as variously coherent and internalized iterations, finding expression and definition from within a broad range of activities and efforts, many of which we have covered in earlier chapters.

It is from within these actions, many having grown into micro-movements in their own right, that we find the most fertile ground from which a compeerist-oriented movement of movements could form. Building on the commoner consciousness that is there, the compeerist aim thus becomes to tie the various commons-oriented forces into a larger whole by creating a basic political consensus around the broad aim of expanding the commons and commoning as an alternative to capital. In this sense, 'the commons' becomes the 'empty signifier' noted by Laclau and Moofe (2014) as the amalgamating idea and discourse that can unify a large, diversified group of people by being able to encompass all of their various concerns, imperatives, and context-specific outlooks (see also Walljasper, 2010; Dardot and Laval, 2014).

In the digital realm, then, promising initiatives to be brought into the fold of a broader mobilization would include hacker and pirating efforts; the production of free, open-source software; reclaiming data; establishing platform co-ops; and the various work geared towards decentralizing and democratizing the internet. Also included here are the broader demands being made for the revision or outright abolishment of copyrights and patents and the push to dismantle the monopolistic/oligopolistic power of the tech giants. In the material realm, common cause can be found in the numerous environmental and justice-oriented efforts seeking a sustainable and fair use of our global material commons; the pursuit of off-grid resilience capabilities; and the various initiatives to expand the urban commons, including the cooperativization and municipalization of key infrastructure. In the actual making of stuff, in turn, obvious synergies exist with the DIY, maker, open-hardware, and open-design movements, which are each motivated in different ways by a desire to exit materially based dependencies on capital with the help of an open-source digital commons. Not least, within the market-engaged production of material goods and services, important allies can be found in commons-oriented cooperatives, open-value-networks, and non-profits across key economic sectors.

In employing the commons and commoning as an underlying 'empty signifier', compeerists hope that the various commoners involved in these visions and actions could be convinced that their work not only has macro-level political insinuations – in that they favour more commons-friendly political-economic conditions – but that their (latent) policy preferences are also shared by a host of compatriots involved in disparate yet similar commons-related doing. Once these aligned political positionalities become self-evident, especially in the face of inevitable clashes with powerful capitalist interests, it becomes possible to see, at least for some, how a wide spectrum of commoners could coalesce into a movement of movements committed to a commons-based future beyond capitalism.

Such a hopeful outlook is, of course, not shared by everyone, and many would dismiss such conjecture as being fundamentally out of touch with the socio-political realities on the ground. While difficult to assess such cynical claims in any objective way, compeerists could push back by first pointing to the vibrancy of the many commons oriented micro-movements that already exist. They could further draw attention to the numerous inroads achieved by commons-based political initiatives, particularly in municipalities across Europe; or note the macro-level waves of counter-capitalist uprisings in the last few decades – from the anti-globalization movement in the 1990s to Occupy Wall Street in the 2000s – which offered a glimpse of the tremendous, albeit still mostly diffuse and untapped, people power that seems to lie just beneath the surface. Also notable has been the strong showing since the turn of the century of upstart political parties and candidates taking a more adversarial stance to capital, as for instance in Greece and Spain (and to some extent Britain and the US). While these formal, electoral efforts (which, we should note, were not explicitly compeerist), ultimately failed to bring about paradigm-shifting policies, the fact that they garnered the support that they did points to underlying counter-capitalist sentiments and an openness to forging a different way forward.

Lastly, it is also important to recognize that the nascent, compeerist-aligned forces that are taking form have the potential to significantly expand as the capital-state nexus flounders to deal with a host of culminating crises rooted in the dominant assemblages/apparatuses of the current political-economy (Varvarousis, 2020). These emerging dysfunctions offer compeerists fertile ground for expanding commoner consciousness and, more specifically, forcing an internal reflection of the repressed irrationalities inherent in the 'middle class' justification of the status quo (De Angelis, 2010). Taking these various points together, compeerism maintains that the eventual formation of a commons-centred, counter-capitalist movement of movement is by no means a far-fetched proposition.

Critically, however, in considering the growing disillusionment towards capitalism's hegemony, we must also acknowledge that compeerism will not inevitably be the embraced response. Indeed, the escalating symptoms of a capitalism in crisis (faltering wellbeing, failing governance regimes, wage stagnation, and rising precarity) could quite readily also give rise to sentiments that are inherently neo-fascist (anti-democratic and xenophobic), which is a trend that is already apparent the world over (Dyer-Witheford, 2015). The challenge facing compeerists here brings to mind De Angelis's insistence that working in common is not the same as commoning, as the latter entails a certain form of commoner consciousness, as outlined earlier. As such, faced with the very real prospect of neo-fascist competition, compeerism must clearly stake out its position with the aim of winning out in the arena of public opinion and, ultimately, politics.

This position will revolve around two intertwined points of contention, reminiscent of the clash between fascists and anarchists of old. The first centres on the question of decision making and how it is best governed. Here the neo-fascist's preference of a patriarchal model of top-down authority is in stark contrast to the compeerists' preference of diluting decision-making power, including in the economy, through maximal distribution. The second is the fundamental moral clash over who should be included in the universe of persons considered worthy of our concern and care, or put in more stark terms, who truly counts as human?

This latter question hits on one of the key irrationalities suppressed by De Angelis's middle class, namely the 'othering' that is internalized to blame a particular, generally powerless grouping of human beings for the loss of any wellbeing and/or security within the community. In doing so, responsibility on the part of the actors within capital and the state, that are actually culpable, is deflected. As long as this 'othering' is maintained, regardless of whether this is in a strictly capitalist or neo-fascist state, any transition along compeerist lines will be thwarted.

For compeerists, then, the undemocratic, neo-fascist framework will need to be effectively debunked as illiberal, patronizing, dishonest, and parasitic; its primary aim being nothing more than the amassing of power (and wealth) in the hands of the few. The compeerist alternative, in turn, must come to be understood as a win-win option that could benefit the so-called 99 per cent of the entire globe, thus making such a pursuit not only empowering, fair, and rational, but also potentially cathartic in its ability to bring about a feeling of being in common, or what Hardt and Negri simply referred to as the 'economic power' of 'love' (Hardt and Negri, 2009, p 180). Yet, for such a discourse (and feeling) to take hold – given a broader context shaped by historical injustices and deeply ingrained sentiments centred on competition and mistrust – will undoubtedly require the patient application of compeerist-aligned care and goodwill. This effort, furthermore, will have to emanate from the bottom up, that is, from the many commons-oriented initiatives and micro-movements on the ground, which is also where any formal, populist-type politics embracing the compeerist message would need to be rooted.

Building on this point of a needed material groundedness from which change must emerge, we should keep in mind Chantal Mouffe's (2005) reformulation of Carl Schmitt's 'friend-enemy' dichotomy, where she makes the convincing case that we can never achieve a discourse-based, enlightened end of history. There will always be declared enemies that cannot see eye to eye, where the limits of rational discussion are laid bare. Consequently, compeerism's prospects for outcompeting a neo-fascist alternative will also come down to its ability to deliver equitably and collaboratively governed commons realms that offer real contributions to overall wellbeing. This includes not only concrete material gains but also the social and psychological rewards that come with being able to take part in social relations involved in commoning. Only by offering such tangible benefits will larger segments of the population begin to open up to the compeerist message more broadly.

In light of this demand, then, an overarching imperative for compeerists must be to establish a positive, snowballing feedback loop in which gains in the commons-based economic realm are leveraged to garner social mobilization and political clout, which is then applied to create even more robust compeerist-aligned economic capabilities and hence yet more social and political power. The effective execution of such a feedback loop as capitalism's challenges come to a head is the only way the compeerist post-capitalist vision can both supplant capital while also ensuring neo-fascist alternatives do not get the upper hand. For such a spiralling process of compeerist economic and social usurpation to materialize, however, will necessitate deft, multi-scalar, political engagement and organization, including, crucially, in relation to 'the state'.

Compeerist politics and engaging the state

Inspired by the P2P theoretical approach, compeerism envisions an expanding and bottom-up driven subeconomy where the realms of the political (municipalities), the civil-social (intentional NGOs and communities), and the entrepreneurial (co-ops and open-value-networks) synergize to create open, collaborative, and democratic forms of economic governance that have the potential to challenge capitalism as the dominant mode of production. The process of getting there, which is understood as indeterminate and evolutionary, would ultimately require a gradual but accelerating transvestment of wealth and resources from capital to the commons. This transvestment would express itself, among other things, as an expanding, municipally supported urban commons; ever-larger, community-centred land trusts; growing market share held by non-capital-based, democratized economic and social entities; increasing decapitalization of critical assets via cooperativization initiatives; and 'hostile' takeovers of corporations by commons-based alternatives (Leung, 2018).

Such a shift in wealth and resources from capital to the commons is essential if existing compeerist-aligned subeconomies are to grow and achieve significant autonomy, meaning that any wealth gained by commons-centred entities can actually be 'kept inside the commons sphere itself' (Bauwens and Kostakis, 2014, p 358; also see Dyer-Witheford, 2012). Accomplishing this level of autonomy, in turn, is a prerequisite for the long-term exodus and replacement of capital. Compeerism, however, understands that getting to this point will require effective organization and strategizing via localized, prefigurative actions, meso-level inter-commons forms of trans-local organization, as well as, in the final analysis, targeted involvement in formal, state-based politics.

Regarding the prefigurative level, we would do well to remind ourselves that compeerism is fundamentally grounded in a (r)evolutionary vision where the economy is run by and for the people (not capital or the state), hence cementing the bottom-up impetus of the compeerist outlook. As such, the progression of compeerism, if it happens at all, will be propelled in fits and starts by the impactful events and innovative economic/social experiments unfolding locally as lines of flight (Dyer-Witheford, 2012; Bauwens and Gerhardt, 2020; Wright, 2021). These lines of flight are also immensely important in that they represent what Deleuze and Guattari (1987) refer to as 'micropolitics', which, by being 'molecular' enactments of a desired future to come (Holloway's 'doing'), foster an ethos of 'becoming-revolutionary' (Reyes, 2020). The becoming-revolutionary quality here is essential, as it serves not only as a force that undermines capital, but also as an inoculation against capital's coopting powers.

In addition to these isolated lines of flight, cracks, or micropolitics, compeerism also insists on a trans-local, meso-level political activism centred on achieving a greater solidarity among commoners themselves. We have referred to this throughout the book as various instantiations of boundary commoning, and these, following compeerism's strategic outlook, would need to see a massive expansion via a blossoming of commoner consciousness and a subsequent movement of movements. One of the key aims of boundary commoning is to cohere the lines of flight into a more concerted force to deal directly with capital. These efforts often have a primarily economic impetus, such as the sharing of resources and information, yet when these also include a push to establish a peer-property regime that intentionally excludes capitalist actors, the prospect of contestation and, hence, politics is not far off. This reality, then, leads to a secondary purpose behind boundary commoning, which is the combining of commons-based interests into organized groupings, such as guilds or cooperative alliances. Here the aim is much more directly political as these entities seek to leverage the power of commoners to contend with contextual challenges, which, in the end, will need to be pursued via the existing governance/government arrangements in place.

Indeed, the acknowledgment of the power that state-based assemblages/apparatuses have over compeerists ability to realize their goals leads directly to the embrace of 'molar' forms of political engagement, or macropolitics (Deleuze and Guattari, 1987). This macro-level of activism broadly denotes those efforts that directly seek to interact with and ultimately influence and shape government. It should be noted that beyond the P2P approach, this embrace of macropolitics as a supplement to the micro has also become adopted in some autonomist literature, from the 'harm reduction' espoused by the Midnight Notes Collective (2009) to the law-focused pressurization on the state backed in the later work by Hardt and Negri (2012). More specifically, and following Kioupkiolis (2020b, p 178), the 'alternative politics' involved in such a macro focus would need to orchestrate 'broad-based political alliances which aggregate their forces, coordinate their action around a common political plan and a new collective identity, and make a concerted effort to reshuffle the decks of power so as to restructure dominant social relations'.

In this sense the embrace of the macropolitical is a clear rejection of the assertion that any engagement with the state, or other reified assemblages/apparatuses, inevitably end up bolstering the very forces that are being targeted for change, as per Holloway (2010). Instead, compeerism's position holds that any such complicity can be overcome if the ethos of 'becoming-revolutionary' manages to also infuse the molar outlook of the movement of movements, meaning that the pursuit of state concessions (such as labour unions demanding a higher minimum wage) are not seen as ends in themselves (Merriman, 2018; Gerhardt, 2019). Rather, such demands must be consciously embraced as means to a much larger end, namely the establishment of a post-capitalist, compeerist society (Firat, 2020).

The perceived need to engage the state in this tactical way aligns well with Slavoj Žižek's provocative argument that refusing such engagement is ultimately a form of capitulation. In a controversial piece entitled 'Resistance is Surrender', Žižek (2007) takes to task the increasingly submissive and resigned attitudes he perceives on the political left. His point is that resistance to capitalism and the state has devolved into a retreat, where the political-economic structures are seen as essentially unassailable, while at the same time viewing engagement with the state as inevitably leading to cooptation. With such a starting point, Žižek argues, we end up with the left making lofty moral arguments that have no chance of actually penetrating state power. Those in charge can thus point to the peaceful, disengaged, and noble dissent on the left as an indication that the system is working, only to proceed unhindered in pursuing devastating economic and geopolitical interests.

For Žižek this arrangement is a cynical and destructive win-win, where the dissenters save their souls while the state (and the capital interests it represents) maintains its unchecked power. Žižek (2007, np) goes on to argue that if you believe a different world is truly possible, as compeerism does, then the thing to do is to actually fight for this world, not by making '"infinite" demands we know those in power cannot fulfill' but rather 'to bombard those in power with strategically well-selected, precise, finite demands', as these cannot be so easily dismissed. This is what we can call a 'hit-and-run' tactic, where the state (and its undergirding assemblages/apparatuses) is recognized as a critical fulcrum of power relevant to the prospects of the commons-based subeconomy. At the same time, this engagement is also understood within a deeper 'becoming-revolutionary' stance, committed to the eventual dissolution of the state's current arrangement with capital.

It is clear from Žižek's comments that his focus was primarily on the national level of politics. Yet, before addressing hit-and-run tactics at this scale, we must acknowledge that compeerists would be inclined, first and foremost, to secure support and buy in on the local level, where 'the state' is often considerably more receptive and penetrable. Such 'municipal activism' is what Bookchin ultimately called for as the most appropriate and effective form of anarchist political action (Bookchin and Vanek, 2001). P2P scholars have similarly homed in on the importance of localized engagement, for instance, calling for the formation of 'assemblies of the commons' where commoners can meet with the aim of supporting locally governed commons, and a 'chamber of the commons' that can lobby for commons-friendly municipal policies (Bauwens et al, 2019). Indeed, such municipal activism is already crystallizing the world over as urban-centred commons movements are increasingly framing their actions as a strategy to 'change the world one city at a time' (Utratel and Troncoso, 2017, np).

An encouraging sign of the potential in such an approach is the considerable expansion of the urban commons and the growing number of pro-commons municipal governments (Thompson, 2020; Vesco, 2020; Zechner, 2020). The Bologna Regulation for the Care and Regeneration of the Urban Commons is an oft-cited example that exemplifies this trend. David Bollier (2015, np) explains this project as follows:

> Instead of seeing the city simply as an inventory of resources to be administered by politicians and bureaucratic experts, the Bologna Regulation sees the city's residents as resourceful, imaginative agents in their own right. Citizen initiative and collaboration are regarded as under-leveraged energies that – with suitable government assistance – can be recognized and given space to work. Government is re-imagined as hosting infrastructure for countless self-organized commons.

In this way over 90 collaborative agreements have been met in Bologna between citizens and the local government, focusing on everything from childcare to urban agriculture.

Nevertheless, the struggle to expand the commons along compeerist lines will inevitably also push up against larger scaled assemblages/apparatuses, which demand more macro-level hit-and-run efforts. To be effective, however, any such engagements with the national state must be well organized and ultimately well-funded. Bauwens and his collaborators, as part of a growing awareness within P2P approaches for the need to engage government, make a compelling case for the commons-based subeconomy to actively support a 'counter-power' to the existing political order at various scales (Bauwens et al, 2019). There are numerous ways this counter-power could be pursued, including through lobbying campaigns, infiltrating political parties, running independent candidates, establishing commons-oriented parties (along the lines of the Pirate Party or a more intentionally counter-capitalist version of the British Co-operative Party), and, not least, creating policy-oriented think tanks and relevant academic fields of study to shape and popularize compeerist-oriented discourses (O'Neil and Broca, 2021).

In a moment, we will turn to how a compeerist counter-power could be put to use to directly pressure and influence government. Yet, the latter point just noted regarding the broader shaping of discourse, and hence public opinion, is worth briefly homing in on. While discourse alone cannot lead to systemic change, it nonetheless makes up a critical component of the overarching superstructural hegemony, or counter-hegemony, that undergirds or challenges any particular political-economic arrangement (Gramsci, 2011). As such, the role of discourse in forming attitudes and manipulating policy decisions should not be underestimated. Indeed, the rise of neoliberalism, at least in terms of the needed execution of its defence, has been linked precisely to the methodical building up of free-market philosophies and narratives emanating from economics departments and a slew of think tanks created precisely for this purpose (Harvey, 2006; Plehwe 2017). It stands to reason that for a compeerist trajectory to unfold, a similar infrastructure would also be needed – the creation of the P2P Foundation is certainly a promising start, but much more would be needed.

As an example of a compeerist-aligned discourse that could have far-reaching impact, we can point to the efforts linked to challenging and rethinking the taken-for-granted use of economic indicators (such as GDP, productivity, unemployment) as the primary gauge of a nation's accomplishments, self-worth, and most critically, overall wellbeing. Making the limits and possible alternatives to these econocentric measures a real topic of debate could prove to be a potent, self-reflective exercise for individuals and society, who may end up demanding the use of more holistic and pertinent indices covering such things as happiness, health, and sustainability (Jackson, 2017). If such non-capitalist indicators were to become fundamentally embedded in the strategic mission and vision of the state, then the capital-oriented hardwiring within its various departments would likely be, at least partially, short-circuited.

Short- and long-term demands

Having established the argument for engaging the state at multiple scales, we can next review the basic policy orientations that would most logically emerge in a compeerist movement of movements. We can make a distinction here between efforts aimed at addressing the more finite, short-term predicament of the commons and commoning and those seeking more *longue-durée*-focused shifts that would lead to significant decapitalizations across the national and even global economy (Troncoso and Utratel, 2015). Given that prior chapters have already offered numerous suggestions for hit-and-run policy targets across multiple economic sectors, we can limit ourselves here to key takeaways while expounding some dimensions that have not yet been fully addressed.

In looking to near-term efforts aimed at supporting current, and often still struggling, commons-based initiatives, especially those seeking to directly compete with capital, a critical focus would naturally centre on the market playing field where big-capital maintains sizable, yet unjustifiable state-sanctioned advantages. Thus, one of the first broad aims of a compeerist movement of movements would, undoubtedly, be to undermine capital's ability to exploit and extract, for instance through stricter environmental and worker welfare regulations and a more commons-friendly governance of digital value. Again, the logic here from a compeerist perspective is that the more capital is forced to internalize negative externalities and heed the 'common good', the less market competitive capital becomes compared to compeerist-oriented alternatives.

A further important levelling of the market could then be pursued by pressuring the state to make more aggressive use of their antitrust laws, especially in the still largely untouched but increasingly top-heavy and rapidly expanding tech sector. Particularly concerning are big tech efforts to establish far-reaching vertical integration, exemplified by Amazon's production-retailing-logistics nexus, which forces lesser, competing actors into market subservience. Breaking up such monopolistic powers, we should add, is critical for the market viability of any smaller, more locally-focused enterprises, not just commons-based ones. Following from this point, it thus also becomes possible to envision the emergence of a political alliance between commons-based market actors and the so called 'petite-bourgeoisie' in their challenging of big-capital. We should note that bringing small-business interests into the fold of progressive, anti-corporate political platforms in this way is not a novel idea and is receiving renewed interest on the left (Mason, 2016; Holmberg and Mitchell, 2020).

Beyond the need to check capital's extractive/exploitative tactics, compeerism is also aware of the important role the state can play to foster the commons more directly. This can include the state's own contributions to the commons through public institutions and, more importantly, establishing laws, subsidies/grants, and purchasing arrangements that would directly bolster the ability of commons-based entities in all economic sectors to function and thrive. With regard to law in particular, the regulation of small-scale, community-oriented production, from energy to food, could be more carefully tailored and decentralized to foster the needs and wishes of local communities without compromising more macro-scaled environmental, labour, and animal welfare standards (Carson, 2010). We can note that this pursuit of more fine-tuned laws/regulations again aligns well with the interests of the petite bourgeoisie.

Turning next to longer term targets, compeerism holds aspirations for far-reaching counter-capitalist measures that can be understood as a macro-level expression of its 'becoming-revolutionary' ethos. In other words, while these policy ideas and demands appear out of reach today, often going hand in hand with a significant breakup of the capital-state nexus, they are nonetheless continuously present, ready to be activated and pushed for whenever the opportunity emerges. We can note that while these more ambitious aims may come across as the 'infinite' demands denounced by Žižek, they ultimately have a different quality to them because they overlap with simultaneous micropolitical engagements, some of which will be directly in the service of laying the groundwork for these more far-reaching ambitions.

One clear long-term focus here pertains to the state's power to decapitalize key assets and means of production. While compeerists are committed to pursuing the goal of decapitalization through a path of transvestment, propelled by a competitive, commons-based economy, it is also recognized that circumstances can emerge that would rightfully compel the state to pursue targeted forms of public repossession. While compeerists are generally sceptical of the 'public' takeover of large-scale economic entities, this does not mean state-based takeovers must revert to privatization. For compeerists, cooperativization remains the preferred goal. For instance, when the US government took ownership of General Motors after the financial crisis of 2007/8, instead of returning the company to private ownership, as was done in 2009, it could instead have been converted to a worker co-op with numerous important community-oriented stakeholders given positions on an empowered governance board. In a similar way, then, in the aftermath of financial meltdowns or in the clear presence of exigencies on the part of the common good, corporate entities within banking, IT, resource extraction, as well as some of the largest internet platforms, could also eventually be bought out by the state and then broken up into federated stakeholder or member cooperatives.

A further important, long-term compeerist aim pertains to the state undoing some of the most restrictive burdens imposed on the commons and commoning via the apparatus of capture and the subsequent commoditization of everything. In this sense, compeerists are generally supportive of greater welfare provisions, with the logic that the more secure people feel in being able to meet their basic needs, the more likely they will be to engage in, and help expand, the commons. However, in recognizing the centrality of the apparatus of capture to capitalism's overall functionality – and homing in especially on the role played in this capture by the current governance of money – compeerism is particularly committed to both instituting a universal basic income (UBI) and finding a replacement for the monetary-banking apparatus, preferably via a commons-friendly state that adopts a sovereign money regime. A UBI, along with the public provision of other basic needs such as health care and education, would release workers from mandatory abstract labour, freeing them to the commons. The embrace of sovereign money, in turn, could bring an end to the unsustainable imperative of debt-based growth and allow a progressively minded state to channel resources more intentionally to address society's most pressing challenges.

A final, *longue-durée* aspiration inherent in compeerism, especially in the wealthy Minority World, is for the logic and execution of statecraft to shift from its current, nationally defined 'us-versus-them' premise to one centred on a commitment to transnational collaboration and solidarity in the pursuit of universal wellbeing (Esposito, 2013; Healy et al, 2021). Such a paradigm shift would then compel these states to redress their past colonial and existing postcolonial relationships. This making of amends would entail a number of concrete commitments. The first would be to devolve control and governance over 'distant' natural resources to regional and local communities along commons-based principles (even if this comes at the cost of capital-based interests within Minority World states). A second area of focus would centre on establishing an expanded and universally accessible digital commons containing vital, fully open-source knowledge/code/data. Finally, there would need to be a transfer of development funds and material resources from the Minority to the Majority World, ideally made directly to commons-based, local actors on the ground.

A fundamental rethinking of the state's identity and overall relation to the rest of the world along these lines is likely the most radical compeerist ambition of all, and to many it will come across as an idealistic fairy tale. Yet, we should keep in mind that the pursuit of a cooperative, peaceful world order is at the heart of many global and regional movements today, whether it is resisting military expansion and aggression, pursuing climate justice, or demanding a more fair and equitable global economic system. There is also a growing engagement with alternative conceptualizations of international relations, for instance ones driven by an ethics of care, that point to emerging lines of flight in the realm of 'foreign policy' (Robinson, 2011; 2018). Indeed, the pursuit of human wellbeing and dignity via the United Nations' millennium development goals, as imperfect or incomplete as this effort may be, is a clear indication that the seeds for such alternative thinking already exist (Fehling et al, 2013).

Democratizing the state

Even with a growing and well organized compeerist movement of movements, translating this political mobilization of the people into favourable state action is another matter. In most 'democratic' states today there are numerous obstacles in place that fundamentally dilute the power that the people actually have over their governments, hence drastically limiting the ability of the populace to harness the state as an agent of change. From a compeerist perspective it is imperative that these obstacles are dismantled, bringing about a much deeper democratization, indeed a commonification, of the various assemblages/apparatuses that make up the state (Laclau and Mouffe, 2014; Kioupkiolis, 2020c; Wright, 2021).

We can begin with issues related to our current execution of representative democracy, where the populace is often excluded and ignored in decision making (Kioupkiolis, 2017). The severity of this problem varies, but the United States is an especially egregious example, with three clear causes of its particular 'electoral dysfunction'. The first is the critical role played by money in elections, where it is generally only the wealthy that can afford to enter public service, meaning there are few politicians 'of the people', and then, once elected, these 'public servants' quickly succumb to the continuous demand to fundraise for re-election. The well documented result of this predicament is that politicians become more beholden to their donors than to their voters, as evidenced in the continuous passing of unpopular legislation and the barring of policy that has popular support (Lessig, 2019).

A second culprit is that the election process is intentionally skewed to disempower specific populations. This is done by using a winner-take-all system for political districts and then gerrymandering these in a way where certain constituents are diluted and hence marginalized. Lastly, there are many hindrances put in place to make voting difficult or impossible, from the disenfranchisement of particular persons (for instance ex-felons and non-citizens) to broad restrictions on when and how a vote can be cast, with subsequently long lines at the polling place. The inevitable consequence of these multiple barriers to effective representation is, in the end, widespread voter resignation. In the US, for example, it is the norm for nearly half of all citizens of voting age to opt out of major elections (McDonald, nd).

There are, however, also relatively straightforward solutions to these electoral dysfunctions, which tend to garner widespread support, making them ideal targets for a compeerist movement of movements (BC, 2022). First, good compensation for all elected officials and serious campaign finance reforms could be instituted, for instance by establishing publicly funded elections and banning special interest donations, which, again in the US, has been given free rein through the infamous Citizens United ruling by the Supreme Court. Next, to enable representation that is actually representative, a more inclusive allotment of legislative seats could be introduced by expanding the number of representatives per district, as per a proportional ranked choice voting arrangement called for in the House of Representatives' Fair Representation Act (2021). Relatedly, any redistricting of political maps would need to be depoliticized and include broad citizen participation to prevent the intentional disenfranchisement of a particular group. Not least, the voting process itself can be made much more accessible by using decentralized, blockchain-enabled polling systems that would allow for easy and secure online voting, as is already being done in Estonia (Mulholland, 2021).

Apart from fixing the most problematic distortions in our representative democracies, compeerism's commitment to much more direct and inclusive forms of governance naturally translates to demands for greater citizen empowerment within the assemblages/apparatuses of the state itself. A first step here would be to make government significantly more understandable and accountable, meaning all the flows of money involved in government, the various processes of deliberation, and the ultimate crafting of budgets and legislation should be made clearly and openly available for review by the public. While efforts to achieve greater transparency have been adopted by some states, much more is needed. This could mean, for instance, the use of public blockchain ledgers to capture and display the detailed chronology of events involved in any specific policy decision (Bollier and Helfrich, 2019).

A next step could then be the formation of citizen councils or committees that serve in an advisory or oversight role in relation to various government activities. The process of selecting citizens for such tasks could proceed via a lottery within a pool of volunteers that are representative of the population. In the US state of Colorado, for instance, such a system has been adopted to create a commission to help in the determination of fair voting jurisdictions and the prevention of gerrymandering (CIRP, 2021). Focusing on even more direct participation and hence commonification, efforts could turn to increasing access to policy through citizen-based referendums (recall the importance of such tools in the energy democracy movement); establishing government issued, regular and meaningful public feedback polls; and, most impactfully, empowering the citizenry with direct up or down votes on important actions or legislation, along the lines of the Swiss model (Frey, 1994).

While these actions are all vital, however, there is nonetheless one further imperative on which their progressive potential ultimately depends, which is the formation of a self-reflective, engaged, and broadly informed citizenry. Although many advocates of the digital commons have espoused the potential of the digital revolution to bring about an enlightened populace, techno-sceptics, backed by unsettling realities on the ground, have effectively cast doubt on such optimism. Apart from issues associated with the digital divide, concerns have focused on how the massive (dis)informationscape unleashed by the internet has led to the eroding of more structured and monitored forms of information/knowledge delivery, especially in the crucial realms of journalism and education. Without such 'professional' and accredited gatekeepers, the argument goes, we are left in a democracy-stifling morass of confusion and mediocrity (Keen, 2015).

Compeerism, which is committed to the overarching principle of devolving the means of production (including that of information) to the people, is nonetheless acutely aware that the internet (and other digital means of communication), as any technology, is malleable, meaning it can also be incorporated into assemblages/apparatuses that lead to negative outcomes. As we have repeatedly seen, compeerism therefore insists on the need to become politically engaged to help shape these assemblages/apparatuses in a more favourable direction, while at the same time seeking to 'abstractly hack' the implicated technology to enable the pursuit of alternative ends. In this sense, then, when it comes to information/education, the compeerist outlook dismisses the techno-determinist notion of an internet-based mass enlightenment, fully embracing the need for well-funded and staffed public schooling (especially considering how citizen empowerment depends on effective civics instruction and the teaching of critical thinking and media-literacy skills) (Neumann, 2017). Similarly, compeerism's embrace of maximizing the production and accessibility of reliable information, makes it sensitive to the significant damage done by the loss of local/regional journalism, and hence committed to finding ways in which such community focused, independent sources of news and research can be retained.

At the same time, however, compeerism also refutes the claim that the information/knowledge sharing that is bubbling forth from the digital commons is inherently inferior or irreparably harmful. More specifically, even with the significant disadvantages faced by commons-based, collaborative efforts in the realm of journalism and education, high-quality production in these areas is rapidly expanding. This includes the quickly evolving field of volunteered wiki journalism and non-profit investigative research and reporting, such as Indymedia, ProPublica, and Reveal, as well as the tremendous growing access to commons-based, peer-produced educational resources, from Wikipedia to the development of P2P University (Lewis and Usher, 2013; Antoniadis and Pantazis, 2021). Furthermore, with the continuing development and release of open-source software and data, the uncovering, curating, and sharing of information/knowledge is becoming ever easier, meaning the range of free and empowering digital resources is likely to keep expanding (Kostakis and Pantazis, 2021).

Given this emerging context of massively available, high-quality educational/informational content – much of it produced within the commons subeconomy – compeerists are prone to ask whether the capital-oriented gatekeepers of old, from large news corporations to for-profit issuers of degrees and certifications, can still be justified. Not only are these entities increasingly superfluous, and burdened with their own quality issues, but they actively work to limit the inherent potential of the informal, bottom-up resources of the digital commons. In doing so, it should be noted, they continue to cement existing wealth and class-based inequalities (Collins, 2019). This does not mean, however, that oversight and accreditation must be abandoned. Instead, the execution of these functions could shift to more compeerist aligned entities – from peer-to-peer centred non-profits to more bureaucratic, government-aligned organizations – whose mission would centre on leveraging and enabling, rather than squashing, the commons-based, digital resources at our disposal.

In this way compeerism offers a different approach to what it nonetheless acknowledges to be a critically important imperative, that is, ensuring quality control within the morass of digital, crowdsourced informational content. Indeed, compeerists can see as well as anyone how the tempest of conflicting 'facts' and increasingly hostile discourses enabled by the internet – now having spread into mass media and culture more broadly – is leading to a fractalization of reality into multiple, mutually incongruent, and antagonistic life worlds. Consequently, the ability to engage in intentional communication and constructive debate, which provides the bedrock and foundation for democracy, let alone radically democratic governance, is dissipating (Slaby, 2021).

Yet, perhaps the most critical question that needs to be addressed here pertains to the scope and depth to which oversight and accreditation mechanisms should be applied, especially when imposed on the realm of free, crowdsourced informational content. This is, of course, a hot button issue that will continue to play out, most immediately in terms of how to regulate speech within the dominant, privately-owned social media platforms. As we are seeing, addressing the festering ailment of mis- and disinformation in this open space (increasingly enabled by AI capabilities) is exceedingly difficult due to powerfully held sentiments related to liberty and free speech, not to mention complex ontological questions regarding truth and reality. In response to this challenge, compeerism is inclined to fall back on its fundamental commitment to pragmatism, seeking a middle ground between the enlightenment-based view of an absolute, rigid truth and the postmodern-rooted embrace of relativism. As such, a broadly accepted dialectical compromise must be found between a critical thinking that questions reality and authority, and an underlying foundation of communally held assumptions that allow for communication and debate.

Only in a society that has mastered such a balance can toxic and intentionally misleading information be effectively dealt with in a constructive manner. Yet, in the end, it will be up to each society to find and execute such a state of self-reflective functionality. For compeerists involved in such a process, the underlying impetus will again be informed by the key principles of sound commons governance, meaning that any established supervision and oversight over our unwieldy digital commons would need to evolve out of, and be maintained by, an inclusive, bottom-up, democratic process. At the same time – and keeping in mind the inevitable clash between friend-enemy juxtapositions pointed out by Chantal Mouffe (2005) – compeerists would do well to acknowledge that when it comes to intentional disinformation and the sowing of confusion, as is a standard tactic within neo-fascist movements, difficult scenarios may also arise requiring carefully-weighed political action that is more decisive and, ultimately, uncompromising in the face of intractable and intentionally perpetrated harm. In other words, radical democratic governance can be open and inclusive towards all positions, except those that are deliberately intolerant and violent.

In sum, then, and in taking a step back to consider the various aspects of compeerism's proposed engagement with the state covered in the latter part of this chapter, we find a political outlook that is ambitious but also results-oriented, with a view to the *longue durée*. Following from this, there will undoubtedly be times when compeerists find themselves bogged down in minor policy battles, up to their neck in the unpleasant process of sausage-making that feels far removed from the ultimate aim of achieving meaningful systemic change. Nevertheless, as unflappable pragmatists, true compeerists will view these macropolitical engagements within a broader becoming-revolutionary attitude, where the demands being made, as minor as they may appear, are recognized as a means to foster more beneficial conditions for the concrete exits and alternatives to capital and other forms of oppression being pursued on the ground.

At the same time, and stepping back even further, we can also see that the variously tiered forms of activism pursued in the name of the commons and commoning are never isolated or unidirectional. There will always need to be a continuous collaboration between the micro-, meso-, and macro-levels of compeerist political engagement. Fuelled by a budding commoner consciousness, a compeerist movement of movements is tasked with inspiring all three levels, and these in turn must enable and facilitate each other. At times one political front may stagnate or experience setbacks, at other times one or the other may go through a massive surge of progress. Ultimately, the success of each in facilitating a transition to a compeerist future will depend on their effective mutual synergies with the others.

10

A Compeerist Society

The most fundamental distinction between compeerism and capitalism is the focus on the production of democratically determined use-value instead of the private pursuit of exchange-value. In other words, it is not simply supply and demand, deeply configured by the distribution of money and privately held property, which will decide what gets produced. Instead, when the means of production are truly commanded by a compeerist society, their use will primarily be employed to expand humanity's capacity to thrive. In preceding chapters we focused on the promise and challenges facing the broad adoption of such a political economy. The context in this exploration, however, was always one in which capital and the capital-state nexus was still firmly in control. In this final chapter, then, we consider what a compeerist mode of production could look like if it actually were to become dominant.

Anarchist and Marxist depictions of a final end-goal economy generally espouse an aim in which, in the words of Kropotkin (1995, p 78), the 'associations of men and women who … work on the land, in the factories, in the mines, and so on, [are] themselves the managers of production'. Yet there is significant variation as to how such an economy would function on a larger scale. In capitalism, money, representing all the tangible value of the world, gives the invisible hand of the market its movement. Using money determines demand while pursuing money motivates supply. What possible and preferable alternatives exist to this arrangement?

In anarcho-communist approaches the answer is to get rid of money, markets, and property altogether. Means of production are owned in common and supply and demand is determined from within the community, with each working according to their ability and everyone receiving according to their needs. In collectivist approaches, in turn, there is again an embrace of mutually-owned production capabilities, yet the role of money is generally revived, at least in the short term, as a labour token. This token, which can be redeemed for communally produced goods, ensures a motivation to work and a means with which to organize distribution, hence addressing two key uncertainties within the anarcho-communist approach.

Alternatively, mutualist outlooks accept money and markets as long as property ownership is conditional, meaning it should not lead to artificial scarcity or be used to exploit labour. In many mutualist understandings, which place a particular emphasis on human liberty, it is the state, using its authority and monopoly on violence, that is the real problem. Without the state handing capital control over property and money, the thinking goes, community-based property regimes benefiting the populace at large would dominate.

Due to its post-ideological stance, compeerism could, in theory, be open to any of the approaches just noted, but there is nonetheless one area where they are considered to fall short. With the state generally removed from each of these proposals, they all struggle to explain how the suggested alternative economies will function as intended. Hence, in contradistinction, and despite its commitment to decentralization and democratic economic production, compeerism takes the position that some form of macro-level governance is still called for (unless we embrace anarcho-primitivism's call to revert to small-scale habitations with minimal technology). Beyond the effective administration of money, property, and markets, there are many other geographically far-reaching issues that ultimately require cooperation and administration at larger scales, several of which have been covered in the previous chapters.

To pursue effective governance in such realms, compeerism embraces Ostrom's governance ideal of maintaining clearly-bounded decision-making jurisdictions, yet where some jurisdictions will have to be trans-local. One political theorization that is in line with this basic outlook can be found in Bookchin's conceptualization of 'libertarian municipalism', which envisions multiple levels of radically democratic decision making in what is often referred to as a confederacy of nested political units (Bookchin, 1991). The tricky part in such an arrangement, however, is determining what power the upper tiers of the nested organization should have.

In his proposal, Bookchin argues that actual policy would be determined by local councils, while the administration of these policies would occur at higher level confederal assemblies. Still, it is hard to imagine how thousands of radically democratic councils could effectively devise policies for the many trans-local/regional issues that are in play in our current socio-economic realities. More to the point, consensus will never be reached, thus forcing the question of how much freedom localized entities should have in going their own way, keeping in mind that local decisions often have geographically far-reaching consequences. When push comes to shove, Bookchin ultimately admits that the confederal assemblies, composed of delegates from lower tiers, would indeed need to have some form of top-down power. One example he offers is how this 'community of communities' could intervene in local cases where 'human rights are violated or where ecological mayhem is permitted' (Bookchin, 1991, np).

A more recent theorization of a post-capitalist, commons-oriented governance arrangement that nonetheless admits a certain degree of transregional decision-making centres on the establishment of a facilitative partner state (Bauwens et al, 2019; Pazaitis and Drechsler 2021). For P2P theorists, who have been actively exploring this idea, a partner state is one that has severed ties with capital, yet instead of becoming the powerful and dominant vanguard of a post-capitalist society, it pursues the more limited aim of simply empowering commons-centred 'autonomous social production' (Troncoso and Utratel, 2015, p 85). Such a 'state', while committed to more radical democracy, would nonetheless maintain the macro-level capability needed in facilitating and assisting the numerous activities involved in managing and expanding a sustainable and justly governed commons across multiple geographical scales. This could include taming market forces, to the extent that these are still in play, and working hand in hand with empowered commons-based actors to help achieve social and environmental wellbeing.

In the end, the nested confederacy model and the partner state conceptualization are not exclusionary and compeerists can be comfortable with both. The former is essentially focused on how best to organize macro governance without losing true democracy, while the latter centres more on what such macro-governance would ultimately be tasked with doing. A further issue that requires additional attention in both, however, pertains to the critical question of how geographically expansive the biggest community of communities is to be, and more to the point, if it is not global, how are these radically democratic forms of governance to interact with external political entities? Perhaps this question is downplayed by some proponents of these governance frameworks because the focus on localization is seen to mute the relevance of so-called 'international relations'. Yet, as we have seen throughout this book, the realization of the compeerist vision will inevitably entail the continuation of global interconnectivities, and these too will need to be managed.

Clearly, given compeerists' commitment to equality and the ability of all humankind to thrive, the embrace of rigid borders, isolation, and autarky are not options, nor is the often directly related embrace of the 'us-versus-them' dichotomy so effectively fomented by current nation-states and radicalized in emerging neo-fascist discourses. In their place, and given the potentialities inherent in humanity's advanced level of technological development, a compeerist partner state would naturally lean towards the broad outlook that sharing, collaboration, and commons-oriented governance offers the most assured path to prosperity, not just for a particular community, but for all. In the previous chapter we addressed what such a reorientation of the state could mean, especially within the Minority World. At the same time, we can also note that compeerism's commitment to decentralized and radical democratic governance aligns well with the position that the upper most tier of any nested governance structure should be limited in size and tailored to the people being governed. The ultimate reach, power, and orientation of this upper tier, will, therefore, need to be endogenously and democratically decided.

While the broad options for pursuing the macro-level governance of a compeerist society presented here are a good starting point, there are still many open questions. Given that compeerism does not offer a singular, prescriptive vision of a post-capitalist world, to satisfy the desire for more detail we can imaginatively explore just one hypothetical example of a future compeerist society. In depicting this scenario, and in contrast to the econocentric focus of classically aligned Marxists, no primacy is given here to the economic and political arrangements in play (the classic structure vs. superstructure construct). Both are seen as evolving together, with each influencing the other. Since we must start somewhere, however, we will commence with a focus on the political.

A hypothetical partner state

Imagine we are in the late 22nd-century and a compeerist 'renaissance' has come about after a prolonged period of environmental and subsequently social and economic upheaval. Most notable on the political front is that the Westphalian order of nation-states has largely been dismantled, giving rise to the predominance of partner states, each consisting of several tiers of governance with distinct jurisdictions. The highest level of political authority within these partner states has been shaped by commons-oriented societies in an effort to create a macro-level governance unit that can facilitate the expansion and management of the commons, yet with significantly less coercive power than the nation-states of old. The territorial reach of these partner states is also more confined, based primarily on the agreed-upon cultural and natural characteristics of the underlying 'bio-region' (Alperovitz, 2005).

Homing in on just one of these, we can envision, for lack of a better name, the Alpha Bioregion (AB), located in North America and with a population of about 35 million people. The region is governed by a nested system of commons-oriented councils, with the highest tier, the federal partner state, maintaining a binding constitution that evolved as a deliberative process of negotiation and compromise. Guided by principles for effective, collaborative commons governance, the constitution lays out the legal organization of the various lower tiers of decision making, as well as the establishment of a bill of rights. This bill enshrines the entitlement to basic individual liberties from coercive authority; rights to the means required for a thriving existence; a commitment to the commons and its democratic governance; and nonhuman rights focused on the humane and enlightened treatment of animals and ecosystems. True to Thomas Jefferson's belief that a constitution should be a living document, however, the AB's constitution is a constant work in progress.

The highest tiered, federal partner state is given jurisdiction over a number of key governance areas that are by their nature geographically expansive. This includes the responsibility of maintaining an effective monetary and judicial system; providing critical transregional infrastructure (broadband, rail, roads, seaports) and services (postal, health, higher education, research); and, more broadly, implementing regulations and guidelines pursuant to the bill of rights. The federal partner state is also responsible for managing relations with political units outside the AB, for instance to negotiate transregional agreements in the areas of trade, immigration, the environment, and space exploration. Yet, despite some similarities, the AB's federal partner state is quite different to the traditional nation-state, as significant power is devolved to lower tiers of governance which range from the six meso-regions directly under the top tier to the thousands of neighbourhood-sized precincts at the lowest level. Each tier is composed of representatives from the tier immediately below it and while each governance level has certain powers that pertain to its specific jurisdiction, significant leeway is given the lower tiers in interpreting and applying any regulations/guidelines coming from further up the nested arrangement.

The governance of the commons in such a political regime is inevitably multi-scalar and characterized by negotiation, collaboration, and the skilful navigation of conflicting interests. The central role of the federal partner state here, as per the constitution, is to pursue the expansion and accessibility of the human-made commons while fostering fair, sustainable, and democratic management over the natural ones. Yet, it is further down the nested governance structure that these macro-level aims are ultimately implemented via targeted policies and oversight procedures. Furthermore, the actual, on-the-ground management of the various commons is then primarily performed by an assortment of partner-state entities, cooperatives, and non-profits that tend to be local in relation to the resources and assets they are overseeing.

To help envision this decentralized partner state, it must be placed within the broader context of a populace that has become well-informed and has largely embraced commons-centric rationales when engaging in governance issues. Moreover, this governance should be understood as being conducted within a society in which compeerism has become the dominant mode of production. In other words, the benefits of win-win strategies have begun to bear fruit, including basic needs/wants being met, the equalization of opportunities to thrive, minimal wealth gaps and, critically, a significant increase in the amount of free time – all of which we will explore in more detail when we cover the economy. Not least, governance itself has been fundamentally transformed by sophisticated big-data capabilities and advanced AI data crunching, making it much easier to execute valid assessments of problems as well as offer data-driven response options.

Still, it would be wrong to conclude that an apolitical technocracy has been established. There will, for example, always be contestation over the stakeholdership, and hence power claims made, over a given commons. Indeed, the question of who gets a seat at the table is always a fraught one. Furthermore, even with excellent, data-based analyses and policy options, difficult decisions still have to be made regarding the underlying values and aesthetics to be pursued, where to set priorities, and what degree of risk is deemed acceptable in any given governance decision. Finally, the collection, processing, and interpretation of data can never be a completely objective process, no matter how smart the AI. In short, politics will remain an integral part of any commons-centred governance regime.

Unlike today, however, the organization of political affairs in the AB is very different due to its decentralized, nested character, which gives much more power to the populace in determining their local realities. In this way, there is generally lively participation in the lower tiers of the partner state, where, within the broad guidelines and overarching goals agreed upon at the higher tiers, a number of important issues are adjudicated, largely in line with the agonistic approach to commons-based politics addressed in the last chapter. Important governance topics include, for instance, land use and the rights/responsibilities of land users; achieving resilience, organizing and implementing educational opportunities; and, not least, resolving contentious issues like the regulation of weapons, drugs, advertisement, and car use. Beyond these localized forums that are part of the multi-scaled partner state's responsibilities, however, commoners are also engaged in numerous economic governance processes involving non-state actors. Cooperatives, open-value-networks, and non-profits have become the norm in the AB's economy and these too, using advanced network democratization platforms (like Loomio today), pursue and facilitate participation and decision making from within and outside the organization regarding its economic mission and operations.

This localized participation then easily feeds into the higher tiers of the partner state, giving rise to a steady stream of qualified 'commons servants' from below. At these higher tiers, governing bodies inevitably become more distant from the populace. Nevertheless, representational politics have here been made significantly more democratic by adopting many of the reform recommendations explored in the last chapter. In this way the upper tiers of the partner state government have managed to achieve high degrees of transparency and fair representation, and, with the help of numerous digitally enabled governance tools, constituents are given multiple opportunities to participate in important decision making.

It should nonetheless be noted that the ideal of consensus is generally rejected within the deliberative bodies of the AB partner state, as such an aspiration carries with it the sense that there is an absolute right to be attained, a position compeerism generally rejects (Mouffe, 2009). Instead, more attention is paid to the process of politics with an emphasis put on avoiding simple win-lose scenarios, for example by employing ranked voting for various policy options. In this way, by arriving at solutions/decisions that are considered 'good enough' by a unanimous majority, there is a greater likelihood of avoiding either stalemate or widespread disgruntlement, both of which are associated with winner-take-all arrangements (Bollier and Helfrich, 2019).

It is also recognized that the monumental sum of continuous, micro-level decision making entailed in governance can never be fully democratized without causing paralysis and governance burnout. Therefore, various forms of common criteria are used in which micro-managers within partner state and other democratic organizations are freed to handle mundane, everyday decisions with the understanding that they maintain full accountability in their charge to abide by the democratically established guidelines that apply. Blockchain-based ledgers are again an effective tool here in maintaining full, detailed transparency and hence accountability in any execution of policy.

In its entirety, then, the governance arrangement within the AB depicted here is a combination of the nested political jurisdictions theorized by Bookchin and the partner state proposed by P2P scholars. The aim of such an organizational structure is to facilitate an engaged and commons-focused populace to run its own affairs at multiple scales in a way that is radically democratic, fair, and practical. In the end, it is nonetheless just one, rough outline; there are many variations possible. Regardless of the governance regimes adopted, however, they must ultimately be understood as both expressions and enablers of the specific commons-based socio-economy being pursued and executed. We can now delve deeper into the form that one such economy might take.

A hypothetical compeerist economy

Any effort to supplant the capitalist mode of production must ultimately ask the fundamental question of how the distribution of resources is to be determined, or put into more personal terms, who gets what? In capitalism this question is answered by privatizing and commoditizing everything, then pitting individuals, all with different starting conditions, against each other in a 'game' of trying to collect as many tokenized claims to consumption (money) as possible. In the hypothetical Alpha Bioregion (AB) an alternative mode of production, using different assumptions and starting conditions, has been established. The aim of this economy is to achieve a just and sustainable society centred on a vibrant digital and material commons that affords everyone the opportunity to thrive.

In basic terms we can establish at the outset that the AB economy is mutualist in nature, meaning that money and markets for the exchange of goods and services are maintained, but within a more collaborative (commons-based) approach to property. As discussed in prior chapters, compeerism holds that using money-enabled markets to help in mediating supply and demand does not of necessity lock societies into exchange-value monopolization. The fundamental question, rather, is how money, property, and market signals can be organized to achieve desired outcomes. It is precisely due to this needed, active organization of the economic environment that a commons-friendly partner state is accepted as an integral part of the AB's mode of production. We can best consider how the active shaping of the most critical pillars of the economy – money, property, and markets – are pursued in the AB by taking each in turn.

Money

With the exception of a few small jurisdictions, the AB's economy is still primarily organized around exchange using money. As such, there are several forms of money in use, yet the dominant currencies of account are still sovereignly issued fiat tender managed by the federal partner state. A distinctive feature of the AB's monetary system, however, is that it uses two forms of money, a demurrage-based currency and standard money.

Demurrage tender, which is entirely digital and can be held in secure digital wallets, is designed to incrementally lose its value over time. To prevent efforts to use this money as a way to store wealth, it may only be used on things that have an immediate or short-term expiration, such as perishable goods, fees, and one-time services. These items, in turn, have limits on how much can be purchased at a time. As such, the demurrage currency is issued with the aim of accounting for some 75 per cent of the economy, with standard money denominating the 25 per cent consisting of durable and semi-durable goods. Given the inherent lack of value storage capacity in demurrage money, and limitations on what can be bought, any exchange with standard money is generally not viable due to the latter's high price. In other words, the demurrage currency's design cannot be circumvented on a large scale.

The AB's dual, sovereign monetary system helps ensure the circulation of wealth and the prevention of crass income inequalities due to the limitation of store-of-value tender, while the partner state's power over the creation and release of both currencies boosts its funding capabilities. More specifically, the AB's monetary arrangement gives the partner state greater control over three crucial, interrelated macroeconomic goals: limiting materially-based economic growth, facilitating a viable universal basic income, and preventing excessive inflation.

The first goal is rooted in the acceptance that wellbeing and security for all, including future generations, requires the abandonment of the exponential growth imperative. The most critical move within the AB in this regard has been the elimination of the fractional reserve banking system that characterized the monetary-banking apparatus under late capitalism. Hence, the issuing of fiat money is no longer rooted in interest-bearing, growth-demanding bank loans. Instead, money is now primarily released into the economy through the spending of various scalar iterations of the partner state. These entities, moreover, largely use this money in the support of commons-based, non-profit, and hence non-growth-oriented entities. Furthermore, the money that is released into the economy is carefully controlled and monitored to ensure it does not spur unsustainable growth, especially when it comes to the standard currency needed for the consumption of durable goods.

Turning to universal basic income, the AB's populace has come to acknowledge that, in a world of incredible AI and robotic-driven productivity gains, combined with the loss of non-productive capitalist jobs that are no longer needed ('bullshit jobs'), formal work should no longer be the basis of the entitlement to consume. The adoption of a universal basic income (UBI) thus manages to break capital's power over labour via the apparatus of capture. The populace of the AB accepts this UBI as the sharing of a collectively achieved wealth, massively amplified through the extraordinary productive capabilities developed over generations. The feeling of oppression linked to the need to earn a wage is therefore overcome, and labour is freed up to be put to use non-coercively, especially in the commons realm.

The AB's federal partner state funds the UBI by making it 90 per cent demurrage currency, meaning that most of the UBI funds can unproblematically be reissued without inflating the money supply. With fully-automated luxury communism remaining outside the realm of possibility, and with the constant shifting of markets and labour behaviour, there is, nonetheless, a continuous and careful tweaking of guaranteed income required. The main objective of this fine-tuning is to allow for both access to the basic resources needed to thrive, even without work, while also maintaining adequate incentives to ensure that the labour still needed in the economy is forthcoming, an issue we will revisit shortly.

Lastly, regarding inflation, the AB manages the issuance of currency through a transparent, representative monetary authority that is designed to be apolitical and as objective as possible. This bureaucratic entity is charged with the pursuit of the two macroeconomic goals just noted (low growth with a UBI), while also ensuring the money supply remains linked to the value it represents in the economy. This latter task is facilitated by the fact that the predominant state-based tender is its demurrage currency, which cannot be stored and hence can be continuously reissued. With regard to standard money, in turn, careful and calculated management is utilized to ensure this money continuously circulates back through the partner state, which is primarily achieved through various forms of intentional, market-shaping fees, taxes, and other forms of income.

Property

Turning next to property, it is the AB's federal partner state that is tasked with maintaining basic guidelines for the fostering of commons-oriented property governance, yet many of the details of this property regime are left to the lower tiers. In broad terms, however, and following collectivist thinking, land and other means of production are considered non-personal, meaning that various limitations, or so called 'usufruct' norms can be placed on them. In this way 'title' to non-personal property, like land, tends to fall under an abandonment criteria, meaning they are void once this 'property' is not actively being used.

Non-personal property titles also do not generally change hands solely on the basis of exchange-value, that is, money. In other words, the issuing of titles entails various conditions and procedures that seek to balance community interests and the rights of current title holders, with heavy emphasis placed on transparency and stakeholder input and voting. This balanced management approach is then used to determine who may take over the property title, under what conditions, and, to the extent that payment is involved, who the recipient of this compensation will be. The issuing of some titles, furthermore, such as for productive land, have expiration dates, meaning they function essentially like lease agreements that regularly need to be renewed.

To be clear, the aim in this non-personal property regime is to democratize the allocation and use of critical physical assets, meaning these are to be governed as a material commons. Importantly, by handing significant control over non-personal property to the populace, extractive capital becomes fundamentally hobbled, as it can only gain access to non-personal land and assets if the community is convinced this is the best option. Consequently, it is a widely adopted norm within the AB that property should not be used for rent seeking or exploitative activities, which then also means that most economic actors are commons-oriented by nature. Where for-profit enterprises still exist, they tend to be smaller operations occupying a market niche that is seen as not effectively filled by commons- or state-based entities.

Personal property within the AB, in turn, applies to individual, material possessions one has acquired through one's own toil or through the purchase of the fruits of someone else's non-coerced labour. While this is a relatively straightforward definition, things can become a bit more complicated in cases where non-personal property, like land, has non-mobile personal property within it, like a house or a production facility. In this sense, each applicable jurisdiction is responsible for finding their own way of dealing with the disentanglement of personal and non-personal property when it comes to issues of rights, limitations, and usufruct requirements.

Importantly, following from the definition of personal property just offered, a person's work also falls within this category, meaning the individual maintains the right to sell their labour. Given the overall macroeconomic structures in place, however, and particularly with the existence of a UBI, no one must feel coerced to work for money. Most paid labour occurs in cooperative arrangements where remuneration is organically determined from within, using various democratic means. Determining what is proportional or fair is nonetheless always a moving target. Hence, within the AB, most of the bigger cooperatives remunerate their workers based on the type of work involved, yet with caps put in place to prevent large wage divides. Within smaller cooperatives, however, it is more common to find labour regimes based on full parity, valued only in terms of time put in.

Nonetheless, when dealing with intellectual and creative work, especially with digitization enabling limitless distribution at practically no cost, the issue of property and labour can again become a bit more problematic. As suggested in Chapter 3, compeerism generally views the fruits of intellectual/creative work to be a blend of personal and commons property; in other words, while these ideas/creations emanate from, and entail the work of, an individual, this individual is also tapping into the broader commons of the general intellect. In the AB there is a concerted effort to fairly manage the dual nature of this work.

For those seeking to garner income from their intellectual/creative labour, the AB does allow for a certain degree of personal property claims, with some piracy restrictions in place. In the same way, peer property is legally protected from exploitation by capital. Yet the rights to profit on self- or enterprise-generated intellectual property are also curtailed in significant ways. For instance, there are much shorter term-limits before intellectual property or patents expire, and if any intellectual property exceeds a certain exchange-value, or is considered of very high use-value (for instance in the field of medicine), a trigger mechanism sets in where this property is automatically commonified. This is done by having the relevant intellectual property bought out for a reasonable sum by an acquisition fund run by the federal partner state.

Even so, it is important to recognize here, given the shift in mentalities and incentives within the AB, that most intellectual/creative work has shifted to non-profit, commons-oriented entities where the labour is performed with the full understanding that it is intended for the commons. While this work is largely driven by inherent reward and community recognition, as most academic work today, some remuneration is also often established. This can take the form of a wage, supported either by the partner state or a community supported non-profit, or through a cooperative or guild-like organization that seeks a balance between commons-contributions and market income.

A good example of the latter within the AB is the commons-based Cultural Workers Guild (CWG). While the CWG opens up all of its digital value to the commons for free after one year, they also issue a demurrage-based cryptocurrency called Culture Coin which is needed to pay for live performances and recently released digital content. A certain amount of Culture Coin is then regularly distributed for free to everyone, yet, to gain access to additional, CWG-sourced value that has not been fully released to the commons, it is necessary to buy additional Culture Coin.

For the CWG, the monetary income gained in this way enables it to pursue its mission of both expanding the cultural commons while also rewarding its members through democratically agreed-upon remuneration protocols. The CWG's ability to look out for its members, its access to an expansive repository of peer-licensed cultural content, and its broad embrace and support from within society more generally, is a strong incentive to become a member. As such, the CWG manages to absorb a large portion of the cultural talent within the AB, leading to an abundant production of diverse cultural value for the commons.

Markets

With the money and property components of the AB economy in place we can lastly turn to the market that is thus enabled. As noted earlier, some leftist scholars reject markets as incompatible with post-capitalism as they are seen to perpetuate exchange-value rationales, which, in their view, will inevitably dominate. Within the AB, however, and in line with market socialist thinking, markets are instead understood as malleable; they can be constrained and guided to subdue extractive/exploitative impulses while fostering commons-oriented forms of economic interaction, such as mutual aid, gifting, pooling, and sharing. In considering how this can be done, we can first point out that the property and monetary governance arrangements outlined in the previous two sections would already have a significant impact, both in terms of demand (now with much more equal, but also more constrained access to consumption) and supply (now with significantly less capital involvement). In addition to these external conditions, however, and keeping in mind that the economic realm will still maintain a mixture of public, private, and commons-based entities, the AB partner state also draws on a number of direct market interventions aimed at facilitating and fostering a compeerist-aligned economy.

First, while not being the agent of a fully planned economy, the AB partner state, in all its scaled iterations, nonetheless remains a significant market participant as a supplier and purchaser of goods/services – similar to the state today, except with much deeper involvement and intentionality. In this way the partner state has substantial power to form markets by either becoming a dominant market participant itself, for instance in health care, or by bolstering cooperatives and non-profits by becoming a key customer for their goods and services. Furthermore, given its sovereign monetary authority, the partner state is able to channel credit and investments in a way that supports commons-based market actors and activities. Then, to further fine-tune supply and demand, standard interventions from the social-democratic toolbox are made use of. Included here are incentivizing tax credits and subsidies, for example to assist households and communities in making resiliency-fostering investments; or disincentivizing fees and taxes that can, for instance, check certain extractive forms of production or limit the consumption of socially or environmentally burdensome goods.

Also noteworthy, however, is the use of highly innovative market-shaping mechanisms aimed at achieving ambitious and far-reaching governance goals. Taking environmental stewardship as an example, the AB partner state issues digital environmental impact tokens (EI tokens) linked to land-, water-, and air-based ecological boundaries, which are then needed, beyond the standard price, to purchase something in the market. The amount of allowable environmental impacts in each of the categories is capped within a determined region. Each product/service is then given impact points based on carefully calculated, geographically specific, and continuously revised environmental-impact assessments. The more points a product/service has, the more tokens are needed to purchase it. We should note that the ability to effectively calculate a region's real-time environmental caps and a product's overall points is made possible via an expansive internet of things and advanced AI capable of processing this big data.

Within this arrangement, then, everyone gets a certain, carefully determined amount of EI tokens issued to their digital wallets every week, which can either be used or traded on the open market. In this way EI tokens work to fundamentally shape consumption away from environmentally impactful goods/services while motivating producers to decrease the EI points attributed to their economic activities. Lastly, to encourage a system where the maximum allowable impact is generally not achieved, an alternative use of EI tokens is created by allowing their use for the payment of some partner-state-issued fees or taxes.

Given this example of sophisticated technology being employed to fundamentally structure supply and demand in the market, a natural question that can be posed here is why such tools could not be even further leveraged to overcome markets altogether. It is a question that deserves a bit more attention, and in answering it, we can also get a better understanding of the AB's approach to markets more generally. To do so, we can first consider the vision of a technologically advanced cybernetic-like system posited by Nick Dyer-Witheford, which he presents as the ultimate execution of communist state planning. It is worth quoting at some length:

> A new cybernetic communism ... would, we have seen, involve some of the following elements: use of the most advanced super-computing to algorithmically calculate labour time and resource requirements, at global, regional and local levels, of multiple possible paths of human development; selection from these paths by layered democratic discussion conducted across assemblies that include socialized digital networks and swarms of software agents; light-speed updating and constant revision of the selected plans by streams of big data from production and consumption sources; the passage of increasing numbers of goods and services into the realm of the free or of direct production as use values once automation, copy-left, peer-to-peer commons and other forms of micro-replication take hold; the informing of the entire process by parameters set from the simulations, sensors and satellite systems measuring and monitoring the species metabolic interchange with the planetary environment. (Dyer-Witheford, 2013, p 20)

Dyer-Witheford's vision clearly overlaps with the compeerist one depicted in the AB. Indeed, the potential promise of utilizing endless streams of real-time big data and the 'advanced super-computing' to process this information into effective problem and policy analyses have been similarly noted in this and previous chapters. Still, in the end, the AB stops well short of seeking the implementation of a fully-fledged, hi-tech, communist technocracy.

For one, humans are considered as simply too complex and variable to allow for their needs, preferences, and whims to be perfectly calculated, even with unfathomable computing power. Thus, the spontaneous, decentralized, self-organizational capacities inherent in markets are still embraced as a better calculating mechanism, with the caveat that these markets are made to function within an equitable society that gives everyone the adequate means to engage in consumption – for instance via a guaranteed income. For the other, in line with compeerism's deep suspicion of hierarchical, top-down micro-management, the AB is simply more trusting of direct, on-the-ground micro-interactions and decisions than it is of a centralized system of economic governance that – even with the inclusion of so-called 'democratic discussions' – could still run roughshod over the wants and desires of individuals and even entire minority communities.

At the same time, and as should be quite clear by now, despite the preference and embrace of micro-level exchange over super-computed state planning, the

Austrian School's insistence that markets must be untouched for their magical calculating power to work is also wholeheartedly rejected. Instead, the AB maintains that markets can never be pure or perfect, they always function in a context of extraneous factors that are never equal or constant, from knowledge and affect to geography and wealth. The aim of the AB, then, is not to pursue an impossible ideal of a 'free' market, but rather to actively employ traditional and high-tech interventions to actively shape the overarching conditions within which the market and its calculating power is asked to operate. These conditions, in turn, are intentionally and collaboratively designed, reviewed, and revised, propelled by the aspiration of creating a rich commons-based economy that can ensure everyone's ability to thrive.

Envisioning post-capitalist production, consumption, and work

With the broad structural components of the hypothetical AB economy in place, we can end by describing in a bit more detail what production/consumption and work would look like. Turning to the former, we find a socially and ecologically sustainable economy that prioritizes use-value production aimed at universally meeting basic needs and wants. While the provision of abundant, high quality free amenities, such as education and health care, is organized primarily by a combination of variously tiered partner state entities and non-profits, additional basic goods and services are mediated through a market that is nonetheless dominated by socially concerned organizations, cooperatives and open-value networks. Due to being deeply democratized, these compeerist-aligned market actors also emphasize the facilitation of use-value access via a focus on 'affordable quality'. Achieving this affordability, and hence access, is ultimately made possible due to limited-profit pressures, the cutting out of middlemen, partner-state subsidies, and expansive boundary commoning, including the ability to freely tap into peer-property licensed value.

When it comes to more desire-based consumption, while the same accessibility-focused compeerist producers/providers are in play (now also competing with a few more profit-oriented entities), we nevertheless hit upon inevitable limits. These are primarily imposed by market structures prioritizing use-value production and then the material confines of our closed, and hence bounded, physical and natural systems. Regarding this latter point, the AB, which is deeply committed to long-term resilience in the face of these limits, has embraced the design global, manufacture and grow local ideal, resulting in a multi-scalar system of nested circular economies with down-scaled production arrangements that tend to have light ecological footprints. This 'less efficient' approach to material production, along with the imposition of environmental tokens and constraints placed on the issuing of standard money, means that the ability to humour an excessive buy-and-discard mentality has been significantly curtailed.

Yet, the reduced consumption of often sub-standard material goods is considered an acceptable cost by most AB residents in return for enhanced product quality and positive community and environmental relations. This attitude is perhaps best explained with the help of a contemporary example in the real world, that is, locally and sustainably sourced craft beer, which is also increasingly organized within worker owned enterprises (Palladino, 2017). Thus, such craft beer may be up to 20 per cent more expensive to produce than that made in a large factory leveraging economies of scale and pursuing extractive production rationales, yet the craft brewery, beyond being more generatively focused in its operations, also offers high quality and greater selection, motivated by localized demands. This local focus often also means the craft brewery puts greater emphasis on community relations, for instance by providing space for consumption and general conviviality. As a result, the higher price (that is, reduced efficiency) is widely accepted as being worth it, which goes a long way to explain the craft beer explosion in the US over the last few decades (BA, 2022).

In the AB, this more comprehensive evaluation of efficiency in relation to 'value' more broadly has been applied to the economy as a whole. One important consequence of this approach, especially with regard to the rejection of throughput-heavy consumption, has been the fostering of positive demand-oriented sentiments. For instance, there are now much greater expectations not only regarding the quality, but also the modularity and repairability of the goods being purchased, helping in the execution of a well-functioning circular economy. A further knock-on effect has been the establishment of extensive collaborative consumption arrangements, like car shares, tool libraries, and real estate time-share cooperatives, which all serve to substantially stretch material constraints.

Relatedly, there is now also a much greater involvement of users/consumers in the production process. These prosumers thus find arrangements to work with local commons-oriented enterprises and open-value-networks to offer certain inputs (labour, ideas, assets) to assist in the production and tailoring of goods they have requested. Small-scale makers and growers have also become commonplace, seeking either greater self-sufficiency or making use of vibrant, digitally supported markets for selling, trading, and sharing individually produced goods and services. This trend has been facilitated by the democratization of the means of production, where widely accessible fab labs and a massive open-source library of digital value has made material and non-material production increasingly feasible. Given this demise of the pure 'consumer', it is not surprising that retailers (essentially middlemen) have been largely sidelined in the AB economy.

In a similar way, there has been a marked breakdown of the client-server type model in the service sector, which, incidentally, is often much less restrained in terms of ecological limits. Here, abundant access to services is not just a result of an economy dominated by commons-oriented enterprises, it is also, again, a result of the empowerment of the prosumer. Thus, while it is still possible to pay for personalized services in the AB, there are now also a wide range of easily accessible free or very low-priced online options based on interaction and input between users and highly capable AI programmes tapping into networked big data. Households and organizations can thus easily access insights, analyses, and tailored solutions ranging from health advice and legal help to architectural design and engineering consultancy, widely supplanting the need for external professionals. The availability of these lower-cost options has meant individuals and households have more means to access other, more human-dependent services, such as frequenting cafes and restaurants or attending live cultural performances.

It is within the broader context of the production/consumption arrangements in place that we must then also understand the general approach to work within the AB, which is shaped by two symbiotic developments. For one, as noted earlier, the AB economy maintains a significantly diminished demand for labour due to very high levels of automation and the loss of meaningless 'bullshit' jobs. For the other, the drive to work in order to boost consumption has been considerably eroded as the concept of prosperity has evolved to become increasingly removed from its connection to material acquisition in relation to others. Indeed, with a greater turn to prosumerism, and the related expunging of corporate power, we find a society in which brands have been increasingly replaced by personal customization and competency, where a person's belongings are no longer a class representation of one's power to shop, but much more an individualized and fair representation of one's ability to make.

With this context in mind, it is therefore not surprising that roughly half of the AB's work-eligible population chooses to rely almost exclusively on the universal basic income to pay for their market-based consumption (as a comparison, the labour force participation rate in the US and EU today stands at about 25 per cent) (OECD, 2021). A significant portion of this non-waged population in the AB, however, also supplements their UBI income via non-monetary forms of barter, as in blockchain-enabled systems for trading skilled labour or goods. For those still receiving a wage, furthermore, the additional money earned is considered by many as a bonus, second to more important factors such as the personal and social rewards that are associated with their work. This sentiment of wanting to work for work's sake is directly linked to greater worker empowerment and the localized manner of production and consumption within the AB, thus largely overcoming the alienation associated with capitalist forms of production.

A critical overall dynamic that then follows from the AB's non-coercive labour market is that a significant amount of time/work is freed up for non-market-based commoning. At the household level this can express itself, for instance, in spending more intentional time parenting, gardening, or cooking; on the local/regional level it could mean participating in a district resource-management initiative or helping to put on a community play; and globally, commons contributions may take the form of coding offered to an open-sourced app within the digital commons, or data collection for a crowdsourced research project spearheaded by a community halfway around the world. Doing this work, which offers fulfilment, camaraderie, and recognition is also a primary contribution to the vibrant, non-market-based forms of exchange and overall resiliency that characterizes life in the AB.

Still, it would be disingenuous to suggest money, and the consumption claims that come with it, have entirely lost their meaning. As noted earlier, there is an ongoing macroeconomic tweaking taking place to create enough of an incentive, given the establishment of a UBI, to find the labour needed for the tasks that still require human time and ability, particularly those remaining jobs that may be considered undesirable. In the end, monetary remuneration remains an important motivator here as the ability to consume beyond a certain point is still largely determined by money. As such, if you wish to access more of the goods and services within the market-mediated economy that exists, you will also have to contribute more to it. Accordingly, even with a cultural shift away from materialistically based perceptions of prosperity and social status, the enticement to work for money still persists, although now the remuneration demanded to do certain things has significantly gone up. As a consequence of this latter point, we should add, it is not uncommon within the AB to see those engaging in the most tedious of jobs, even if they do not require special skills or talents, maintaining the highest levels of consumption.

In sum, then, the hypothetical AB region of the future presented here offers a vision of a political and economic organization of society that enables universal opportunities for individual and community thriving. In this way, the value of environmental and social sustainability permeates the political-economic arrangements in place leading to what can be termed an 'apparatus of compeerist capture', centred not on the commodification of everything, as in the capitalist apparatus of capture, but rather on its commonification, where labour is set free, rents are largely abolished, and value is understood, measured, and operationalized in multiple ways, not just via markets.

Moreover, the specific applications and interpretations of value(s) will vary from one locale to another. Indeed, one of the benefits of the AB partner state's form is that it offers many avenues for communities at various scales to pursue their own preferred conditions for thriving. This approach is in line with the limited experiences we have had of radically decentralized forms of governance within non-capitalist contexts in the past. During the Spanish Revolution initiated in 1936, for instance, eastern Spain was a medley of different anarchist and communist economic systems, with some areas maintaining strictly regulated markets while others abandoned money altogether (Bolloten, 1991). We should note that beyond variations in property, money, and market management, technology too can be approached in different ways. Even if most, along compeerist lines, will likely choose to fully maximize the potential of technology and the geographical interconnectedness that this embrace facilitates and requires, some may opt for a more low-tech, isolated, self-sufficient form of living, which , in the end, can also be accommodated within compeerism's broader post-ideological foundation.

Lastly, underlying the choices pursued in terms of overall economic and technological governance, there also reside significant divergences in aesthetic and cultural preferences. Following Iris Marion Young's (1990) vision of the ideal urban environment, however, this diversity does not have to mean compartmentalization through starkly demarcated boundaries that spell a sudden shift from one way of being to another. Rather, a well-functioning diverse society will be characterized by a continuous, open, and tolerant exchange between identities and modes of organization, expressed in a material landscape composed of a multitude of interstitial, blended spaces that make up the smooth transition between what are otherwise quite distinct neighbourhoods, counties, and regions. In short, it would be a landscape revealing a broad spectrum of possibilities for being, where anyone can find their ideal habitat for flourishing.

Conclusion

Today, humanity possesses wealth, knowledge, and productive capabilities that are truly immense, the thing of fantasies just one hundred years ago. And yet, we live in a world characterized by massive inequality, widespread poverty, environmental collapse, and political instability and conflict. Given what humanity has to work with, it is hard to imagine that a better outcome is not possible. Consider, for instance, that contemporary global per-capita GDP is roughly on par with that of Costa Rica, Thailand, or Serbia (or the US of the 1950s). Human development indices show that countries that have achieved this range of economic production can manage very high human development, with health, education, and environmental/social sustainability scores that are comparable to those of rich countries (Jackson, 2017). In fact, if we home in only on happiness and life satisfaction, the correlation between wellbeing and GDP begins to fall apart after the world's average economic output is achieved. Costa Rica, for instance, has repeatedly ranked as one of the fifteen happiest countries in the world (Garrigues, 2019).

Next, consider that the averaged global wealth per adult, that is, overall net worth, currently stands at around US$80,000 (Hechler-Fayd'herbe, 2021). If this wealth were equitably distributed and added to the global average per capita GDP, we would reach affluence levels significantly higher than mid-range countries like Costa Rica. If we then further assume a significant reduction in prices that could be achieved in many critical goods and services by shifting from a profit-seeking form of production that fosters artificial scarcity to one centred on expanding the abundance of use-value, then these affluence levels would rise even higher. In other words, taking all of these considerations into account, it is fair to conclude that humanity easily has the means to establish a Minority World, middle class life for essentially everyone on the planet, with perhaps somewhat less quantity in the material things consumed but with a greater access to product quality and the ubiquitous availability of top-notch, basic and supplementary services.

The fact that such an achievement appears as distant as ever, however, should give pause regarding the current organization of our productive capabilities and its political defence. Indeed, we started the book by challenging the resigned conviction that there can be no alternative to capitalism. We then proceeded to explore such an alternative, under the label of compeerism – that is, a proposed, still nascent form of democratized production that prioritizes use-value and the pursuit of social and environmental resilience by fostering collaboration, openness, and solidarity. A commons-based order is here envisioned as a potential that could grow from within the shell of capitalism, finding exits and alternatives to capital dependence until a post-capitalist society is achieved.

In prior chapters, various examples of compeerist economic activity and thought were presented as lines of flight that point to alternative social relations and forms of production. Yet, as we have also seen, in existing conditions these still evolving non- and counter-capitalist efforts are often controlled and subverted by capital in numerous ways. As such these lines of flight can come across as insignificant, errant streaks that quickly fall back to earth. Yet behind these faint stirrings are also some very big potentialities – we can identify four in all – that go to the very heart of capitalism's weaknesses. Many may still dismiss these latent potencies as being too inconsequential. From a compeerist perspective, however, such estimations fail to take into account the possibility of these distinct pieces of the transition puzzle coming together and synergizing to form a unified whole. In such a scenario, compeerism holds, we would, indeed, be looking at a truly powerful culmination of forces, or 'generalized conjunction', capable of delivering a systemic shift to a post-capitalist future.

The first piece of the compeerist transition puzzle centres on freeing the general intellect by expanding the digital commons, guarding it from capital cooptation via expansive peer-licensing regimes, and taking back the internet from capital. The second piece focuses on a commonification of the material economy by expanding and strengthening sound, commons-based forms of control and management in infrastructure, manufacturing, and primary production. Within this piece there is an imperative to strive towards greater decentralization/localization where possible, in pursuit of community empowerment and far-thinking environmental stewardship/rehabilitation. The third piece, then, aims at challenging the monopoly of exchange-value and thus dismantling the apparatus of capture. The imperative demanded here is to exit the current bank-centred governance of money and replace it with one that allows for, and even fosters, alternative forms of valuation within production.

We should note that in all three of these pieces there is an underlying strategy of not only making compeerist-aligned economic activities more viable, but making them capable of engaging in a steadily growing transvestment of assets and wealth from capital to the commons. A corollary of this strategy is that such a transvestment will necessitate compeerists actively engaging markets with the aim to outcompete capital. It is only in this way, given the rejection of violent revolution, that a commons-based subeconomy can expand, grow, and eventually displace capital's dominance across the economy.

The final piece of the puzzle is also the only piece that can bind the puzzle into a whole, while still depending on the other pieces to find its form. This is the mobilization of a massive movement of movements that demands a commons-centred mode of production as the most rational arrangement through which to pursue our individual and collective thriving. This piece comes with two interlinked underpinnings, one stipulates the need to foster and expand an intentional, counter-capitalist and pro-commons consciousness, and the other insists that prefigurative micropolitics and meso-level inter-commons solidarity must be accompanied with a more macro-centred political engagement aimed at influencing and ultimately reforming the state. This latter imperative is rooted in the conviction that the ability to successfully execute a compeerist transition is closely tied to the overarching socio-economic-political contexts in place, and these, in turn, are most directly and consequentially shaped by state-based policies and initiatives.

For most, it is this fourth piece dealing with a mass mobilization, the lynchpin of the entire puzzle, which is the most elusive or difficult to envision. The likely reason for this is that societies appear to be stuck in a certain paradigm, or what some would argue, a capital-serving hegemony. As with our view of exchange-value that becomes our dominant lens for seeing the world (the water that the fish swims in), we are generally stuck in a host of preconceptions and assumptions that prevent the populace from finding their way to an intentional and mobilizing commoner consciousness. The task, therefore, which is immense, is nothing less than the dawn of an entirely new meaning system, with different rules and parameters and hence differing goals and strategies. In other words, a different game must be proposed and internalized.

The game metaphor is fitting because games are essentially meaning-creation assemblages/apparatuses; they offer an unambiguous explanation or story of a given context, present rigid guidelines and parameters for acting in this provided setting, and then present a clear end-goal. As such, games create an enclosed space of order and purpose within a chaotic universe of uncertainty/futility, and when groups are involved in the game, they can also foster a compelling sense of identity and belonging. We can see the power of games at work, for instance, when masses of fans become transfixed and highly impassioned by big sporting events. Yet the same game dynamics can be seen to unfold in actual life, now at a much larger scale and with much higher stakes. The most obvious example here is nationalism, in which case the guidelines stipulate clear 'us versus them' parameters within a context of scarcity, where winning can take various forms, including, in its most escalated iteration, on the battlefield.

Yet, more subtly, a mode of production can also be seen through the lens of games, as it too provides an overarching story and guidelines, as well as an end goal that gives purpose. In capitalism the rules are quite simple with a starting point of 'every man for himself' (but with options for alliances), the final aim being to amass more wealth than one's opponents. Scarcity is again a defining part of the context, and where one starts on the playing board (the accident of birth) plays a big role in one's chances of success. Importantly, and keeping the meaning-creating power of games in mind, once becoming a full participant in the life-encompassing, capitalist game, amassing wealth represents much more than simply increasing one's ability to consume, it becomes the meaning-giving end of 'winning' at life itself.

In this sense, compeerism can ultimately be seen as the proposition of a compelling, alternative game to capitalism, hence offering an entirely new way of making sense of the economic world and our purpose in it. As such, the compeerist game is more nuanced, has more rules, and, most significantly, it is cooperative in nature. The aim is to collaborate in order to create the most enabling, diverse, and beautiful commons possible, the reward of which is increased prosperity and wellbeing for all players.

To shed some more light on the rationale behind this cooperative focus, and why it should be adopted, imagine a competitive game where, quite suitably, the goal is to accumulate more tokens than any other player. Such competitive games usually succumb to what is termed a 'Nash equilibrium' in game theory, which means that players pursue a very narrow strategy based on the assumption that everyone else is a rival pursuing their own self-interest in winning the game. By proceeding in this way, the total collective amount of tokens achieved tends to be significantly below the higher ranges of what is possible. In other words, the competitive goal of trying to win more tokens than one's opponents means that strategies are employed that seek to limit token access to other players, and vice versa.

Now consider, however, that an alternative, collaborative playing of this game, where the goal is to gain the greatest number of tokens collectively, not only results in achieving higher total token amounts but also, generally, more per player. Let us say 99 per cent of players achieve better end-game token amounts in a collaborative, sharing scenario than in a competitive one. In such a case, given the slim odds of doing better by taking the competitive route, the strategically sound decision lies in adopting collaboration. It is this strategic preference that ultimately sums up the compeerist outlook: instead of committing to a competitive game with few winners, we should agree to play by the cooperative rules, with the goal of achieving the greatest collective prosperity possible, which, as it turns out, also ends up being the most beneficial for the overwhelming majority of individuals.

Even if collaboration is the most logical strategy, however, actually convincing the populace to switch their approach and understanding of the real-life game of token acquisition, that is, capitalism, can be exceedingly difficult. This is because the compeerist change being proposed challenges the very foundation of the hegemonic economic narrative that has become internalized into our sense of being and purpose. A foundational mental shift of this magnitude, therefore, would entail more than just a political or economic upheaval; it would of necessity also constitute a cultural, philosophical, and psychological one as well.

Just as the Enlightenment accompanied capitalism, offering a completely new way of seeing the self and the world, so too compeerism will need to be supplemented by a new *Weltanschauung*. Importantly, such a mental/conceptual outlook would not be in causal relation to the nascent, compeerist mode of production; rather it would exist as a co-evolving and mutually shaping force entwined with it. In this sense there is much that can still be done to bring the work and thoughts of social scientists across disciplines to bear on what a compeerist-aligned worldview would entail and how it could be promoted. Still, one important component of any such mental framework seeking to challenge the status quo – for instance by demanding a world that is fair, sustainable, and prosperous – is the conviction that such a world *is* actually achievable. This book has tried to contribute to this task by arguing that, indeed, it is. Humanity just needs to find the right inspiration, resolve, and political prowess to change the underlying logic and rules of the game.

References

Abell, H., 2014. Worker cooperatives: Pathways to scale – project equity. Project-Equity. Available at: https://www.project-equity.org/wp-content/uploads/2017/02/Worker-Cooperatives-Pathways-to-Scale.pdf [Accessed 3 April 2022].

Adkins, L., Cooper, M. and Konings, M., 2020. *The Asset Economy: Property Ownership and the New Logic of Inequality*, Cambridge: Polity Press.

Adorno, T.W., 2015. *Negative Dialectics*. London: Routledge.

AFT, 2021. Saving American Farmland: 2017 Nationwide Survey of Land Trusts that Protect Farm and Ranch Land, *FIC*. Available at: https://farmlandinfo.org/publications/2017-nationwide-survey-of-land-trusts-that-protect-farm-and-ranch-land/ [Accessed 30 November 2022].

Agamben, G., 2009. *What is an Apparatus? and Other Essays*, Stanford, CA: Stanford University Press.

Agrarian Trust, 2021. About Agrarian Trust. Available at: https://www.agrariantrust.org/about/ [Accessed 6 April 2022].

Akuno, K., 2019. Building a solidarity economy in Jackson, Mississippi. Cooperation Jackson. Available at: https://cooperationjackson.org/blog/2019/10/10/building-a-solidarity-economy-in-jackson-mississippi [Accessed 3 April 2022].

Alam, S., 2008. Majority world: Challenging the West's rhetoric of democracy. *Amerasia Journal*, 34(1), pp 88–98.

Alexander, F.H., 2018. *Benefit Corporation Law and Governance: Pursuing Profit with Purpose*, Oakland, CA: Berrett-Koehler.

Alperovitz, G., 2005. *America Beyond Capitalism: Reclaiming our Wealth, our Liberty, and our Democracy*, Hoboken, NJ: John Wiley & Sons.

Alves, W., Ferreira, P. and Araújo, M., 2019. Mining co-operatives: A model to establish a network for sustainability. *Journal of Co-operative Organization and Management*, 7(1), pp 51–63.

Angel, J., 2016. Towards an energy politics in-against-and-beyond the state: Berlin's struggle for Energy Democracy. *Antipode*, 49(3), pp 557–576.

Antoniadis, P. and Pantazis, A., 2021. P2P Learning. In M. O'Neil, C. Pentzold and S. Toupin, eds. *The Handbook of Peer Production*. Hoboken, NJ: Wiley-Blackwell, pp 197–210.

Arvidsson, A., 2020. Capitalism and the Commons. *Theory, Culture, and Society*, 37(2), pp 3–30.

Arvidsson, A. and Peitersen, N., 2016. *The Ethical Economy: Rebuilding Value After the Crisis*, New York, NY: Columbia University Press.

Atkinson, R.D., Correa, D.K. and Hedlund, J.A., 2008. Explaining international broadband leadership. Information Technology and Innovation Foundation. Available at: https://itif.org/publications/2008/05/01/explaining-international-broadband-leadership [Accessed 29 June 2022].

BA, 2022. National beer sales and production data. *Brewers Association*. Available at: https://www.brewersassociation.org/statistics-and-data/national-beer-stats/ [Accessed 10 April 2022].

Badgley, C., Moghtader, J., Quintero, E., Zakem, E., Chappel, M., Avilés-Vázquez, K., et al, 2007. Organic agriculture and the global food supply. *Renewable Agriculture and Food Systems*, 22(2), pp 86–108.

Baig, R., Roca, R., Freitag, F., Navarro, L., 2015. Guifi.net, a crowdsourced network infrastructure held in common. *Computer Networks*, 90, pp 150–165.

Banov, M., 2018. An Operating System for Collective Intelligence (White Paper). *DAOstack*. Available at: https://daostack.io/ [Accessed 7 July 2022].

Baringa, E. and Ocampo, J., 2019. *FairCoop: The Global Cooperative and its Collaborative Cryptocurrency*, Frederiksberg: Copenhagen Business School.

Barnes, H., 2020. Microsoft and open source: An unofficial timeline. *Box of Cables*. Available at: https://boxofcables.dev/microsoft-and-open-source-an-unofficial-timeline/ [Accessed 1 April 2022].

Bass, T., Sutherland, E. and Symons, T., 2018. Reclaiming the Smart City: Personal Data, Trust and the New Commons. *Nesta*. Available at: https://media.nesta.org.uk/documents/DECODE-2018_report-smart-cities.pdf [Accessed 2 April 2022].

Batterham, R.J., 2017. The mine of the future – even more sustainable. *Minerals Engineering*, 107, pp 2–7.

Bauwens, M., 2005. The political economy of peer production. *CTheory*. Available at: https://journals.uvic.ca/index.php/ctheory/article/view/14464 [Accessed 30 March 2022].

Bauwens, M., 2009. Class and capital in peer production. *Capital & Class*, 33(1), pp 121–141.

Bauwens, M. and Gerhardt, H., 2020. A commons-based peer to peer path to post-capitalism: An interview with Michel Bauwens. *Antipode Online*. Available at: https://antipodeonline.org/2020/02/19/interview-with-michel-bauwens/ [Accessed 6 April 2022].

Bauwens, M. and Kostakis, V., 2014. From the communism of capital to capital for the commons: Towards an open co-operativism. *tripleC*, 12(1), pp 356–361.

Bauwens, M. and Kostakis, V., 2015. Towards a new reconfiguration among the state, civil society and the market. *Journal of Peer Production*, (7). Available at: http://peerproduction.net/issues/issue-7-policies-for-the-commons/peer-reviewed-papers/towards-a-new-reconfiguration-among-the-state-civil-society-and-the-market/ [Accessed 5 May 2023].

Bauwens, M. and Niaros, V., 2017. Value in the commons economy: Developments in open and contributory value accounting. *Commons Transition*. Available at: https://commonstransition.org/value-commons-economy/ [Accessed 1 April 2022].

Bauwens, M. and Pantazis, A., 2018. The ecosystem of commons-based production and its transformation dynamics. *The Sociological Review*, 66(2), pp 302–319.

Bauwens, M. and Ramos, J.M., 2018. Re-imagining the left through an ecology of the Commons: Towards a post-capitalist commons transition. *Global Discourse*, 8(2), pp 325–342.

Bauwens, M., Kostakis, V. and Pazaitis, A., 2019. *Peer to Peer: The Commons Manifesto*, London: University of Westminster Press.

Bauwens, M., Kostakis, V., Trancoso, S., Utradel, A.M., 2017. *Commons Transition and P2P: A Primer*, Amsterdam: Transnational Institute.

Bauwens, T., 2021. Are the circular economy and economic growth compatible? A case for post-growth circularity. *Resources, Conservation and Recycling*, 175, p 105852.

BBC, 2013. Berlin energy grid nationalisation fails in referendum. *BBC News*. Available at: https://www.bbc.com/news/world-europe-24800129 [Accessed 23 June 2022].

BC, 2022. Momentum for Democracy Reform across the country. Brennan Center for Justice. Available at: https://www.brennancenter.org/our-work/research-reports/momentum-democracy-reform-across-country [Accessed 11 May 2022].

Benkler, Y., 2002. Intellectual property and the organization of information production. *International Review of Law and Economics*, 22(1), pp 81–107.

Benkler, Y., 2006. Commons-based Agricultural Innovation: Innovations case discussion: CAMBIA-BiOS. *Innovations: Technology, Governance, Globalization*, 1(4), pp 58–65.

Benkler, Y., 2006b. *The Wealth of Networks: How Social Production Transforms Markets and Freedom*, New Haven, CT.: Yale University Press.

Benkler, Y., Shaw, A. and Hill, B.M., 2015. Peer production: A form of collective intelligence. In T.W. Malone and M.S. Bernstein, eds. *Handbook of Collective Intelligence*. Cambridge, MA: MIT Press, pp 175–204.

Bernie, 2017. High-speed internet for all. Bernie Sanders Official Website. Available at: https://berniesanders.com/issues/high-speed-internet-all/ [Accessed 3 April 2022].

Bernstein, J., 2021. What can you actually buy with Bitcoin? *The New York Times*. Available at: https://www.nytimes.com/2021/02/03/style/what-can-you-actually-buy-with-bitcoin.html [Accessed 3 July 2022].

Berry, D.M., 2019. Against infrasomatization: towards a critical theory of algorithms. In D. Bigo, E. Isin and E.S. Ruppert, eds. *Data Politics Worlds, Subjects, Rights*. London: Routledge, pp 43–63.

Birkinbine, B.J., 2018. Commons praxis: Toward a critical political economy of the Digital Commons. *tripleC*, 16(1), pp 290–305.

Birkinbine, B.J., 2021. Political Economy of Peer Production. In O.N. Mathieu, P. Christian and T. Sophie, eds. *The Handbook of Peer Production*. Hoboken, NJ: Wiley-Blackwell, pp 33–43.

Blum, A., 2019. *Tubes: A Journey to the Center of the Internet*, New York, NY: Ecco, an imprint of HarperCollins Publishers.

BOAI, 2022. Budapest Open Access Initiative. Available at: https://www.budapestopenaccessinitiative.org/ [Accessed 1 April 2022].

Boggs, C., 1977. Marxism, prefigurative communism, and the problem of workers' control. *Radical America*, 11(6), pp 99–122.

Bollier, D., 2015. Bologna, a laboratory for Urban Commoning. David Bollier news and perspectives on the commons. Available at: http://www.bollier.org/blog/bologna-laboratory-urban-commoning [Accessed 9 April 2022].

Bollier, D., 2017. *Think Like a Commoner: A Short Introduction to the Life of the Commons*, Gabriola Island, BC: New Society Publishers.

Bollier, D. and Conaty, P., 2016. Democratic Money and Capital for the Commons. The Heinrich-Böll-Stiftung. Available at: https://www.boell.de/sites/default/files/democratic_money_capital_for_the_commons_report_january2016.pdf [Accessed 7 April 2022].

Bollier, D. and Helfrich, S., 2015. *Patterns of Commoning*, Amherst, MA: Levellers Press.

Bollier, D. and Helfrich, S., 2019. *Free, Fair, and Alive the Insurgent Power of the Commons*, Gabriola Island, BC: New Society Publishers.

Bolloten, B., 1991. *The Spanish Civil War: Revolution and Counterrevolution*, Chapel Hill, NC: The University of North Carolina Press.

Bongiovanni, J. and Switzer, H., 2021. Public banking on the PBI model: Why not? Alliance For Just Money. Available at: https://www.monetaryalliance.org/public-banking-on-the-pbi-model-why-not/ [Accessed 8 April 2022].

Bookchin, M., 1991. Libertarian municipalism: An overview. *Green Perspectives*, (24). Available at: http://dwardmac.pitzer.edu/Anarchist_Archives/bookchin/gp/perspectives24.html [Accessed 9 April 2022].

Bookchin, M. and Vanek, D., 2001. Murray Bookchin interview. *Harbringer*, 2(1). Available at: https://social-ecology.org/wp/2001/10/harbinger-vol-2-no-1-%E2%80%94-murray-bookchin-interview/ [Accessed 9 April 2022].

Bowyer, A. and Olliver, V.O., 2016. The official history of the reprap project. *All3DP*. Available at: https://all3dp.com/history-of-the-reprap-project/ [Accessed 3 April 2022].

Bozuwa, J., 2018. Public ownership for Energy Democracy. *The Democracy Collaborative*. Available at: https://democracycollaborative.org/learn/publication/public-ownership-energy-democracy [Accessed 2 April 2022].

Brand, S. ed., 1985. Keep designing. *Whole Earth Review*, pp 44–55.

Brastaviceanu, T., 2016. Open value networks. *Open*. Available at: https://open.coop/2016/06/15/open-value-networks/ [Accessed 1 April 2022].

Brastaviceanu, T. and Bergeron, F., 2015. Sensorica Business Plan 3.0.

Bregman, R., 2016. Nixon's basic income plan. *Jacobin Magazine*. Available at: https://www.jacobinmag.com/2016/05/richard-nixon-ubi-basic-income-welfare/ [Accessed 8 April 2022].

Brenner, R., 2006. *The Economics of Global Turbulence: The Advanced Capitalist Economies From Long Boom to Long Downturn, 1945–2005*, London: Verso.

Brock, A., 2016. Beyond blockchain: Simple scalable cryptocurrencies. *Medium*. Available at: https://medium.com/holochain/beyond-blockchain-simple-scalable-cryptocurrencies-1eb7aebac6ae [Accessed 28 June 2022].

Brock, A., 2018. Building responsible cryptocurrencies. *Medium*. Available at: https://medium.com/h-o-l-o/building-responsible-cryptocurrencies-d45d7d2173ed [Accessed 8 April 2022].

Brock, A., 2021. Holochain. *Holochain – P2PWiki*. Available at: https://wiki.p2pfoundation.net/Holochain [Accessed 3 April 2022].

Broumas, A., 2020. *Intellectual Commons and the Law: A Normative Theory for Commons-Based Peer Production*, London: University of Westminster Press.

Brown, D., 2021. Crypto tax: 'Miamicoin' has made the city $7 million so far, a potential game-changer for revenue collection. *The Washington Post*. Available at: https://www.washingtonpost.com/technology/2021/09/30/crypto-miamicoin/ [Accessed 8 April 2022].

Burke, M.J. and Stephens, J.C., 2018. Political Power and Renewable Energy Futures: A critical review. *Energy Research & Social Science*, 35, pp 78–93.

Caffentzis, G., 2010. The future of 'the commons': Neoliberalism's 'plan B' or the original disaccumulation of capital? *New Formations*, 69(69), pp 23–41.

Caffentzis, G. and Federici, S., 2014. Commons against and beyond capitalism. *Community Development Journal*, 49(1), pp 92–105.

Cammaerts, B., 2015. Pirates on the liquid shores of liberal democracy: Movement frames of European pirate parties. *Javnost – The Public*, 22(1), pp19–36.

Carlsson, L.G. and Sandström, A.C., 2007. Network governance of the commons. *International Journal of the Commons*, 2(1), pp 33–54.

Carroll, W.K., 2010. Crisis, movement, counter-hegemony. *Interface*, 2(2), pp 168–198.

REFERENCES

Carson, K., 2009a. Cost-plus markup and mandatory overhead. *Center for a Stateless Society*. Available at: https://c4ss.org/content/253 [Accessed 6 April 2022].

Carson, K., 2009b. Industrial policy: New wine in old bottles. *Center for a Stateless Society*. Available at: https://c4ss.org/content/23567 [Accessed 4 April 2022].

Carson, K., 2010. *The Homebrew Industrial Revolution: A Low-Overhead Manifesto*, Charleston, SC: BookSurge.

Castle, S., 2020. Boulder ends 10-year municipalization effort as voters OK historic deal with Xcel. *Boulder Beat*. Available at: https://boulderbeat.news/2020/11/04/boulder-xcel-franchise-muni-history/ [Accessed 3 April 2022].

CBO, 2020. The 2020 long-term budget outlook. Congressional Budget Office. Available at: https://www.cbo.gov/system/files/2020-09/56516-LTBO.pdf [Accessed 8 April 2022].

Chandler, D.L., 2016. 3 questions: Neil Gershenfeld and the spread of Fab Labs. *MIT News*. Available at: https://news.mit.edu/2016/3-questions-neil-gershenfeld-fab-labs-0104 [Accessed 3 April 2022].

Chapman, J., 2015. *Emotionally Durable Design: Objects, Experiences and Empathy*, London: Routledge.

Chaves, F., 2021. How to embrace open source in design. Awkbit. Available at: https://www.awkbit.com/en/blog/how-embrace-open-source-design [Accessed 1 April 2022].

Cheney, G., Santa Cruz, I., Peredo, A.M., Nazareno, E., 2014. Worker cooperatives as an organizational alternative: Challenges, achievements and promise in business governance and ownership. *Organization*, 21(5), pp 591–603.

Chomsky, N., 2006. *Failed States: The Abuse of Power and the Assault on Democracy*, New York, NY: Metropolitan Books/Henry Holt.

Choulet, C., 2016. German Sparkassen: A model to follow? BNP Paribas. Available at: https://economic-research.bnpparibas.com/html/en-US/German-Sparkassen-model-follow-4/29/2016,28761 [Accessed 5 July 2022].

Circles, 2020. Whitepaper: Circles UBI: Handbook. *Circles Handbook*. Available at: https://handbook.joincircles.net/docs/developers/whitepaper/ [Accessed 8 April 2022].

CIRP, 2021. Commissioner selection process. Colorado Independent Redistricting Commissions. Available at: https://redistricting.colorado.gov/content/commissioner-selection-process [Accessed 9 April 2022].

Claeys, G., Demertzis, M. and Efstathiou, K., 2018. Crypto currencies and monetary policy. Euro Parliament. Available at: https://www.europarl.europa.eu/cmsdata/150000/BRUEGEL_FINAL%20publication.pdf [Accessed 8 April 2022].

Cohen, J., 2021. 4 companies control 67% of the world's cloud infrastructure. *PCMAG*. Available at: https://www.pcmag.com/news/four-companies-control-67-of-the-worlds-cloud-infrastructure [Accessed 28 June 2022].

Cohen, N., 2021b. Wikipedia is finally asking Big Tech to pay up. *WIRED*. Available at: https://www.wired.com/story/wikipedia-finally-asking-big-tech-to-pay-up/ [Accessed 13 April 2022].

Collins, R., 2019. *The Credential Society: An Historical Sociology of Education and stratification*, New York, NY: Columbia University Press.

Commons Transition, 2014. FLOK Society. *Commons Transition*. Available at: https://commonstransition.org/flok-society/ [Accessed 7 April 2022].

Corcoran, H. and Wilson, D., 2010. The Worker Co-operative Movements in Italy, Mondragon and France: Context, Success Factors, and Lessons. *Community-Wealth*. Available at: https://community-wealth.org/sites/clone.community-wealth.org/files/downloads/paper-corcoran-wilson.pdf [Accessed 3 April 2022].

Cornell, A., 2016. *Unruly Equality: US Anarchism in the 20th Century*, Berkeley, CA: University of California Press.

Couldry, N. and Mejias, U.A., 2019. *The Costs of Connection: How Data is Colonizing Human Life and Appropriating it for Capitalism*, Stanford, CA: Stanford University Press.

Coxworth, B., 2018. LSEV claimed to be world's first mass-producible 3D-printed electric car. *New Atlas*. Available at: https://newatlas.com/lsev-3d-printed-car/53897/ [Accessed 4 April 2022].

CSE, 2022. How much does a typical residential solar electric system cost? *Center for Sustainable Energy*. Available at: https://sites.energycenter.org/solar/homeowners/cost [Accessed 23 June 2022].

CUNA, 2021. The state of small credit unions today. Ohio Credit Unions. Available at: https://ohiocreditunions.org/wp-content/uploads/2021/08/State-of-Small-credit-unions.pdf [Accessed 8 April 2022].

CUToday, 2019. Total CU membership rises to 36.2% of U.S. population. *CUToday*. Available at: https://www.cutoday.info/Fresh-Today/Total-CU-Membership-Rises-to-36.2-of-U.S.-Population [Accessed 8 April 2022].

Dafermos, G., 2012. Authority in peer production: The emergence of governance in the FreeBSD Project. *Journal of Peer Production*, (1). Available at: http://peerproduction.net/issues/issue-1/peer-reviewed-papers/authority-in-peer-production/ [Accessed 1 May 2022].

Daly, H., 2019. A journey of no return, not a circular economy. Steady State Herald. Available at: https://steadystate.org/a-journey-of-no-return-not-a-circular-economy/ [Accessed 16 April 2022].

Dardot, P. and Laval, C., 2014. *Commun: Essai sur la Révolution au XXIe Siècle*, Paris: La Découverte.

Davies, J., 2016. Uh-oh: AD blocking forecast to cost $35 billion by 2020. Digiday. Available at: https://digiday.com/media/uh-oh-ad-blocking-forecast-cost-35-billion-2020/ [Accessed 2 April 2022].

Dawson, C., 2014. Shale Boom helps North Dakota Bank earn returns Goldman would envy. *The Wall Street Journal*. Available at: ahttps://www.wsj.com/articles/shale-boom-helps-north-dakota-bank-earn-returns-goldman-would-envy-1416180862 [Accessed 8 April 2022].

De Angelis, M., 2007. *The Beginning of History: Value Struggles and Global Capital*, London: Pluto Press.

De Angelis, M., 2010. The production of commons and the 'explosion' of the middle class. *Antipode*, 42(4), pp 954–977.

De Angelis, M., 2012. Crises, movements, and commons. *borderlands*, 11(2). Available at: https://webarchive.nla.gov.au/awa/20130514051053/http://www.borderlands.net.au/vol11no2_2012/deangelis_crises.htm [Accessed 30 April 2022].

De Angelis, M., 2017a. Grounding social revolution: Elements for a systems theory of commoning. In G. Ruivenkamp and A. Hilton, eds. *Perspectives on Commoning: Autonomist Principles and Practices*, London: Zed Books, pp 213–256.

De Angelis, M., 2017b. *Omnia Sunt Communia: On the Commons and the Transformation to Postcapitalism*, London: Zed books.

de Graaf, F., 2017. Smart Integrated Decentralised Energy (side) systems. Metabolic. Available at: https://www.metabolic.nl/publications/side-systems-pdf/ [Accessed 2 April 2022].

De Moor, T., 2008. The silent revolution: A new perspective on the emergence of Commons, guilds, and other forms of corporate collective action in Western Europe. *International Review of Social History*, 53(S16), pp 179–212.

Deleuze, G. and Guattari, F., 1987. *A Thousand Plateaus: Capitalism and Schizophrenia*, Minneapolis, MN: University of Minnesota Press.

Deng, Y.Y., Haigh, M., Pouwels, W., Ramaekers, L., Brandsma, R., Schimschar, S., et al, 2015. Quantifying a realistic, worldwide wind and solar electricity supply. *Global Environmental Change*, 31, pp 239–252.

Densmore, O., nd. Open source research, a quiet revolution. *Backspaces*. Available at: https://backspaces.net/research/opensource/OpenSourceResearch.html [Accessed 4 July 2022].

DGRV, 2020. Energy Cooperatives in Germany State of the Sector 2020 Report. DGRV. Available at: https://www.dgrv.de/wp-content/uploads/2020/07/20200708_State-of-the-sector-2020.pdf [Accessed 2 April 2022].

Di Mento, M., 2019. Foundation assets top $1 trillion, but signs point to slump. *Foundation Financial Research*. Available at: https://foundationfinancialresearch.com/Foundation%20Assets%20Top%20One%20Trillion%20Dollars.pdf [Accessed 7 April 2022].

Dobusch, L., 2020. German public broadcaster ZDF releases dozens of videos under CC Licenses. Creative Commons. Available at: https://creativecommons.org/2020/06/16/german-public-broadcaster-zdf-releases-dozens-of-videos-under-cc-licenses/ [Accessed 1 April 2022].

Duarte, M.E., 2017. *Network Sovereignty: Building the Internet Across Indian Country*, Seattle, WA: University of Washington.

Durden, T., 2020. The soaring value of intangible assets in the S&P 500. ZeroHedge. Available at: https://www.zerohedge.com/markets/soaring-value-intangible-assets-sp-500 [Accessed 31 March 2022].

Dyer-Witheford, N., 1999. *Cyber-Marx: Cycles and Circuits of Struggle in High-Technology Capitalism*, Urbana, IL: University of Illinois Press.

Dyer-Witheford, N., 2012. The circulation of the common. Global Project. Available at: https://www.globalproject.info/it/in_movimento/nick-dyer-witheford-the-circulation-of-the-common/4797 [Accessed 1 May 2022].

Dyer-Witheford, N., 2013. Red plenty platforms. *Culture Machine*, 14, 1–27. Available at: https://culturemachine.net/wp-content/uploads/2019/05/511-1153-1-PB.pdf [Accessed 4 April 2022].

Dyer-Witheford, N., 2015. *Cyber-Proletariat: Global Labour in the Digital Vortex*, London: Pluto Press.

Dykstra, G., 2012. Pragmatism on the prairie. *The New York Times*. Available at: https://www.nytimes.com/2012/03/31/opinion/pragmatism-on-the-prairie.html [Accessed 4 April 2022].

EC, 2019. Market brief organic farming in the EU. EU Agricultural Markets Briefs. Available at: https://ec.europa.eu/info/sites/default/files/food-farming-fisheries/farming/documents/market-brief-organic-farming-in-the-eu_mar2019_en.pdf [Accessed 6 April 2022].

Edelman, M., Weis, T., Baviskar, A., Borras Jr, S.M., Holt-Giménez, E., Kandiyoti, D., et al, 2014. Introduction: Critical perspectives on food sovereignty. *The Journal of Peasant Studies*, 41(6), pp 911–931.

Engels, F., 2000. *Engels to Franz Mehring, Marx-Engels Correspondence 1893*. Marxists.org. Available at: https://www.marxists.org/archive/marx/works/1893/letters/93_07_14.htm [Accessed 14 May 2022].

Enspiral, 2021. Home. Enspiral. Available at: https://www.enspiral.com/ [Accessed 5 July 2022].

Esposito, R., 2013. *Terms of the Political Community, Immunity, Biopolitics*, New York, NY: Fordham University Press.

Fair Representation Act, 2021. H.R.3863, 117th Cong. Available at: https://www.congress.gov/bill/117th-congress/house-bill/3863/text [Accessed 11 May 2022].

FairCoin, 2018. FairCoin 2: Revision of one of the most promising cryptocurrencies. *fair-coin*. Available at: https://fair-coin.org/en/faircoin-2-revision-one-most-promising-cryptocurrencies [Accessed 8 April 2022].

Fairphone, 2021. Longevity. Available at: https://www.fairphone.com/en/impact/long-lasting-design/ [Accessed 6 April 2022].

FairShares, 2017. Home. FairShares. Available at: http://www.fairshares.coop/ [Accessed 1 April 2022].

Fama, M., Fumagalli, A. and Lucarelli, S., 2019. Cryptocurrencies, monetary policy, and new forms of monetary sovereignty. *International Journal of Political Economy*, 48(2), pp 174–194.

Farm Hack, 2016. Get started. Farmhack.org. Available at: https://farmhack.org/wiki/getting-started [Accessed 6 April 2022].

Federici, S., 2012. Feminism and the politics of the commons. In D. Bollier and S. Helfrich, eds. *The Wealth of the Commons: A World Beyond Market and State*, Amherst, MA: Levellers Press, pp 45–54.

Federici, S., 2019. *Re-enchanting the World: Feminism and the Politics of the Commons*. Oakland, CA: PM Press.

Fehling, M., Nelson, B.D. and Venkatapuram, S., 2013. Limitations of the millennium development goals: A literature review. *Global Public Health*, 8(10), pp 1109–1122.

Feldman, D., Ramasamy, V., Ran, F., Ramdas, A., Desai, J., Margolis, R., 2021. U.S. Solar Photovoltaic System and Energy Storage Cost Benchmark: Q1 2020. *NREL*. Available at: https://www.nrel.gov/docs/fy21osti/78882.pdf [Accessed 2 April 2022].

Fennell, L.A., 2011. Ostrom's law: Property rights in the Commons. *International Journal of the Commons*, 5(1), pp 9–27.

Ffwd, 2022. Tech nonprofits, accelerated exclusively by fast forward. Fast Forward. Available at: https://www.ffwd.org/about/ [Accessed 1 April 2022].

Firat, B.Ö., 2020. Global movement cycles and commoning movements. *Commons*. Available at: https://commons.sehak.org/2018/12/07/global-movement-cycles-and-commoning-movements-begum-ozden-firat/ [Accessed 9 April 2022].

Fisher, M., 2009. *Capitalist Realism: Is There No Alternative*, Winchester: O Books.

Flynn, C. and Yamasumi, E., 2021. *Peoples' Climate Vote*, Oxford: University of Oxford. Available at: file:///C:/Users/hgerhard/Downloads/UNDP-Oxford-Peoples-Climate-Vote-Results.pdf [Accessed 6 April 2022].

Foster, J.B., Clark, B. and York, R., 2010. Capitalism and the curse of energy efficiency: The return of the Jevons paradox. *Monthly Review*, 62(6). Available at: https://monthlyreview.org/2010/11/01/capitalism-and-the-curse-of-energy-efficiency/ [Accessed 6 April 2022].

Foucault, M., 1980. *Power/Knowledge: Selected Interviews and Other Writings*, Brighton: The Harvester Press.

Franzoni, C., Poetz, M. and Sauermann, H., 2021. Crowds, citizens, and science: A multi-dimensional framework and agenda for future research. *Industry and Innovation*, 29(2), pp 251–284.

Frey, B.S., 1994. Direct democracy: Politico-economic lessons from Swiss experience. *The American Economic Review*, 84(2), pp 338–342.

Friedman, T.L., 2005. *The World Is Flat: A Brief History of the Twenty-First Century*, New York, NY: Farrar, Straus and Giroux.

Fritsch, F., Emmet, J., Friedman, E., Kranjc, R., Manski, S., Zargham, M., et al, 2021. Challenges and approaches to scaling the Global Commons. *Frontiers in Blockchain*, 4. Available at: https://www.frontiersin.org/articles/10.3389/fbloc.2021.578721/full [Accessed 8 April 2022].

Garrigues, L.G., 2019. Why Costa Rica tops the happiness index. *YES! Magazine*. Available at: https://www.yesmagazine.org/issue/climate-action/2019/01/31/why-costa-rica-tops-the-happiness-index [Accessed 19 April 2022].

Garrod, J.Z., 2016. The real world of the decentralized autonomous society. *tripleC*, 14(1), pp 62–77.

Gaspar, V., Medas, P. and Perrelli, R., 2022. Global debt reaches a record $226 trillion. *IMF Blog*. Available at: https://blogs.imf.org/2021/12/15/global-debt-reaches-a-record-226-trillion/ [Accessed 8 April 2022].

Genter, J.T., 2022. How airlines make billions from monetizing frequent flyer programs. *Forbes Magazine*. Available at: https://www.forbes.com/sites/advisor/2020/07/15/how-airlines-make-billions-from-monetizing-frequent-flyer-programs/ (Accessed 4 April 2022).

Gerhardt, H., 2019. Engaging the non-flat world: Anarchism and the promise of a post-capitalist Collaborative Commons. *Antipode*, 52(3), pp 681–701.

Gerhardt, H., 2020. Blockchains: Building blocks of a post-capitalist future? *ROAR Magazine*. Available at: https://roarmag.org/essays/blockchains-post-capitalism/ [Accessed 6 April 2022].

Gershenfeld, N., 2012. How to make almost anything: The digital fabrication revolution. *Foreign Affairs*, 91(6), pp 42–57.

Gibson-Graham, J.K., 2003. Enabling ethical economies: Cooperativism and class. *Critical Sociology*, 29(2), pp 123–161.

Gibson-Graham, J.K., 2010. *The End of Capitalism (As We Knew It): A Feminist Critique of Political Economy*, Minneapolis, MN: University of Minnesota Press.

Giotitsas, C., 2019. *Open Source Agriculture: Grassroots Technology in the Digital Era*, Basingstoke: Palgrave Macmillan.

Giotitsas, C., Nardelli, P.H.J., Kostakis, V., Narayanan, A., 2020. From private to public governance: The case for reconfiguring energy systems as a Commons. *Energy Research & Social Science*, 70. Available at: https://www.sciencedirect.com/journal/energy-research-and-social-science/vol/70/suppl/C [Accessed 2 April 2022].

GNU, 2021. What is free software? GNU Operating System. Available at: https://www.gnu.org/philosophy/free-sw.en.html [Accessed 1 April 2022].

Gordon, C., 2021. We don't have to keep shoveling money to Big Ag. *Jacobin*. Available at: https://jacobin.com/2021/01/big-ag-farm-subsidies-agriculture/ [Accessed 17 November 2022].

Gorz A., 2010. *The Immaterial: Knowledge, Value and Capital*, London: Seagull Books.

Graeber, D., 2011. *Debt: The First 5,000 Years*, New York, NY: Melville House.

Graeber, D., 2019. *Bullshit Jobs: A Theory*, London: Penguin Books.

Gramsci, A., 2011. *Prison Notebooks*, New York, NY: Columbia University Press.

Graziano, V. and Trogal, K., 2019. Repair matters. *ephemera*, 19(2), pp 203–227.

Grimley, M., 2020. Just how Democratic are rural electric cooperatives? *Institute for Local Self-Reliance*. Available at: https://ilsr.org/just-how-democratic-are-rural-electric-cooperatives/ [Accessed 3 April 2022].

Gritzas, G. and Kavoulakos, K.I., 2016. Diverse economies and alternative spaces: An overview of approaches and practices. *European Urban and Regional Studies*, 23(4), pp 917–934.

Gurumurthy, A. and Chami, N., 2020. Data governance and the new frontiers of resistance. *ROAR*. Available at: https://roarmag.org/essays/intelligent-corporation-platform-capitalism/ [Accessed 1 April 2022].

Gutberlet, J., ed., 2019. *Urban Recycling Cooperatives: Building Resilient Communities*, London: Routledge.

Hagel, J., Brown, J.S., Kulasooriya, D., Giffi, C., Chen, M., 2015. The future of manufacturing. Deloitte Insights. Available at: https://www2.deloitte.com/content/dam/Deloitte/za/Documents/manufacturing/ZA_Future_of_Manufacturing_2015.pdf [Accessed 4 April 2022].

Hardt, M., 2010. The common in communism. *Rethinking Marxism*, 22(3), pp 346–356.

Hardt, M. and Negri, A., 2001. *Empire*, Cambridge, MA: Harvard University Press.

Hardt, M. and Negri, A., 2005. *Multitude: War and Democracy in the Age of Empire*, New York, NY: The Penguin Press.

Hardt, M. and Negri, A., 2009. *Commonwealth*, Cambridge, MA: Harvard University Press.

Hardt, M. and Negri, A., 2012. *Declaration*, New York, NY: Argo-Navis.

Hardt, M. and Negri, A., 2017. *Assembly*, Oxford: Oxford University Press.

Harvey, D., 2005. *A Brief History of Neoliberalism*, Oxford: Oxford University Press.

Harvey, D., 2006. Neo-liberalism as creative destruction. *Geografiska Annaler: Series B, Human Geography*, 88(2), pp 145–158.

Harvey, D., 2013. *The New Imperialism*, Oxford: Oxford University Press.

Harvey, D., 2015. *Seventeen Contradictions and the End of Capitalism*, Oxford: Oxford University Press.

Hawken, P., 2021. Reduced food waste. *Project Drawdown*. Available at: https://www.drawdown.org/solutions/reduced-food-waste [Accessed 6 April 2022].

Healy, S., Borowiak, C., Pavloskaya, M., Safri, M., 2021. Commoning and the politics of solidarity: Transformational responses to poverty. *Geoforum*, 127, pp 306–315.

Hechler-Fayd'herbe, N., 2021. Global Wealth Report. Credit Suisse. Available at: https://www.credit-suisse.com/about-us/en/reports-research/global-wealth-report.html [Accessed 19 April 2022].

Hill, B.M. and Monroy-Hernández, A., 2012. The remixing dilemma: The trade-off between generativity and originality. *American Behavioral Scientist*, 57(5), pp 643–663.

Hill, K., 2021. I cut the 'big five' tech giants from my life and it was hell. *Gizmodo Australia*. Available at: https://www.gizmodo.com.au/2021/06/i-cut-the-big-five-tech-giants-from-my-life-it-was-hell/ [Accessed 1 April 2022].

Hirsch, J. and Hsu, T., 2014. Elon Musk opens up Tesla patents to everyone. *Los Angeles Times*. Available at: https://www.latimes.com/business/autos/la-fi-tesla-open-source-20140613-story.html [Accessed 1 April 2022].

Holloway, J., 2010. Cracks and the crisis of labor. *Antipode*, 42(4), pp 909–923.

Holloway, J., 2012. *Crack Capitalism*, London: Sage.

Holloway, J., 2019. *Change the World Without Taking Power: The Meaning of Revolution Today*, London: Pluto Press.

Holmberg, S.R. and Mitchell, S., 2020. Why the left should ally with small business. *The Nation*. Available at: https://www.thenation.com/article/society/democrats-labor-business-monopoly/ [Accessed 9 April 2022].

Holtz-Eakin, D., Bosch, D., Gitis, B., Goldbeck, D., Rossetti, P., 2021. The green new deal: scope, scale, and implications. American Energy Forum. Available at: https://www.americanenergyforum.org/post/the-green-new-deal-scope-scale-and-implications [Accessed 8 April 2022].

Hoskins, S.M., 2011. Consumer bankruptcy and household debt. Congressional Research Service. Available at: https://crsreports.congress.gov/product/pdf/RS/RS20777/38 [Accessed 8 April 2022].

Howell, C. and West, D.M., 2022. The internet as a human right. Brookings. Available at: https://www.brookings.edu/blog/techtank/2016/11/07/the-internet-as-a-human-right/ [Accessed 3 April 2022].

Huber, J., 2014. Modern money theory and new currency theory: A comparative discussion. *Real-World Economics Review*, (66), pp 38–57. Available at: http://www.paecon.net/PAEReview/issue66/whole66.pdf [Accessed 8 April 2022].

Huber, J., 2017. *Sovereign Money: Beyond Reserve Banking*, Basingstoke: Palgrave Macmillan.

Hyde, L., 2012. *Common as Air: Revolution, Art, and Ownership*, London: Union.

ICA, 2018. Cooperative identity, values and principles. *International Cooperative Alliance*. Available at: https://www.ica.coop/en/cooperatives/cooperative-identity [Accessed 21 June 2022].

IEA, 2022. The role of critical minerals in clean energy transitions. *IEA*. Available at: https://energycentral.com/system/files/ece/nodes/481551/theroleofcriticalmineralsincleanenergytransitions.pdf [Accessed 6 April 2022].

IMF, 2021. Household debt, loans and debt securities. *International Monetary Fund*. Available at: https://www.imf.org/external/datamapper/HH_LS@GDD/SWE [Accessed 8 April 2022].

Irfan, U., 2012. Edison's revenge: Will direct current make a comeback in the U.S.? *Scientific American*. Available at: https://www.scientificamerican.com/article/edisons-revenge-will-direct-current-make-a-comeback-in-us/ [Accessed 2 April 2022].

IS, 2021. Mission. *Internet Society*. Available at: https://www.internetsociety.org/mission/ [Accessed 3 April 2022].

ITF, 2015. The carbon footprint of global trade. International Transport Forum. Available at: https://www.itf-oecd.org/sites/default/files/docs/cop-pdf-06.pdf [Accessed 5 April 2022].

ITU, 2021. Internet use. International Telecommunication Union. Available at: https://www.itu.int/itu-d/reports/statistics/2021/11/15/internet-use/ [Accessed 3 April 2022].

IUPUI, 2018. Giving USA 2018: The Annual Report on Philanthropy for the Year 2017, Chicago, IL: Giving USA Foundation.

Jackson, T., 2017. *Prosperity Without Growth: Foundations for the Economy of Tomorrow*, London: Routledge.

Jameson, F., 1996. *The Seeds of Time*, New York, NY: Columbia University Press.

Jiménez, A., 2020. The silicon doctrine. *tripleC*, 18(1), pp 322–336.

Jones, J.M. and Saad, L., 2019. U.S. support for more government inches up, but not for socialism. *Gallup*. Available at: https://news.gallup.com/poll/268295/support-government-inches-not-socialism.aspx [Accessed 20 May 2022].

Kalischer-Coggins, A., 2021. How Detroit residents are building their own internet. *The Hill*. Available at: https://thehill.com/changing-america/video/555961-how-detroit-residents-are-building-their-own-internet [Accessed 3 April 2022].

Kavlak, G., McNerney, J. and Trancik, J.E., 2018. Evaluating the causes of cost reduction in photovoltaic modules. *Energy Policy*, 123, pp 700–710.

Keen, A., 2015. *The Internet is Not the Answer: Why the Internet has been an Economic, Political and Cultural Disaster – And How It can be Transformed*, London: Atlantic Books.

Kelly, G. and Massena, S., 2009. Mondragón worker-cooperatives decide how to ride out a downturn. *YES! Magazine*. Available at: https://www.yesmagazine.org/issue/new-economy/2009/06/06/mondragon-worker-cooperatives-decide-how-to-ride-out-a-downturn [Accessed 4 April 2022].

Kelton, S., 2021. *The Deficit Myth: Modern Monetary Theory and the Birth of the People's Economy*, New York, NY: Hatchette Book Group.

Kennedy, M.I. and Kennedy, D., 1995. *Interest and Inflation Free Money: Creating an Exchange Medium that Works for Everybody and Protects the Earth*, Philadelphia, PA: New Society Publishers.

Keynes, J.M., 1973. *Essays in Persuasion*. London: Macmillan.

Kioupkiolis, A., 2017. Common democracy: Political representation beyond representative democracy. *Democratic Theory*, 4(1), pp 35–58.

Kioupkiolis, A., 2020a. *Common and Counter-hegemonic Politics: Re-thinking Social Change*, Edinburgh: Edinburgh University Press.

Kioupkiolis, A., 2020b. Heteropolitics: Refiguring the Common and the Political. Report 1. Heteropolitics. Available at: http://heteropolitics.net/ [Accessed 9 April 2022].

Kioupkiolis, A., 2020c. Heteropolitics: Refiguring the Common and the Political. Report 2. Heteropolitics. Available at: http://heteropolitics.net/ [Accessed 9 May 2022].

Kioupkiolis, A., 2021. Digital commons, the political and social change: Towards an integrated strategy of counter-hegemony furthering the commons. *ephemera*. Available at: https://ephemerajournal.org/contribution/digital-commons-political-and-social-change-towards-integrated-strategy-counter [Accessed 27 February 2023].

Kiva, 2016. About us. *Kiva*. Available at: https://www.kiva.org/about [Accessed 8 April 2022].

Kleiner, D., 2010. *The Telekommunist Manifesto*, Amsterdam: Institute of Network Cultures.

Kleiner, D., 2016. What economy? Profit versus sustainability (II). RedefineSchool.com. Available at: https://redefineschool.com/dmytri-kleiner/ [Accessed 31 March 2022].

Kobie, N., 2019. The complicated truth about China's Social Credit System. *WIRED UK*. Available at: https://www.wired.co.uk/article/china-social-credit-system-explained [Accessed 2 April 2022].

Koebler, J., 2016. The city that was saved by the internet. *VICE*. Available at: https://www.vice.com/en/article/ezpk77/chattanooga-gigabit-fiber-network [Accessed 28 June 2022].

Koivusalo, A. and Mansour, M., 2018. Comparison of performance between social and conventional banks. Umea. Available at: https://www.diva-portal.org/smash/get/diva2:1229140/FULLTEXT01.pdf [Accessed 2 July 2022].

König, T., Duran, E., Fessler, N. and Alton, R., 2018. The proof-of-cooperation blockchain FairCoin. FairCoin. Available at: https://fair-coin.org/sites/default/files/FairCoin2_whitepaper_V1.2.pdf [Accessed 17 April 2022].

Korinek, A. and Stiglitz, J.E., 2021. Covid-19 driven advances in automation and artificial intelligence risk exacerbating economic inequality. *BMJ*. Available at: https://pubmed.ncbi.nlm.nih.gov/33722806/ [Accessed 8 April 2022].

Kostakis, V. and Bauwens, M., 2019. How to create a thriving Global Commons economy. TheNextSystem.org. Available at: https://thenextsystem.org/learn/stories/how-create-thriving-global-commons-economy [Accessed 1 April 2022].

Kostakis, V. and Bauwens, M., 2014. *Network Society and Future Scenarios for a Collaborative Economy*, New York, NY: Palgrave Macmillan.

Kostakis, V. and Pantazis, A., 2021. Is 'deschooling society' possible? Notes from the field. *Postdigital Science and Education*, 3(3), pp 686–692.

Kostakis, V., Latoufis, K., Liarokapis, M., Bauwens, M., 2018. The convergence of digital commons with local manufacturing from a degrowth perspective: Two illustrative cases. *Journal of Cleaner Production*, 197, pp 1684–1693.

Kostakis, V., Niaros, V., Dafermos., G., Bauwens, M., 2015. Design global, manufacture local: Exploring the contours of an emerging productive model. *Futures*, 73, pp 126–135.

Kreiss, D., Finn, M. and Turner, F., 2010. The limits of peer production: Some reminders from Max Weber for the Network Society. *New Media & Society*, 13(2), pp 243–259.

Krook, J. and Baas, L., 2013. Getting serious about mining the technosphere: A review of recent landfill mining and urban mining research. *Journal of Cleaner Production*, 55, pp 1–9.

Kropotkin, P., 1975. The spirit of revolt. In E. Capouya and K. Tompkins, eds. *The Essential Kropotkin*. London: Macmillan, pp 3–9.

Kropotkin, P., 1995. *Evolution and Environment*, Montreal, QC: Black Rose.

Kropotkin, P., 2022. *Mutual Aid: A Factor of Evolution*, New York, NY: Penguin Classics.

Kucinich, D., 2011. H.R.2990 – 112th congress (2011–2012): National Emergency Employment Defense Act of 2011. Congress.gov. Available at: https://www.congress.gov/bill/112th-congress/house-bill/2990 [Accessed 8 April 2022].

Kuipers, D., 2021. Can farm collectives challenge Big Ag? *The Nation*. Available at: https://www.thenation.com/article/environment/collective-farming-agriculture/ [Accessed 29 June 2022].

Kukura, J., 2021. SF still determined to buy local PG&E grid, demands an appraisal. *SFist*. Available at: https://sfist.com/2021/07/27/sf-still-determined-to-buy-local-pg-e-grid-demands-an-appraisal-so-they-can-bid/ [Accessed 23 June 2022].

Kuneva, M., 2009. Keynote speech: Roundtable on online data collection, targeting, and profiling. European Commission. Available at: https://ec.europa.eu/commission/presscorner/detail/en/SPEECH_09_156 [Accessed 22 June 2022].

Labour, 2019. Manifesto: A Green Industrial Revolution. The Labour Party. Available at: https://labour.org.uk/manifesto-2019/a-green-industrial-revolution/ [Accessed 3 April 2022].

Laclau, E. and Mouffe, C., 2014. *Hegemony and Socialist Strategy: Towards a Radical Democratic Politics*, London: Verso.

Langley, P. and Leyshon, A., 2017. Platform capitalism: The intermediation and capitalization of digital economic circulation. *Finance and Society*, 3(1), pp 11–31.

Larivière, V., Haustein, S. and Mongeon, P., 2015. The oligopoly of academic publishers in the Digital Era. *PLOS ONE*, 10(6). Available at: https://doi.org/10.1371/journal.pone.0127502 [Accessed 1 April 2022].

Latoufis, K., 2014. Reinforcing resilience and self-reliance of communities in degrowth: The case study of the renewable energy workshop of 'Nea Guinea'. Degrowth conference Leipzig 2014. Available at: https://degrowth.community/conference2014/scientific-papers/3509 [Accessed 3 April 2022].

Legg, S., 2011. Assemblage/Apparatus: Using Deleuze and Foucault. *Area*, 43(2), pp 128–133.

Lessig, L., 2004. The creative commons. *Montana Law Review*, 65(1). Available at: https://scholarworks.umt.edu/mlr/vol65/iss1/ [Accessed 1 April 2022].

Lessig, L., 2009. *Remix: Making Art and Commerce Thrive in the Hybrid Economy*, New York, NY: Penguin Books.

Lessig, L., 2019. *They Don't Represent Us: Reclaiming Our Democracy*, New York, NY: Dey Street.

Leung, M., 2018. The cooperative hostile takeover. Grassroots Economic Organizing. Available at: https://geo.coop/story/cooperative-hostile-takeover [Accessed 9 April 2022].

Levy, S., 2010. *Hackers: Heroes of the Computer Revolution*, Sebastopol, CA: O'Reilly.

Lewis, M. and Conaty, P., 2012. *The Resilience Imperative: Cooperative Transitions to a Steady-State Economy*, Gabriola Island, BC: New Society Publishers.

Lewis, S.C. and Usher, N., 2013. Open source and journalism: Toward new frameworks for imagining news innovation. *Media, Culture & Society*, 35(5), pp 602–619.

REFERENCES

Lindsey, B. and Teles, S.M., 2017. *The Captured Economy: How the Powerful Enrich Themselves, Slow Down Growth, and Increase Inequality*, New York, NY: Oxford University Press.

Liotard, I., 2017. FabLab – a new space for commons-based peer production. Available at: https://hal.archives-ouvertes.fr/hal-01555978/document [Accessed 3 April 2022].

Loomio, nd. About. Loomio. Available at: https://www.loomio.com/about/ [Accessed 2 July 2022].

Losey, J. and Meinrath, S.D., 2016. In defense of the digital craftsperson. *Journal of Peer Production*, (9). Available at: http://peerproduction.net/issues/issue-9-alternative-internets/peer-reviewed-papers/in-defense-of-the-digital-craftsperson/ [Accessed 30 April 2022].

Lovink, G. and Rossiter, N., 2018. *Organization after Social Media*, Brooklyn, NY: Autonomedia.

Lowrey, A., 2018. *Give People Money: How Universal Basic Income Could Change the Future*, New York, NY: Crown.

LTA, 2022. Gaining Ground United States. Land Trust Alliance. Available at: https://findalandtrust.org/land-trusts/gaining-ground/united-states [Accessed 26 July 2022].

Lund, A., 2017. A critical political economic framework for peer production. *Journal of Peer Production*, (10). Available at: http://peerproduction.net/editsuite/issues/issue-10-peer-production-and-work/peer-reviewed-papers/a-critical-political-economic-framework-for-peer-productions-relation-to-capitalism/ [Accessed 9 April 2022].

Lund, A. and Venäläinen, J., 2016. Monetary materialities of peer-produced knowledge: The case of Wikipedia and its tensions with paid labour. *tripleC*, 14(1), pp 78–98.

Luxemburg, R., 2011. *Reform or Revolution*, New York, NY: Pathfinder.

Lynch, C.R., 2019. Contesting digital futures: urban politics, alternative economies, and the movement for technological sovereignty in Barcelona. *Antipode*, 52(3), pp 660–680.

Lyon, D., 2019. Surveillance capitalism, surveillance culture and data politics. In D. Bigo, E. Isin and E.S. Ruppert, eds. *Data Politics Worlds, Subjects, Rights*. London: Routledge, pp 64–78.

MacKay, D., 2009. Think big on renewables scale. *The Guardian*. Available at: https://www.theguardian.com/environment/cif-green/2009/apr/29/renewable-energy-david-mackay [Accessed 27 November 2022].

Madsbjerg, S., 2017. It's Time to Tax Companies for Using Our Personal Data. *The New York Times*. Available at: https://www.nytimes.com/2017/11/14/business/dealbook/taxing-companies-for-using-our-personal-data.html [Accessed 2 April 2022].

Magdoff, H. and Sweezy, P.M., 1987. *Stagnation and the Financial Explosion*, New York, NY: Monthly Review Press.

Maine, 2021. Governor Mills urges legislature to further consider consumer owned utility. State of Main Office: Governor Janet T. Mills. Available at: https://www.maine.gov/governor/mills/news/governor-mills-urges-legislature-further-consider-consumer-owned-utility-2021-07-13 [Accessed 23 June 2022].

Marketcap, 2022. Largest companies by market cap. Companies Market Cap. Available at: https://companiesmarketcap.com/ [Accessed 16 May 2022].

Marques, R.C. and da Cruz, N.F., 2018. *Recycling and Extended Producer Responsibility: The European Experience*, London: Routledge.

Marx, K., 1973. *Grundrisse: Foundations of the Critique of Political Economy*, London: Penguin .

Marx, K., 1992. *Capital: A Critique of Political Economy, Vol 1*, New York, NY: Penguin Classics.

Marx, K., 1993. *Capital: A Critique of Political Economy, Vol. 3*, New York, NY: Penguin Classics.

Marx, K. and Engels, F., 1965. *The German Ideology*, London: Lawrence & Wishart.

Mason, P., 2016. *Postcapitalism: A Guide to Our Future*, London: Penguin Books.

Massey, D., 1996. Power-geometry and a progressive sense of place. In J. Bird, B. Curtis, T. Putnam, L. Tickner, eds. *Mapping the Futures: Local cultures, global change*, London: Routledge, pp 59–69.

Mazzucato, M., 2015. *The Entrepreneurial State: Debunking Public vs. Private Sector Myths*, London: Anthem Press.

McDonald, M., nd. Voter turnout data. United States Elections Project. Available at: https://www.electproject.org/election-data/voter-turnout-data [Accessed 11 May 2022].

McLuhan, M., 1964. *Understanding Media*, New York, NY: McGraw-Hill.

Meaker, M., 2022. Europe's Digital Markets Act takes a hammer to big tech. WIRED. Available at: https://www.wired.com/story/digital-markets-act-messaging/ [Accessed 2 April 2022].

Meissner, D., Sarpong, D. and Vonortas, N.S., 2018. Introduction to the special issue on 'Innovation in state owned enterprises: Implications for technology management and industrial development'. *Industry and Innovation*, 26(2), pp 121–126.

Merriman, P., 2018. Molar and molecular mobilities: The politics of perceptible and imperceptible movements. *Environment and Planning D: Society and Space*, 37(1), pp 65–82.

Midnight Notes Collective, 2009. Promissory notes: From crisis to commons. Midnight Notes. Available at: http://www.midnightnotes.org/Promissory%20Notes.pdf [Accessed 9 May 2022].

Milham, M. and Klein, A., 2019. Be the change you seek in science. *BMC Biol*, 17(27). Available at: https://doi.org/10.1186/s12915-019-0647-3 [Accessed 19 June 2022].

Miremadi, M., Musso, C. and Weihe, U., 2018. How much will consumers pay to go green? McKinsey & Company. Available at: https://www.mckinsey.com/business-functions/sustainability/our-insights/how-much-will-consumers-pay-to-go-green [Accessed 6 April 2022].

Mitchell, S. and Knox, R., 2021. Fact sheet: How Amazon exploits and undermines small businesses, and why breaking it up would revive American entrepreneurship. Institute for Local Self-Reliance. Available at: https://ilsr.org/fact-sheet-how-breaking-up-amazon-can-empower-small-business/ [Accessed 22 June 2022].

Morozov, E. and Bria, F., 2018. Rethinking the Smart City: Democratizing Urban Technology. RLS-NYC. Available at: https://rosalux.nyc/rethinking-the-smart-city/ [Accessed 2 April 2022].

Morrison, S., 2021. Google is done with cookies, but that doesn't mean it's … . *Vox*. Available at: https://www.vox.com/recode/2021/3/3/22311460/google-cookie-ban-search-ads-tracking [Accessed 2 April 2022].

Mosse, D., 2005. *Cultivating Development: An Ethnography of Aid Policy and Practice*, London: Pluto Press.

Mouffe, C., 2005. *On the Political*, London: Routledge.

Mouffe, C., 2009. *The Democratic Paradox*, London: Verso.

Mouw, S., 2020. 2020 state of curbside recycling. The Recycling Partnership. Available at: https://recyclingpartnership.org/wp-content/uploads/dlm_uploads/2020/02/2020-State-of-Curbside-Recycling.pdf [Accessed 6 April 2022].

Mulholland, P., 2021. Estonia leads world in making digital voting a reality. *Financial Times*. Available at: https://www.ft.com/content/b4425338-6207-49a0-bbfb-6ae5460fc1c1 [Accessed 9 April 2022].

Muller, A., Schader, C., Scailabba, N.E., Brüggemann, J., Isensee, A., Erb, K., et al, 2017. Strategies for feeding the world more sustainably with Organic Agriculture. *Nature Communications*, 8(1). Available at: https://www.nature.com/articles/s41467-017-01410-w [Accessed 6 April 2022].

Nail, T., 2015. *Returning to Revolution: Deleuze, Guattari and Zapatismo*, Edinburgh: Edinburgh University Press.

NAL, 2021. Community supported agriculture. National Agricultural Library. Available at: https://www.nal.usda.gov/legacy/afsic/community-supported-agriculture [Accessed 6 April 2022].

NCN, 2019. Nonprofit impact matters. Available at: https://www.nonprofitimpactmatters.org/site/assets/files/1/nonprofit-impact-matters-sept-2019-1.pdf [Accessed 7 April 2022].

Neumann, R., 2017. American democracy in distress: The failure of social education. *Journal of Social Science Education*, 16(1), pp 5–16.

NGO, 2022. About us. Energy Cooperative. Available at: https://myenergycoop.com/about/ [Accessed 13 July 2022].

Nield, D., 2021. What is google floc and how does it affect privacy? *howtogeek*. Available at: https://www.howtogeek.com/devops/what-is-google-floc-and-how-does-it-affect-privacy/ [Accessed 22 June 2022].

NRECA, 2021. Electric co-op facts and figures. NRECA America's Electric Cooperatives. Available at: https://www.electric.coop/electric-cooperative-fact-sheet [Accessed 2 April 2022].

Ntoutsi, E., Fafalios, P., Gadiraju, U., G., Losifidis, V., L., Nejdl, W., Vidal, M., et al, 2020. Bias in data-driven artificial intelligence systems—an introductory survey, *WIREs Data Mining and Knowledge Discovery*, 10(3). Available at: https://doi.org/10.1002/widm.1356 [Accessed 13 July 2022].

O'Dwyer, R., 2013. Spectre of the commons: Spectrum regulation in the communism of capital. *Ephemera*, 13(3), pp 497–526.

OECD, 2021. Employment – labour force participation rate – OECD data. OECD. Available at: https://data.oecd.org/emp/labour-force-participation-rate.htm [Accessed 10 April 2022].

OFN, 2022. About Us, Open Food Network. Available at: https://openfoodnetwork.org/about-us/ [Accessed 30 November 2022].

OMD, 2022. Budget of the U.S. Government 2022. White House Office of Management and Budget. Available at: https://www.whitehouse.gov/wp-content/uploads/2021/05/budget_fy22.pdf [Accessed 4 July 2022].

O'Neil, M. and Broca, S., 2021. Peer production and social change. In M. O'Neil, C. Pentzold and S. Toupin, eds. *The Handbook of Peer Production*. Hoboken, NJ: Wiley-Blackwell, pp 285–298.

O'Neil, M., Pentzold, C. and Toupin, S. eds., 2021. *The Handbook of Peer Production*, Hoboken, NJ: Wiley-Blackwell.

Orrock, D., 2011. Pro & con: Do Georgia's electric co-ops need better oversight? AJC. Available at: https://www.ajc.com/news/opinion/pro-con-georgia-electric-ops-need-better-oversight/aXmcgp3p1XCt6YwnJ2o9hM/ [Accessed 23 June 2022].

Orsi, C., 2009. Knowledge-based society, peer production and the common good. *Capital & Class*, 33(1), pp 31–51.

OSDD, 2013. Vision and mission. Open-Source Drug Discovery. Available at: http://www.osdd.net/about-us/vision-mission [Accessed 1 April 2022].

OSE, 2014. Machines: Global village construction set. *Open Source Ecology*. Available at: https://www.opensourceecology.org/gvcs/ [Accessed 1 April 2022].

OSE, 2019. Local Motors. *Open Source Ecology*. Available at: https://wiki.opensourceecology.org/wiki/Local_Motors [Accessed 1 April 2022].

Ostrom, E., 2009. *Understanding Institutional Diversity*, Princeton, NJ: Princeton University Press.

REFERENCES

Ostrom, E., 2015. *Governing the Commons: The Evolution of Institutions for Collective Action*, Cambridge: Cambridge University Press.

P2PF Wiki, 2018. Emilia-Romagna. P2P Wiki. Available at: https://wiki.p2pfoundation.net/Emilia-Romagna [Accessed 4 April 2022].

P2PF Wiki, 2019a. Backfeed. *P2P Wiki*. Available at: http://wiki.p2pfoundation.net/Backfeed [Accessed 3 April 2022].

P2PF Wiki, 2019b. Coopyright. *P2P Wiki*. Available at: https://wiki.p2pfoundation.net/Coopyright [Accessed 1 April 2022].

P2PF Wiki, 2021. FLOK Society Project. *P2P Wiki*. Available at: https://wiki.p2pfoundation.net/FLOK_Society_Project [Accessed 6 April 2022].

Palladino, L., 2017. Employee ownership of Craft Breweries: Great Beer that benefits those who produce it and those who drink it. Jason Wiener. Available at: https://jrwiener.com/employee-ownership-of-craft-breweries-great-beer-that-benefits-those-who-produce-it-and-those-who-drink-it/ [Accessed 10 April 2022].

Papadimitropoulos, V., 2018. Reflections on the contradictions of the commons. *Review of Radical Political Economics*, 50(2), pp 317–331.

Pazaitis, A. and Drechsler, W., 2021. Peer production and state theory: Envisioning a cooperative partner state. In M. O'Neil, C. Pentzold and S. Toupin, eds. *The Handbook of Peer Production*. Hoboken, NJ: Wiley-Blackwell.

Pazaitis, A., De Filippi, P. and Kostakis, V., 2017. Blockchain and value systems in the sharing economy: The illustrative case of backfeed. *Technological Forecasting and Social Change*, 125, pp 105–115.

Peels, J. and Haye, G., 2021. Interview with Greg Haye of local motors about co-creation and 3D printing. 3DPrint.com. Available at: https://3dprint.com/235395/interview-with-greg-haye-of-local-motors-about-co-creation-and-3d-printing/ [Accessed 4 April 2022].

Peet, R., 1975. Inequality and poverty: A Marxist-geographic theory. *Annals of the Association of American Geographers*, 65(4), pp 564–571.

Pentzold, C., 2021. Social norms and rules in peer production. In M. O'Neil, C. Pentzold and S. Toupin, eds. *The Handbook of Peer Production*. Hoboken, NJ: John Wiley & Sons, Inc., pp 44–55.

Pew, 2021. Public trust in government: 1958–2021. *Pew Research Center*. Available at: https://www.pewresearch.org/politics/2021/05/17/public-trust-in-government-1958-2021/ [Accessed 18 May 2022].

Piore, M.J. and Sabel, C.F., 2000. *The Second Industrial Divide: Possibilities for Prosperity*, New York, NY: Basic Books.

Piques, C. and Rizos, X., 2017. *Peer to Peer and the Commons: A Path Towards Transition 2 The Commons Economy in Practice*, Amsterdam: P2P Foundation. Available at: https://welcome-cdn1.p2pfoundation.net/wp-content/uploads/2017/10/Report-P2P-Thermodynamics-VOL_2-web_2.0.pdf [Accessed 28 August 2022].

Pitts, F.H., 2018a. *Critiquing Capitalism Today: New Ways to Read Marx*, New York, NY: Springer.

Pitts, F.H., 2018b. A crisis of measurability: Critiquing post-operaismo on labour, value and the basic income. *Capital and Class*, 42(1), pp 3–21. Available at: https://doi.org/10.1007/978-3-319-62633-8_8.

Plehwe, D., 2017. Neoliberal think tanks and the crisis. In R. Backhouse, B.W. Bateman and T. Nishizawa, eds. *Liberalism and the Welfare State: Economists and Arguments for the Welfare State*, New York, NY: Oxford University Press, pp 192–211.

Preukschat, A. and Reed, D., 2021. *Self-sovereign Identity: Decentralized Digital Identity and Verifiable Credentials*, Shelter Island, NY: Manning.

Proudhon, P.-J., 2011. To patriots. In *Property is Theft!: A Pierre-Joseph Proudhon Anthology*. Edinburgh: AK Press, pp 319–322.

Provost, C. and Kennard, M., 2014. Hamburg at forefront of global drive to reverse privatisation of City Services. *The Guardian*. Available at: https://www.theguardian.com/cities/2014/nov/12/hamburg-global-reverse-privatisation-city-services [Accessed 2 April 2022].

Radu, R., 2019. *Negotiating Internet Governance*, Oxford: Oxford University Press.

Ramos, J.M., 2017. Cosmo-localization and leadership for the future. *Journal of Future Studies*, 21(4), pp 65–84.

Ramos, J.M., 2020. The structural, the post-structural and the commons: new practices for creating change in a complex world. In B. Pease, ed. *Doing Critical Social Work*, New York, NY: Routledge, pp 310–325.

Rancière Jacques, 2016. *Dissensus on Politics and Aesthetics*, London: Bloomsbury Academic.

Rayner, T., 2013. Lines of flight: Deleuze and nomadic creativity. Philosophy for Change. Available at: https://philosophyforchange.wordpress.com/tag/lines-of-flight/ [Accessed 31 March 2022].

Reyes, R.S.M., 2020. *Deleuze and Guattari's Philosophy of 'Becoming-revolutionary'*, Newcastle: Cambridge Scholars Publishing.

Rifkin, J., 2013. *The Third Industrial Revolution: How Lateral Power is Transforming Energy, the Economy, and the World*, New York, NY: Palgrave Macmillan.

Rifkin, J., 2015. *The Zero Marginal Cost Society: The Internet of Things, the Collaborative Commons, and the Eclipse of Capitalism*, New York, NY: St. Martin's Griffin.

Rigi, J., 2014. The coming revolution of peer production and revolutionary cooperatives. A response to Michel Bauwens, Vasilis Kostakis and Stefan Meretz. *tripleC*, 12(1), pp 390–404.

Robinson, F., 2011. *The Ethics of Care: A Feminist Approach to Human Security*, Philadelphia, PA: Temple University Press.

Robinson, F., 2018. *Globalizing Care: Ethics, Feminist Theory, and International Relations*, New York, NY: Routledge.

REFERENCES

Rodale, 2018. Farming Systems Trial. *Rodale Institute*. Available at: https://rodaleinstitute.org/science/farming-systems-trial/ [Accessed 6 April 2022].

Rogers, J., 2019. Building cars in the 21st Century. Manufacturing Tomorrow. Available at: https://www.manufacturingtomorrow.com/article/2019/07/building-cars-in-the-21st-century/13706 [Accessed 4 April 2022].

Rosen, N., 2014. Off-grid living: It's time to take back the power from the energy companies. *The Guardian*. Available at: https://www.theguardian.com/lifeandstyle/2014/apr/11/power-energy-companies [Accessed 2 April 2022].

Rotman, D., 2020. Why we will need genetically modified foods. *MIT Technology Review*. Available at: https://www.technologyreview.com/2013/12/17/112585/why-we-will-need-genetically-modified-foods/ [Accessed 6 April 2022].

Rotz, S., Duncan, E., Small, M., Botschner, J., Dara, R., Mosby, I., et al, 2019. The politics of digital agricultural technologies: A preliminary review. *Sociologia Ruralis*, 59(2), pp 203–229.

Ruivenkamp, G.T. and Hilton, A. eds., 2017. *Perspectives on Commoning: Autonomist Principles and Practices*, London: Zed Books.

Ryan, J., 2018. The Bank of Canada should be reinstated to its original mandated purposes. Canadian Dimension. Available at: https://canadiandimension.com/articles/view/the-bank-of-canada-should-be-reinstated-to-its-original-mandated-purposes [Accessed 8 April 2022].

Sagisi, J., 2019. Trading energy: Will the Brooklyn Microgrid Disrupt the energy industry? Medium. Available at: https://medium.com/cryptolinks/trading-energy-will-the-brooklyn-microgrid-disrupt-the-energy-industry-a15186f530b6 [Accessed 2 April 2022].

Salamon, L.M. and Newhouse, C.L., 2020. The 2020 Nonprofit Employment Report. *Nonprofit Economic Data Bulletin*, 48. Available at: ccss.jhu.edu. [Accessed 1 April 2022].

Salman, T., Carrillo, F. and Soruco, C., 2015. Small-scale mining cooperatives and the state in Bolivia: Their histories, memories and negotiation strategies. *The Extractive Industries and Society*, 2(2), pp 360–367.

Sandvine, 2018. 2018 global internet phenomena report. Sandvine. Available at: https://www.sandvine.com/hubfs/downloads/phenomena/2018-phenomena-report.pdf [Accessed 28 June 2022].

Satariano, A., 2019. How the internet travels across oceans. *The New York Times*. Available at: https://www.nytimes.com/interactive/2019/03/10/technology/internet-cables-oceans.html [Accessed 28 June 2022].

Scherrer, C., 1988. Mini-Mills: A new growth path for the U.S. Steel Industry? *Journal of Economic Issues*, 22(4), pp 1179–1200.

Schismenos, A., Niaros, V. and Lemos, L., 2020. Cosmolocalism: Understanding the transitional dynamics towards post-capitalism. *tripleC*, 18(2), pp 670–684.

Scholz, T., 2017. *Uberworked and Underpaid: How Workers are Disrupting the Digital Economy*, Cambridge, MA: Polity Press.

Schor, J.B., 1998. *The Overspent American: Why We Want What We Don't Need*, New York, NY: Harper Perennial.

Schor, J.B., 2010. *Plenitude: The New Economics of True Wealth*, New York, NY: Penguin.

Schweickart, D., 2011. *After Capitalism*, Lanham, MD: Rowman & Littlefield Publishers.

Seetharaman, D. and Grind, K., 2018. Facebook considered charging for access to User Data. The Wall Street Journal. Available at: https://www.wsj.com/articles/facebook-considered-charging-for-access-to-user-data-1543454648 [Accessed 2 April 2022].

Seifert, T., Sievers, S., Bramsiepe, C., Schembecker, G., 2012. Small scale, modular and continuous: A new approach in plant design. *Chemical Engineering and Processing: Process Intensification*, 52, pp 140–150.

Seva Exchange, 2021. Home, Seva Exchange. Available at: https://www.sevaexchange.com/ [Accessed 18 October 2022].

Simons, J. and Ghosh, D., 2020. Utilities for democracy: Why and how the Algorithmic Infrastructure of Facebook and Google must be regulated. Brookings. Available at: https://www.brookings.edu/research/utilities-for-democracy-why-and-how-the-algorithmic-infrastructure-of-facebook-and-google-must-be-regulated/ [Accessed 30 April 2022].

Slaby, M., 2021. *For All the People: Redeeming the Broken Promises of Modern Media and Reclaiming Our Civic Life*, New York, NY: Disruption Books.

Slow Money, 2017. Slow money. Slow Money. Available at: https://slowmoney.org/ [Accessed 8 April 2022].

Smiers, J. and van Schijnde, M., 2009. *Imagine There is No Copyright and No Cultural Conglomerates Too*, Amsterdam: Institute of Network Cultures.

Smith, A., 2015. Tooling up: Civic Visions, FabLabs, and grassroots activism. The Guardian. Available at: https://www.theguardian.com/science/political-science/2015/apr/04/tooling-up-civic-visions-fablabs-and-grassroots-activism [Accessed 3 April 2022].

Somjee, A.H. and Somjee, G., 1978. Cooperative dairying and the profiles of Social Change in India. *Economic Development and Cultural Change*, 26(3), pp 577–590.

Southall, N., 2011. A multitude of possibilities: The strategic vision of Antonio Negri and Michael Hardt. Dissertation. Available at: https://ro.uow.edu.au/theses/3274/ [Accessed 31 March 2022].

Spaeth, S. and Niederhöfer, S., 2021. User motivation in peer production. In M. O'Neil, C. Pentzold and S. Toupin, eds. *The Handbook of Peer Production*. Hoboken, NJ: Wiley-Blackwell, pp 123–136.

Springer, S., 2016. *The Anarchist Roots of Geography: Toward Spatial Emancipation*, Minneapolis, MN: University of Minnesota Press.

Stallman, R., 2021. Copyleft: Pragmatic idealism. GNU Operating System. Available at: https://www.gnu.org/philosophy/pragmatic.html [Accessed 21 June 2022].

Stavrides, S., 2016. *Common Space: The City as Commons*, London: Zed Books.

Stavrides, S., 2019. *Common Spaces of Urban Emancipation*, Manchester: Manchester University Press.

Stewart, M., 2020. Programming fairness in algorithms. Medium. Available at: https://towardsdatascience.com/programming-fairness-in-algorithms-4943a13dd9f8 [Accessed 2 April 2022].

Stone, M., 2021. Why France's New Tech 'repairability index' is a big deal. *WIRED*. Available at: https://www.wired.com/story/frances-new-tech-repairability-index-is-a-big-deal/ [Accessed 3 September 2022].

Stone, P., Brooks, R., Brynjolfsson, E., Calo, R., Etzioni, O., Hager, G., et al, 2016. Artificial Intelligence and Life in 2030. Stanford University. Available at: https://ai100.stanford.edu/2016-report [Accessed 8 April 2022].

Swan, M., 2015. *Blockchain: Blueprint for a New Economy*, Sebastopol, CA: O'Reilly.

Swedberg, R., 2005. Towards an economic sociology of capitalism. *L'Année Sociologique*, Vol. 55(2), pp 419–449.

Switched On, nd. About us. Switched On London. Available at: http://switchedonlondon.org.uk/about-us/ [Accessed 12 July 2022].

Sylvester-Bradley, O., 2019. Hullcoin: Can blockchain unlock the hidden value in hull's economy? open coop. Available at: https://open.coop/2018/04/23/hullcoin-can-blockchain-unlock-hidden-value-hulls-economy/ [Accessed 8 April 2022].

Taylor, A., 2005. *ZIZEK!*, New York, NY: Zeitgeist Films.

Taylor, K., 2018. Swedish election highlights decline of center-left parties across Western Europe. *Pew Research Center*. Available at: https://www.pewresearch.org/fact-tank/2018/09/12/swedish-election-highlights-decline-of-center-left-parties-across-western-europe/ [Accessed 18 May 2022].

Telalbasic, I., 2017. Redesigning the concept of money: A service design perspective on complementary currency systems. *Journal of Design, Business & Society*, 3(1), pp 21–44.

Teng, A. and Czinger, K., 2018. How to recapture the soul of American Manufacturing? *Medium*. Available at: https://medium.com/@Divergent3D/how-to-recapture-the-soul-of-american-manufacturing-e9eeffb8d993 [Accessed 4 April 2022].

Terranova, T., 2014. Red stack attack! Algorithms, capital and the automation of the common. *EuroNomade*. Available at: http://www.euronomade.info/?p=2268 [Accessed 30 April 2022].

Thomas, H.M., 2019. Community-owned energy: How Nebraska became the only state to bring everyone power from a public grid. *YES! Magazine*. Available at: https://www.yesmagazine.org/economy/2015/01/30/nebraskas-community-owned-energy [Accessed 3 April 2022].

Thompson, C., 2018. The future of 'Fab lab' fabrication. WIRED. Available at: https://www.wired.com/story/the-future-of-fab-lab-fabrication/ [Accessed 3 April 2022].

Thompson, M., 2020. What's so new about new municipalism? *Progress in Human Geography*, 45(2), pp 317–342.

Timmermann, C., 2014. An assessment of prominent proposals to amend intellectual property regimes using a human rights framework. *Revista La Propiedad Inmaterial*, 18. Available at: https://papers.ssrn.com/sol3/papers.cfm?abstract_id=2535830 [Accessed 20 June 2022].

Toner, A., 2007. Copyfarleft: An anarchist Gema? kNOw Future Inc. Available at: https://knowfuture.wordpress.com/2007/11/22/copyfarleft-an-anarchist-gema/ [Accessed 1 April 2022].

Toupin, S., 2021. Peer production and collective action. In M. O'Neil, C. Pentzold and S. Toupin, eds. *The Handbook of Peer Production*. Hoboken, NJ: Wiley-Blackwell, pp 299–310.

Townson, N.J., 2021. Can a worker's co-op thrive in big tech? *Early Magazine*. Available at: https://www.earlymagazine.com/articles/can-a-workers-co-op-thrive-in-big-tech [Accessed 1 April 2022].

Toyota, 2021. Mazda Toyota manufacturing begins production on 2022 Corolla Cross, Toyota USA Newsroom. Available at: https://pressroom.toyota.com/mazda-toyota-manufacturing-begins-production-on-2022-corolla-cross/ [Accessed 8 December 2022].

Troncoso, S. and Utratel, A.M. eds., 2015. *Commons Transition: Policy Proposals for an Open Knowledge Commons Society*, Amsterdam: P2P Foundation. Available at: https://commonstransition.org/wp-content/uploads/2014/11/Commons-Transition_-Policy-Proposals-for-a-P2P-Foundation.pdf [Accessed 9 April 2022].

Trostle, H., Kienbaum, K., Andrews, M., Razafindrabe, N.O., Mitchell, C., 2022. Cooperatives fiberize rural America: A trusted model for the internet era. ILSR. Available at: https://ilsr.org/wp-content/uploads/2020/05/2020_05_19_Rural-Co-op-Report.pdf [Accessed 3 April 2022].

UNCTAD, 2019. Digital Economy Report 2019. *UNCTAD*. Available at: https://unctad.org/webflyer/digital-economy-report-2019 [Accessed 1 April 2022].

US PIRG, 2019. Small dollar donors are winning! (for now). PIRG. Available at: https://uspirg.org/blogs/blog/usp/small-dollar-donors-are-winning-%C2%A0now [Accessed 7 April 2022].

Utratel, A.M. and Troncoso, S., 2017. Opinion: Promoting the commons in the time of monsters. *Common Dreams*. Available at: https://www.commondreams.org/views/2017/06/03/promoting-commons-time-monsters [Accessed 9 April 2022].

Vadén, T. and Suoranta, J., 2009. A definition and criticism of cybercommunism. *Capital & Class*, 33(1), pp 159–177.

van de Sande, M., 2015. Fighting with tools: Prefiguration and radical politics in the twenty-first century. *Rethinking Marxism*, 27(2), pp 177–194.

van Dijck, J., Nieborg, D. and Poell, T., 2019. Reframing platform power. *Internet Policy Review*, 8(2). Available at: https://policyreview.info/articles/analysis/reframing-platform-power [Accessed 30 April 2022].

van Haute, E. ed., 2011. *Party Membership in Europe: Exploration Into the Anthills of Party Politics*, Bruxelles: Université de Bruxelles.

Varvarousis, A., 2020. The rhizomatic expansion of commoning through social movements. *Ecological Economics*, 171, p 106596.

Vercellone, C., Brancaccio, F., Giuliani, A., Puletti, F., Rocchi, G., Vattimo, P., 2019. Data driven disruptive commons-based models. DECODE. Available at: https://decodeproject.eu/publications/data-driven-disruptive-commons-based-models-0.html [Accessed 31 March 2022].

Vesco, A., 2020. Heteropolitics: Refiguring the Common and the Political. Report 4. Heteropolitics. Available at: http://heteropolitics.net/ [Accessed 9 May 2022].

Volpicelli, G.M., 2022. Miamicoin is crashing, but it won't go away. WIRED. Available at: https://www.wired.com/story/miami-crypto-miamicoin/ [Accessed 2 July 2022].

von Busch, O. and Palmås Karl, 2006. *Abstract Hacktivism: The Making of a Hacker Culture*, London: Open Mute.

Wallace, A., 2020. Executive Summary. Open GLAM. Available at: https://openglam.pubpub.org/pub/executive-summary/release/2 [Accessed 1 April 2022].

Walljasper, J., 2010. *All That We Share: A Field Guide to the Commons*, New York, NY: The New Press.

Watkins, D., 2018. LibreOffice: A history of document freedom. *Opensource.com*. Available at: https://opensource.com/article/18/9/libreoffice-history [Accessed 1 April 2022].

WEC, 2016. Five environmentally friendly companies that are changing the world. *World Economic Forum*. Available at: https://www.weforum.org/agenda/2016/12/5-environmentally-friendly-companies-that-are-changing-the-world/ [Accessed 18 October 2022].

Weiss, C.C., 2015. World's first 3D-printed supercar aimed at shaking up the auto industry. *New Atlas*. Available at: https://newatlas.com/divergent-microfactories-blade-first-3d-printed-supercar/38201/ [Accessed 4 April 2022].

Werner, R.A., 2014. Can banks individually create money out of nothing?. *International Review of Financial Analysis*, 36, pp 1–19.

White, R.J. and Williams, C.C., 2016. Beyond capitalocentricism: Are non-capitalist work practices 'alternatives'? *Area*, 48(3), pp 325–331.

Widerquist, K., 2017. The cost of basic income: Back-of-the-envelope calculations. *Basic Income Studies*, 12(2). Available at: https://works.bepress.com/widerquist/75/ [Accessed 3 July 2022].

Wiens, K., 2015. IFixit app pulled from Apple's app store. *IFixit News*. Available at: https://www.ifixit.com/News/7401/ifixit-app-pulled [Accessed 3 July 2022].

WikiHouse, 2022. Wikihouse. *WikiHouse*. Available at: https://www.wikihouse.cc/ [Accessed 3 April 2022].

Wikimedia, 2022. Frequently asked questions. Wikimedia Foundation. Available at: https://donate.wikimedia.org/wiki/FAQ [Accessed 21 June 2022].

Wikipedia, 2022. *Wikipedia*. Available at: https://en.wikipedia.org/wiki/Wikipedia [Accessed 19 June 2022].

Wilkinson, R.G. and Pickett, K., 2010. *The Spirit Level: Why Equality is Better for Everyone*, London: Penguin Books.

Wilson, M. and Kleiner, D., 2013. Luddite cybercommunism: An email exchange. *Anarchist Studies*, 21(1), pp 73–84.

WIPO, 2017. World Intellectual Property Report 2017: Intangible Capital in Global Value Chains, Geneva: World Intellectual Property Organization. Available at: https://www.wipo.int/publications/en/details.jsp?id=4225 [Accessed 4 April 2022].

WIRED, 2014. Startup of the week: Figshare. WIRED. Available at: https://www.wired.co.uk/article/figshare [Accessed 1 April 2022].

Woodcock, J., 2021. *The Fight Against Platform Capitalism an Inquiry into the Global Struggles of the Gig Economy*, London: University of Westminster Press.

World Bank, 2021. Market capitalization of listed domestic companies (% of GDP). Available at: https://data.worldbank.org/indicator/cm.mkt.lcap.gd.zs [Accessed 31 March 2022].

Wright, E.O., 2021. *How to be an Anticapitalist in the Twenty-first Century*, London: Verso.

Young, I.M., 1990. *Justice and the Politics of Difference*, Princeton, NJ: Princeton University Press.

Zaleski, A., 2016. The 3D printing revolution that wasn't. *WIRED*. Available at: https://www.wired.com/2016/12/the-3d-printing-revolution-that-wasnt/ [Accessed 1 April 2022].

Zarlenga, S., 2002. *The Lost Science of Money: The Mythology of Money, the Story of Power*, Valatie, NY: American Monetary Institute.

Zechner, M., 2020. Heteropolitics: Refiguring the Common and the Political. Report 6. Heteropolitics. Available at: http://heteropolitics.net/ [Accessed 9 May 2022].

Zhang, Y., Wang, L. and Duan, Y., 2016. Agricultural information dissemination using icts: A review and analysis of information dissemination models in China. *Information Processing in Agriculture*, 3(1), pp17–29.

Žižek, S., 2007. Resistance is surrender: What to do about capitalism. *London Review of Books*, 29(22). Available at: https://www.lrb.co.uk/the-paper/v29/n22/slavoj-zizek/resistance-is-surrender [Accessed 2 July 2022].

Zugasti, I., 2019. Humanity at work. Mondragon Corporation. Available at: https://www.bedc.bm/wp-content/uploads/2019/02/Mondragon-Social-Transformation-Briefing-by-Ibon-Zugasti-Apr.-2018.pdf [Accessed 4 April 2022].

Index

A

abstract hacktivism 32–33, 88, 95, 153
abstract labor 176, 191
Access to Knowledge movement 191
accident of birth 220
Agamben, Giorgio 23
agonism 180, 203
algorithms *see* artificial intelligence.
alienation 18, 123, 214
Alphabet (Google) 52, 57, 58, 61, 65, 68, 70, 85
Amazon 58, 61, 85, 171, 190
anarchism 22, 27, 28, 178, 187, 216
anarcho-communism 198
anarcho-primitivism 199
apparatus of capture 23–25, 31, 138
  and labour 43–44, 50, 143, 147, 176
  and guaranteed income 159–160, 191
apparatus of compeerist capture 215
artificial intelligence (AI) 60, 158–159, 165, 203
  and algorithms 68–69, 70
Austrian School 212
automation 2, 19, 159, 206
autonomist Marxism (autonomists) 10, 26–28, 176–179, 186

B

Bank of Canada 161
Bank of North Dakota 149
Barcelona 71, 99
Bauwens, Michel 7, 63, 133, 188
becoming revolutionary 185, 186–187, 190
Benkler, Yochai 3, 13–14, 25, 28, 44
Big Ag 125, 129
big data 59–61, 66–67, 165, 211
Bitcoin 87, 152, 153, 166, 167, 172
blockchain 4–5, 87, 151–152, 153
Bologna Regulation for the Care and Regeneration of the Urban Commons 187–188
the Borg 24
Bookchin, Murray 187, 189, 204
boundary commoning 50, 63–64, 95, 109, 111, 128–129
  and finances 148, 150, 153
  and politics 111–112, 185–186
Budapest Open Access Initiative 40–41
bullshit jobs 163, 206, 214

C

capitalist realism 1, 7, 54
care (ethics of care) 184, 192
Carson, Kevin 101
censorship *see* disinformation
Centre for the Application of Molecular Biology to International Agriculture (CAMBIA) 128
charities 141–142
Circles 167–168
circular economy 115–119, 213
city cryptos 152
collectivism 198, 207
commoditization 18, 100, 191
commodity fetishism 18, 31, 138–139
commoner consciousness 33, 139, 177–181, 219
Commonification 8, 10, 144–145, 215
  and data 66–71
  and digital value 40–55
  and government 192–194
  and infrastructure 79–84, 86–92
  and manufacturing 95, 104–112, 213
  and natural resources 113–114, 119–121, 124–126
commoning 3, 33, 52, 139, 141, 151, 215
  and political mobilization 176–177, 178–184
commons-based governance 84, 119–120, 124–125
commons-based peer production 3, 5, 28, 36, 40, 63–64
  and shortcomings 6, 7–8, 30, 95, 194–195
communism 138, 206, 211
community sponsored agriculture (CSA) 126
complementary currencies 151–154, 166–168
  see also Circles; city cryptos; freigeld
confederal assemblies *see* nested confederacy
Co-operative Party 118
cooperative accumulation 147–148

INDEX

cooperatives (coops) 29, 45, 46, 143, 145, 208
  in agriculture 128–129
  in banking (credit union) 148, 149–150
  and digital value 45, 53–54, 67
  in infrastructure 80–82, 83–84, 88, 91
  in manufacturing 98, 106–109, 111–112
  in retail 126
  and raw materials 120–121
  stakeholder 91, 92
cooperativization 80, 88, 91, 106
Copyfair 52
copyleft *see* General Public License; creative commons
copyright 20, 49
cosmo-localism 133
Costa Rica 217
Couchsurfing 62–63, 141
counter-hegemony 188
collaboration 2–3, 29, 64, 179, 220
collaborative consumption 140, 213
craft beer 213
creative commons licensing (CC) 38–39, 52
credit union *see* cooperative banking
crowdsourcing 36, 37, 97, 195–196
  and capital cooptation 2–21, 48, 54
cryptocurrency 151–154, 166–172
  and value 152–153
  and regulation 171–172
  as means of exchange 166–170
  as store of value 167, 169–170
  and incentivization 87, 152–153
  corporate 171–172
  see also Bitcoin; Circles; FairCoin
cyber estate 57, 61–62, 69, 70–71
cybernetics 211

D

3D printing 94, 97, 101–102
data colonialism 60, 64–69
DeAngelis, Massimo 50, 176–179
decentralization *see* localization
decentralized autonomous organizations 46, 146
Deleuze and Guattari 23–24, 26, 185–186
demurrage 151, 164, 205
digital abundance 4–6, 29, 56
digital revolution 2–3, 5, 28, 56, 194
Digital Markets Act 70
disinformation 194, 195–196
diverse economies 31
divestment *see* exodus from capital
do it yourself (DIY) 42, 97, 100, 116–117, 182

E

economic democratization 9, 75–76, 95, 106, 116–117, 145, 213–214
  in agriculture 123, 131

economies of scale 96, 102, 104, 213
electoral dysfunction 192–193
Emilia Romagna 101, 103, 108
enclosure 20–21, 22
  of digital commons 4–5, 37–38, 47–48, 57–58
energy democracy 79–82
equality 179, 200
ethical banking 149–150
evolutionary change 26, 29, 33, 185–186
exchange value 8, 23, 155, 198
  as a frame of mind 18, 31, 137–139
exodus (exit) from capital 10, 26, 33, 41, 116, 140–141, 185
  and banking 146–150
  and data 64–66, 71
  through digital commons 35–43, 71
  and energy 76–84
  and the internet 61–64, 86–91
  and money 139–141, 143, 151–154, 166–172
  and production 95–98, 99–101
  and resources 117–121, 124–125, 127–128
extended producer responsibility 118
externalized costs 18, 96, 112

F

fablabs *see* makerspaces
Faircoin 154, 169–170
Fairtrade 132–133
Farm Hack 127
fiat money 19, 23–24, 156, 205
Fictitious capital 21
financialization 20, 21, 157
flexible specialization 95
food sovereignty 126, 130
fully automated luxury communism 206
fractional reserve banking 19, 149, 156–157
friend-enemy dichotomy 184, 196
Free Libre Open Knowledge Project (FLOK) 133–134
freigeld 151

G

galleries, libraries, archives, and museums *see* GLAM
games (as metaphor) 219–221
General Data Protection Regulation (EU) 70
general intellect 2, 39, 42, 56, 71
  efforts to liberate 48, 49, 134, 218
  enclosure of 4–5, 20–21, 22, 133
General Public License (GPL) 36–37, 48, 50
genetically modified organism (GMO's) 123–124, 128
gifting 44, 47, 141–143, 152, 153
gig economy 4, 45
  workers 22, 58, 62
GLAM 44–45, 49
'good enough' governance 204

Google *see* Alphabet
Green New Deal 158, 160
growth imperative 18–19, 115–116, 156–158, 160
guaranteed basic income 159–161, 164, 167–168, 191, 206, 214
guilds 50, 111–112, 209

H

happiness 189, 217
Hardt and Negri 26–27, 29, 178, 184, 186
Harvey, David 95
hegemony 34, 189, 219
Heteropolitics 180
hit and run tactics 187, 189–190
Holloway, John 176–177, 186
Holochain 87–88, 90, 153

I

IBM 37
In-built obsolescence 116
inflation *see* money
intellectual property 4, 20, 41, 49, 110, 129, 208
internalizing costs 112, 129, 189
international relations *see* the state
internet of things 59–60

J

Jefferson, Thomas 202

K

Karatani, Kojin 30
Keynes, John Maynard 159
Kleiner, Dmytri 52, 56–57

L

Laclau and Mouffe 181
land ownership 124–125, 131, 207–208
land trusts 125–126, 185
Lessig, Lawrence 38, 39
libertarian municipalism 199
lines of flight 24–25, 27, 33, 175, 185–186, 218
Local Motors 47–48, 102
localization (decentralization) 3–4, 9, 75–76, 114, 218
  in agriculture 121–124, 127–130
    limitations 130–134
  in data 65–66
  in energy 76–80
    limitations 79, 82–84
  and the environment 115–119
  in governance 33–34, 46, 187–188, 199–200, 203–204
  and the internet 62–63, 86–89
    limitations 89–91
  in production 95, 98–104, 213–214
  and raw materials 119–127

longue-durée 33, 118, 143, 189
Loomio 146, 148
Luxemburg, Rosa 29, 47, 109–110, 144

M

Majority World 10, 130, 132–134
Makerbot 48
maker culture *see* do it yourself (DIY)
makerspaces 98–101
markets 8–9, 31–32, 69, 137–138, 198–199
  commons-based competitiveness in 28–29, 144, 146
  and digital value 47–48, 53–54
  and the internet 63, 64–65, 67
  and natural resources 119, 127–129
  and production 100–101, 102–104, 107, 109–112
  corrupting power of 29, 107–108, 144–146
  need to engage with 6, 29, 52, 141, 143–144
  regulating and shaping of 70, 109, 129–130, 189–191, 205, 209–212
  see also exchange value
Mason, Paul 27–28, 165
Marx, Karl 2, 17–19, 21
McLuhan, Marshall 76, 77
Meta *see* Facebook
Metcalfe's law 62
Micropolitics 185, 190, 219
Microsoft 37, 61, 65, 85
mining sector 119–121
Minority World 10, 84, 130–134, 191–192
Modern Monetary Theory (MMT) 162, 163
modularity 97, 102, 114, 116
Mondragon Corporation 106–108, 145, 170–171
monetary-banking apparatus 155–156
monetary reform *see* the state
money 23, 155–156, 198–199
  and debt 19, 146–147, 155, 156–157
  commons-based options for accessing 141–150
  supply 19, 161–163
  and inflation 162–165, 168, 206–207
  role in valuation 5–6, 8, 31, 138–139, 141
  sovereign control over 161–163, 165, 205–207
  and non-state currency 167–169, 171–172
  see also complementary currency; cryptocurrencies; exchange value; monetary-banking apparatus
Mouffe, Chantal 196
movement of movements 177, 181–183, 197, 219
multitude 26, 27, 178
municipal activism 187–188
municipalization 80–81, 88, 91, 145
Musk, Elon 41
mutual aid 27, 139, 140, 179
mutualism 31, 199, 205

INDEX

N

Nash equilibrium 220
National Emergency Employment Defense Act 165
nationalization 33, 83, 90, 190–191
neo-fascism 183–184, 196, 200
neoliberalism 20, 95, 161, 188
nested confederacy 199, 200–201, 202–203
New Deal 80, 92, 120
non-fungible tokens (NFTs) 5
non-personal property 207–208
non-governmental organizations (NGOs) *see* non-profits
non-profits 52, 67, 111, 141–142, 143, 145, 202
North Dakota Mill and Elevator 106

O

Occupy Wallstreet 178, 182
open cooperativism 63–64, 110, 111
open database Licence (ODbL) 67–68, 71
Open Food Network 128
open source/access 3, 71, 133, 181–182, 191–192
  data 66–69
  design 41–42, 46, 47–48
  education 39, 195
  hardware 42, 96–97, 110, 127
  information/knowledge 39, 40–41, 43, 127, 195–196
  research/science 40, 42–43, 128
  software (FOSS) 3, 35–38, 63–64
  see also creative commons, general public license, open value networks
Open Source Drug Discovery 42–43, 49
Open-Source Ecology 42, 97, 110
open value networks 45–46, 99, 111, 148
organic agriculture 122–123, 125
Ostrom, Elinor 9, 25, 54, 84, 114, 120, 179, 199
  and property 50, 125–126
othering 177, 183
overcapacity 18–19

P

P2P Foundation 3, 30, 133, 189
patents 20, 41–42, 49, 128, 208
partner state 34, 200, 201–204, 205
peer property (licensing) 48, 50–55, 64, 68, 111, 128, 186
personal property 207–208
petit bourgeoisie 108, 190
pirating 38, 53–54, 140, 208
Pirate Party 49, 188
platform cooperatives 61–64, 69, 87
postcolonialism 121, 132–134, 191–192
post-ideology 181, 199, 216
power geometries 131–132, 134, 179

pragmatism 33, 66, 92, 143, 196
prefiguration 24–25, 27, 33
productivity 2, 19, 158–159, 206
proportional rank choice voting 193
prosumer 11, 39, 58, 78, 116, 213–214

R

recycling 115, 117–119
repairability 103, 116–117, 119, 129
remuneration 6, 42–44, 45, 50, 57, 208–209, 215
rent extraction 4, 23, 86, 207
resilience 113–114, 140
revolution 7, 22–23, 26–27, 176
rivalrous resources 54

S

Sanders, Bernie 90, 142
scarcity 5, 54, 76, 134, 219–220
  and capitalism 4, 8, 58
  artificial 2, 20–22, 47–48, 86, 177
self sovereign ID (SSI) 65–66, 68, 70
Sensorica 46, 47
smart city 66–67, 99
smart contract 20, 46, 56, 152
Snowden, Edward 66
social economy 52, 63–64, 109, 112, 143
Social Credit System (China) 59
Socialism 105, 106, 161
  as a political movement 1, 28
  democratic 27–28
  market 31, 33, 209
solar energy 77, 79, 82, 84, 104
solidarity 45, 179, 185
  international 84, 191
solidarity economy *see* social economy
Spanish Revolution 216
Stallman, Richard 35–36, 36–37, 43
the state 6–7, 22, 27–28, 31, 199
  and agriculture 124–125, 126, 129–130
  and banking 149, 150, 156–158
  and cryptocurrencies 167, 171–172
  and data 59, 60, 66, 70–71
  and democracy 192–197
  and digital value production 44–45, 47, 48–49
  and energy 83–84, 91–92
  and fiscal constraints 157–158, 160
  and grants 142–143
  and international relations 134, 191–192, 200–201
  and the internet 90–92
  and manufacturing 105–106, 109, 112
  and monetary reform 156, 160–165
  and market interventions 189–191, 209–212
  the need to engage 33–34, 186–188, 199, 219
  nexus with capitalism 28, 34, 134, 183
  and raw materials 116, 118–121

and research 40, 42–43, 45
see also nationalization, universal basic income
supply-based economy 103, 116
surplus labour 17, 19
sustainability 54, 189, 215

T

tadpole 154
technocracy 203, 211
techno-determinism 32, 194
technological sovereignty 71
thriving (human) 180, 198, 215–216, 219
TimeBanks 140
tiny house movement 77, 178
trade 84, 120, 130–134, 169
transvestment 29, 125, 144, 168–169, 185
Tribal Digital Village 88–89

U

Uber 57, 58, 70, 71
unemployment 18, 158–159, 162
United Nations 89, 192

universal basic income (UBI) *see* guaranteed basic income
urban waste mine 117–119
us versus them 134, 191, 200, 219
use-value 9, 21, 75, 122, 163, 212

V

vanguardism 179, 200
values 31–32, 45, 52, 110, 138, 144–145, 203
    specific compeerist-aligned 8–9, 105, 176, 179

W

Weltanschauung 221
Westphalian order 201
win-lose dynamics 204
win-win dynamics 84, 130, 184, 202
Wikimedia Foundation 52–53
Wikipedia 3, 39, 44, 54
    and labor 43–44, 53

Y

Young, Iris Marion 216

Z

Žižek, Slavoj 1, 186–187

www.ingramcontent.com/pod-product-compliance
Lightning Source LLC
Chambersburg PA
CBHW051534020426
42333CB00016B/1916